INTERNATIONAL COURTS AND TRIBUNALS SERIES

General Editors

RUTH MACKENZIE
CESARE P. R. ROMANO
MIKAEL RASK MADSEN

Balancing International Judicial Independence

INTERNATIONAL COURTS AND TRIBUNALS SERIES

A distinctive feature of modern international law and society is the increased role played by international courts and tribunals. **The International Courts and Tribunals Series** is the dedicated home for scholarly works which address, in critical and analytical fashion, the legal and policy aspects of the functioning of international courts and tribunals. The series encourages both legal analysis of the institutional, substantive, and procedural aspects of international courts, and socio-legal studies that explore the issues these courts are called to address and how they are influenced by global developments. We publish both comparative works involving multiple courts and single-court studies.

Balancing International Judicial Independence

Legal and Political Constraints in Regional Courts

AIDA TORRES PÉREZ

Pompeu Fabra University (Barcelona)

OXFORD
UNIVERSITY PRESS

OXFORD
UNIVERSITY PRESS

Great Clarendon Street, Oxford, OX2 6DP,
United Kingdom

Oxford University Press is a department of the University of Oxford.
It furthers the University's objective of excellence in research, scholarship,
and education by publishing worldwide. Oxford is a registered trade mark of
Oxford University Press in the UK and in certain other countries.

Published in the United States of America by Oxford University Press
198 Madison Avenue, New York, NY 10016, United States of America.

British Library Cataloguing in Publication Data
Data available

Library of Congress Control Number: 2026934685

ISBN 978-0-19-885254-4

DOI: 10.1093/oso/9780198852544.001.0001

Printed and bound by
CPI Group (UK) Ltd., Croydon, CR0 4YY

The manufacturer's authorized representative in the EU for product safety is
Oxford University Press España S.A. of Parque Empresarial San Fernando de Henares,
Avenida de Castilla, 2 – 28830 Madrid (www.oup.es/en or product.safety@oup.com).
OUP España S.A. also acts as importer into Spain of products made by the manufacturer.

MIX
Paper | Supporting
responsible forestry
FSC® C013604
FSC
www.fsc.org

To Joan and Caterina

Contents

Introduction ix

PART 1 INTERNATIONAL JUDICIAL INDEPENDENCE

1. From Domestic to International Judicial Independence 3
   1. Introduction 3
   2. The Reach of State Consent 5
      2.1. The origin and design of international courts 6
      2.2. Compulsory jurisdiction 7
      2.3. Enforcement and compliance 9
   3. Between Common Standards and Institutional Diversity 10
   4. The Principle of Judicial Independence as Instrumental and Relative 18
      4.1. The aims of international judicial independence 18
      4.2. Constrained international judicial independence 22

PART 2 LEGAL AND POLITICAL CONSTRAINTS

2. Judicial Accountability in the International Sphere 27
   1. Introduction 27
   2. The Legal Accountability of Regional Judges 30
      2.1. Standards of judicial conduct 31
      2.2. The consequences of failure to meet standards of conduct 34
      2.3. The judges' accountability holders 35
      2.4. The disciplinary regime in practice 38
   3. Trade-offs in Institutional Design: Internal and External Judicial Independence 41
   4. International Codes of Judicial Conduct and Ethics 46
3. A Checks and Balances Approach to Political Constraints on Regional Courts 52
   1. Introduction 52
   2. Framing Judicial Independence: Functional Separation and Institutional Constraints 53
   3. A Checks and Balances Approach to International Judicial Independence 59
      3.1. Global constitutionalism: pursuing the rule of law in the international sphere 59

3.2. From judicial independence to interdependence 63
a) The multiplicity of spheres and actors 65
b) Dynamic perspective 66
c) Institutional mutual recognition and respect as precondition 67
d) Coping with indeterminacy: how to justify the allocation of power constraints 70

PART 3 CHECKS AND BALANCES: INSTITUTIONAL ACTORS AND MECHANISMS

4. Sources of Institutional Constraint 75
1. Introduction 75
2. Governmental Institutions 76
2.1. Intergovernmental bodies and judicial governance 77
2.2. Between state sovereignty and democratic legitimacy 80
3. Parliamentary Institutions 84
3.1. The role of regional and domestic parliaments 84
3.2. Democratic legitimacy, deliberation, and transparency 86
4. Domestic and International Judiciary 91
4.1. Patterns of collaboration and resistance 92
4.2. Epistemic and deliberative values through judicial dialogue 98

5. Judicial Selection and Appointment 103
1. Introduction 103
2. Selecting Regional Judges: The Legal Framework and Practice 106
3. Advisory Expert Panels 110
4. Transparency 117
5. Tenure, Reappointment, and Dissenting Opinions 122

6. Political Override and Non-Compliance 127
1. Introduction 127
2. Forms of Political Override of Regional Courts' Judgments 128
2.1. Treaty amendment 131
2.2. Legislative override 134
2.3. Substantive and structural override 136
3. Non-Compliance 139

Afterword 145
Bibliography 149
Index 157

Introduction

As international and regional courts have proliferated across the globe,[1] their growing influence over domestic law and policy has sparked concerns about their legitimacy.[2] The normative legitimacy of international and regional courts as institutions vested with the power of adjudication is heavily grounded on their independence.[3] Their legitimacy, furthermore, may well also be contingent on other factors, such as democratic rule[4] or effectiveness.[5] Notwithstanding, judicial independence lies at the core of the justification of the courts' power to adjudicate, in a way that is distinct from the power exercised by other public authorities. While judicial independence is essential for these courts to function legitimately, unchecked judicial power can be equally troubling. Courts that enjoy absolute independence may be just as problematic as ones that are completely subservient.[6] To find the right balance, a much more nuanced understanding of judicial independence is needed, one that goes beyond simply shielding judges from external pressures and incorporates appropriate mechanisms for accountability and oversight. This book offers a novel normative framework on the delicate balance between judicial independence and power constraints on regional courts.

From the perspective of classic international law, however, governmental control over international courts is not categorically regarded illegitimate, but

[1] Karen J Alter, 'The Multiplication of International Courts and Tribunals After the End of the Cold War' in Cesare PR Romano, Karen J Alter, and Yuval Shany (eds), *The Oxford Handbook of International Adjudication* (Oxford University Press 2014); Andreas Follesdal and Geir Ulfstein (eds), *The Judicialization of International Law* (Oxford University Press 2018).

[2] Samantha Besson and others, 'Legal Philosophical Issues of International Adjudication: Getting Over the Amour Impossible between International Law and Adjudication', *The Oxford Handbook of International Adjudication* (Oxford University Press 2013); Armin von Bogdandy and Ingo Venzke, *In Whose Name? A Public Law Theory of International Adjudication* (Oxford University Press 2016) 67; Harlan Grant Cohen and others, 'Legitimacy and International Courts – A Framework' in Nienke Grossman and others (eds), *Legitimacy and International Courts* (Cambridge University Press 2018).

[3] Philippe Sands and Ruth Mackenzie, 'International Courts and Tribunals and the Independence of the International Judge' (2003) 44 Harvard International Law Journal 271; Joe McIntyre and James Crawford, 'The Independence and Impartiality of the "International Judiciary"' in Christopher Forsyth and Shimon Shetreet (eds), *The Culture of Judicial Independence* (Brill 2011).

[4] Bogdandy and Venzke (n 2).

[5] Yuval Shany, *Assessing the Effectiveness of International Courts* (Oxford University Press 2014); Cohen (n 2) 6, 8–9.

[6] Andreas Follesdal, 'Independent yet Accountable: Stress Test Lessons for the European Court of Human Rights' (2017) 24 Maastricht Journal of European and Comparative Law 484.

Balancing International Judicial Independence. Aida Torres Pérez, Oxford University Press.
 DOI: 10.1093/oso/9780198852544.001.0001

then we still might question the extent to and axes along which international courts are or should enjoy a margin of independence. In a well-known debate, Posner and Yoo teamed up, on one side, to argue that dependent (politically controlled) international courts were more effective.[7] In response, Helfer and Slaughter co-wrote a piece explaining why they believed independent international courts might better serve states' interest.[8] Primarily leaning on political science literature, Helfer and Slaughter held that delegating authority to independent international courts serves the interests of the states to the degree that such delegation enhances the credibility of the states' international commitments.[9] Yet they also pointed out that states face a second level of design decisions where they can include control mechanisms in order to exert some influence over the courts.[10] Helfer and Slaughter formulated a theory of 'constrained independence' in which the creation of independent international courts, particularly in multilateral regimes, in coordination with fine-grained structural, political, and discursive mechanisms to limit the potential for judicial overreaching could well serve state interests.[11] While truly enlightening, their work focused overtly on controlling mechanisms in the hands of state governments, and they took a descriptive rather than normative approach towards a theory of constrained independence.

As international courts, and in particular regional courts, increasingly depart from a narrow dispute settlement model and assume more functions similar to those of constitutional courts,[12] scholars have increasingly examined them through constitutional lenses.[13] This clash of competing normative perspectives is the motivation for the elaboration of a suitable framework for conceptualizing judicial independence and constraints on international regional courts. Our aim is to elaborate an appropriate normative theoretical framework for conceptualizing the independence of regional courts and concordant mechanisms for power constraint.

While the independence of domestic courts has been thoroughly analysed in an extensive body of literature, it has only been in the last decades that a

[7] Eric A Posner and John C Yoo, 'Judicial Independence in International Tribunals' (2005) 93 California Law Review 1.

[8] Laurence R Helfer and Anne Marie Slaughter, 'Why States Create International Tribunals: A Response to Professors Posner and Yoo' (2005) 93 California Law Review 899, who also challenged the variables and data used by Posner and Yoo.

[9] ibid 33–34.

[10] ibid 44.

[11] ibid 1.

[12] Karen J Alter, *The New Terrain of International Law: Courts, Politics, Rights* (Princeton University Press 2014); Bogdandy and Venzke (n 2) 9–17.

[13] Anne Peters, 'The Merits of Global Constitutionalism' (2009) 16 Indiana Journal of Global Legal Studies 397.

group of scholars has devoted increasing attention to the independence of the international judiciary.[14] In general, current attempts to operationalize judicial independence at the international level overly focus on the role of state governments in the operations of a single regional or international court. However valuable the insights provided by these studies are, the research on international judicial independence and power constraints remains undertheorized, underdeveloped, and fragmented. This book addresses that gap with a novel normative framework that strikes a nuanced balance between judicial independence and legitimate constraints on the power of regional courts. The theoretical and practical difficulties of constraining judicial power without undermining judicial independence lie at the core of this study.

The book is structured in three parts. First, Chapter 1 offers a conceptual framework for international judicial independence that is sensitive to the unique institutional and political contexts in which regional courts operate and avoids uncritical transposition of domestic models. The comparative analysis will focus on a selection of regional human rights and integration courts in Europe and America: the European Court of Human Rights (ECtHR), the Court of Justice of the European Union (CJEU), the Inter-American Court of Human Rights (IACtHR), and the Andean Tribunal of Justice (ATJ).

The second part of the book investigates normative grounds for legitimate constraints on judicial power. Chapter 2 examines mechanisms implemented to ensure legal accountability upon which Chapter 3 builds by exploring whether the principle of checks and balances, a central pillar to prevent undue concentration of power in domestic governance, can be adapted to the international sphere. Political constraints on regional courts, it will be argued, raise serious concerns but cannot be rejected outright. Indeed, they can be conceived as useful forms of institutional interdependence under a refined version of the checks and balances principle.

The third part of the book will tackle the implications of deploying the checks and balances principle as a normative justification for certain political

[14] Posner and Yoo (n 7); Helfer and Slaughter (n 8); Daniel Terris, Cesare Romano, and Leigh Swigart, *The International Judge: An Introduction to the Men and Women Who Decide the World's Cases* (Oxford University Press 2007); Erik Voeten, 'The Impartiality of International Judges: Evidence from the European Court of Human Rights' (2008) 102 The American Political Science Review 417; Paul Mahoney, 'The International Judiciary—Independence and Accountability' (2008) 7 The Law and Practice of International Courts and Tribunals 313; McIntyre and Crawford (n 3); Eyal Benvenisti and George W Downs, 'Prospects for the Increased Independence of International Tribunals' (2011) 12 German Law Journal 1057; Shany (n 5); Bogdandy and Venzke (n 2); Tom Ginsburg, 'Political Constraints on International Courts' in Cesare PR Romano, Karen J Alter, and Yuval Shany (eds), *The Oxford Handbook of International Adjudication* (Oxford University Press 2014); Dominik Zimmermann, *The Independence of International Courts: The Adherence of the International Judiciary to a Fundamental Value of the Administration of Justice* (Nomos 2014).

constraints on regional courts. Chapter 4 will examine institutions that might provide sources of constraints on regional courts based on the values that those institutions embody. Then Chapters 5 and 6 will focus on specific crucial constraining mechanisms: judicial selection and political override, which will be critically examined in light of the checks and balances principle.

Ultimately, the novel normative framework proposed by the book reconciles the needs, often in stark tension, for legitimate checks on judicial power and judicial independence. The book's legal analysis is informed by the political science and sociological literature on international courts and fills a significant gap in the existing literature, which largely remains descriptive and insufficiently attentive to the theoretical foundations of and normative justification for constraints on regional courts.

I am deeply grateful to my colleagues and friends for their intellectual generosity and illuminating insights, which were crucial in writing this book. My deepest thanks go to Armin von Bogdandy, Rafael Bustos Gisbert, Ana Carmona Contreras, Marc Carrillo, Monica Claes, Gabriel Doménech Pascual, Victor Ferreres Comella, Owen Fiss, Bradley Hayes, Marisa Iglesias, Nico Krisch, Mikael Madsen, Juan Antonio Mayoral, Luis Alejandro Ramírez, María Ángeles Rueda, Rosario Serra Cristóbal, Neus Torbisco Casals, Alejandro Saiz Arnaiz, Joan Solanes Mullor, Roberto Toniatti, and Bruno de Witte.

This book was completed in the peaceful and inspiring environment of Oxford University. I am grateful to Freya Baetens, Mathew Dyson, Louise Fawcett, Eduardo Posada, and Iyola Solanke for their invaluable help and warm hospitality. I would also like to thank the ICREA Academia program for providing the funding that made this project possible.

Finally, Jorge's love and support were the constant force that sustained me on this journey. This book is dedicated to our two joys, Joan and Caterina, who grew from wide-eyed infants into wonderfully curious and cheerful children as I wrote on these pages. It is also for my father, Joan Torres, in loving memory, whose inspiration will always remain with me.

PART 1

INTERNATIONAL JUDICIAL INDEPENDENCE

1

From Domestic to International Judicial Independence

1. Introduction

In a seminal 2003 article on the independence of the international judiciary, Mackenzie and Sands reaffirmed the importance of judicial independence for the credibility and legitimacy of international courts and tribunals while questioning whether it would be 'appropriate to treat the independence of the international judiciary as one would that of national judges', or if 'something qualitatively different about international law and courts' meant that 'different (lesser) standards should apply in the international setting'[1] For their part, Crawford and McIntyre have claimed that 'the increased intermingling of politics and law, and the fragility of the institutions, might seem to demand *more* rather than *less* stringent application of these principles [of independence and impartiality]'.[2] Should standards of judicial independence for international courts be less or more stringent than for national courts? Rather than approaching the matter as a question of degree, several considerations must be made for the specificities of the international setting in which international courts operate and the great diversity of international courts that exist.

While interest in and concern surrounding international judicial independence is a relatively new phenomenon, the amount of doctrinal analysis on the independence of domestic courts is overwhelming.[3] The abundant literature may be why applying a domestic frame of reference to the international sphere is so tempting. However, given the diverging institutional and political frameworks of domestic and international courts, the principles developed

[1] Ruth Mackenzie and Philippe Sands, 'International Courts and Tribunals and the Independence of the International Judge' (2003) 44 Harvard International Law Journal 271, 275.

[2] James Crawford and Joe McIntyre, 'The Independence and Impartiality of the "International Judiciary"' in Christopher Forsyth and Shimon Shetreet (eds), *The Culture of Judicial Independence* (Brill 2011) 205–06.

[3] Dating back to the eighteenth century, Charles Louis de Secondat de Montesquieu, *The Spirit of the Laws* (Anne M Cohler, Basia Carolyn Miller, and Harold Samuel Stone eds, Cambridge University Press 1989); Alexander Hamilton and others, *The Federalist Papers* (New American Library 1961).

Balancing International Judicial Independence. Aida Torres Pérez, Oxford University Press.
 DOI: 10.1093/oso/9780198852544.003.0001

at the domestic level cannot be automatically transposed to the international sphere.[4] However important it is to draw lessons from studies focusing on domestic courts,[5] we must also consider how differences between domestic and international judiciaries affect the conception and implementation of judicial independence at the respective level.[6]

As a normative ideal, independence requires the freedom for judges to deploy their adjudicative power without undue influence or pressure from outside actors that might distort the decision-making process. To borrow the wording of the *Burgh House Principles on the Independence of the International Judiciary*, 'The court and the judges shall exercise their functions free from direct or indirect interference or influence by any person or entity'.[7] Every definition of judicial independence shares, in fact, the common element of freedom from the preferences of other actors,[8] yet what judicial independence means and requires in the international sphere remains contested. There is little agreement on what judicial independence boils down to or how much of it is required, in particular when it comes to international courts. The goal of this chapter is to bring attention to some conceptual factors that could contribute to an analytical framework for international judicial independence.

First, since governments are the key actors at the international level, we will start by reflecting upon the relevance and limits of state consent for the prospects of international judicial independence. Second, it bears emphasizing that this work does not aim to formulate a single model of judicial independence that will fit all international and regional courts. The efforts at providing common standards of international judicial independence must take into consideration the great diversity of international courts without flattening the

[4] McIntyre and Crawford (n 2) 205–06.

[5] Stephen Burbank and Barry Friedman, *Judicial Independence at the Crossroads: An Interdisciplinary Approach* (SAGE Publications 2002); Vicki C Jackson, 'Judicial Independence: Structure, Context, Attitude' in Anja Seibert-Fohr (ed), *Judicial Independence in Transition*, vol 233 (Springer Berlin Heidelberg 2012); Shimon Shetreet and Christopher Forsyth (eds), 'The Culture of Judicial Independence: Conceptual Foundations and Practical Challenges' (2013) 76 The Modern Law Review 181.

[6] Paul Mahoney, 'The International Judiciary—Independence and Accountability' (2008) 7 The Law and Practice of International Courts and Tribunals 313; McIntyre and Crawford (n 2).

[7] Study Group of the International Law Association, 'Burgh House Principles on the Independence of the International Judiciary' (2005) art 1(1) <https://docs.pca-cpa.org/2020/04/ef1f0fb6-burgh-house-principles.pdf> accessed 19 March 2026.

[8] Lewis A Kornhauser, 'Is Judicial Independence a Useful Concept?' in Stephen Burbank and Barry Friedman, *Judicial Independence at the Crossroads: An Interdisciplinary Approach* (SAGE Publications 2002) 48; Erik Voeten, 'International Judicial Independence' in Jeffrey L Dunoff and Mark A Pollack (eds), *Interdisciplinary Perspectives on International Law and International Relations: The State of the Art* (Cambridge University Press 2012) 422; Dominik Zimmermann, *The Independence of International Courts: The Adherence of the International Judiciary to a Fundamental Value of the Administration of Justice* (Nomos 2014) 51–52.

differences. Third, we understand that judicial independence is not a value in and of itself[9] and that, as a principle, it is not absolute. We must always be attuned to the values that judicial independence is to serve at the international level and to the principles that may justify constraints on the action of international courts.

2. The Reach of State Consent

The judiciary is one of the three branches of power provided for in state liberal democratic constitutions, which usually establish the main principles of the judiciary's structure and composition. Within the constitutional structure, domestic courts enjoy compulsory jurisdiction and coercive powers to enforce their decisions. In stark contrast, the creation of international and regional courts, their jurisdiction, and the enforcement of their decisions are all conditioned upon state consent.[10] Hence, at least from an institutional perspective, international courts are largely dependent on the states that created them. Several authors, in view of that dependence, have demanded enhanced protection for the judicial independence of international courts. For instance, Mahoney has asserted that the dependence on state consent, 'when coupled with the fact that in the international arena the interplay between law and politics is necessarily more heightened than at national level, makes the position of the international judge more uncomfortable'.[11]

In what follows, we will take a closer look at the role of state consent to assess the prospects of international judicial independence.[12] State consent is relevant, if not determinant, in at least three different junctures: at the origin and design of international courts; when the terms for acceptance of compulsory jurisdiction are set; and for the enforcement and compliance of international courts' decisions. It will be argued that, despite the leading role still played by state governments in international politics, state consent for framing a conceptual understanding of international judicial independence is declining from its former pervasiveness.

[9] Stephen B Burbank and Barry Friedman, 'Reconsidering Judicial Independence' in Stephen Burbank and Barry Friedman, *Judicial Independence at the Crossroads: An Interdisciplinary Approach* (SAGE Publications 2002) 11.

[10] Crawford and McIntyre (n 2) 190–91.

[11] Mahoney (n 6) 317–18.

[12] This analysis stems from Aida Torres Pérez, 'In Nobody's Name: A Checks and Balances Approach to International Judicial Independence' in Hélène Ruiz Fabri and others (eds), *International Judicial Legitimacy* (Nomos Verlagsgesellschaft mbH & Co KG 2020) 49–54.

2.1. The origin and design of international courts

The states party to international treaties creating international and regional courts determine their design. Expecting those states to create and design independent international courts poses a puzzling problem from the perspective of state sovereignty that has not escaped scholarly attention.[13] Helfer and Slaughter have reasoned that states favour independent tribunals over dependent ones when the problems they face require multilateral, as opposed to bilateral cooperation, which, for instance, would be the case when treaties create rights for private parties.[14] Yet Helfer and Slaughter also pointed out a second level of design decisions where states are able to set up control mechanisms that give them some influence over the courts.[15] The authors advanced a typology of mechanisms that distinguishes between formal and political mechanisms for state control (*ex ante* and *ex post*) and various constraints coming from the global community, more loosely identified.[16] Helfer and Slaughter compellingly showed how creating independent international courts, particularly in multilateral regimes, together with mechanisms to ensure a measure of control, can be in the states' interests. This is not to dismiss outright the prospects for judicial independence at the international level, but rather to understand it as necessarily constrained.

Thus, some forms of influence over the design of international courts by state governments might be retained, both the appointment of judges and the financing of the court being examples. Nonetheless, the practical impact of these avenues of influence might be overestimated, given the difficulty or cost of activating them, especially those that require the cooperation of other states, entail reputational costs, or might generate opposition from other states or other international or domestic actors.[17] Moreover, in the end, their effectiveness depends on contextual factors. For instance, governments may retain the power to appoint judges, but in those courts in which the number of judges is less than the number of states, compromises must be reached. And while states might seek to amend the corresponding treaty to oppose a judgment they

[13] Andrew Moravcsik, 'The Origins of Human Rights Regimes: Democratic Delegation in Postwar Europe' (2000) 54 International Organization 217, 219; Laurence Helfer and AM Slaughter, 'Why States Create International Tribunals: A Response to Professors Posner and Yoo' (2005) 93 California Law Review 899, 33.

[14] Helfer and Slaughter (n 13) 41–42.

[15] ibid 44.

[16] ibid 45–46.

[17] ibid 44.

dislike, success will usually require unanimous backing of all the parties, compounding the difficulty.

2.2. Compulsory jurisdiction

One of the primary differences between the national and international judiciary is compulsory jurisdiction. While the jurisdiction of domestic courts is compulsory, in that a lawsuit can be filed without the consent of the defendant, the jurisdiction of international courts is conditioned upon state consent.[18] Nonetheless, as Romano argued, a paradigm shift from consensual to compulsory jurisdiction has begun. While the principle of state consent still stands, its practical significance has been reduced: 'The expression of consent has become so removed in time and substance from the exercise of jurisdiction that one may question whether consent continues to serve a significant function in the international order.'[19] At present, acceptance of several of these courts' jurisdiction is a prerequisite for entry to the corresponding international organization or legal regime, thus all state parties are subject to the compulsory jurisdiction of the respective court, which include the European Court of Human Rights (ECtHR),[20] the Appellate Body of the World Trade Organization (WTO AB), the Court of Justice of the European Union (CJEU), the Andean Tribunal of Justice (ATJ), and the Caribbean Court of Justice (CCJ), among others.[21]

In other cases, states may wait until after becoming parties to an international organization to decide whether to accept the jurisdiction of the corresponding court through an additional protocol or declaration. This is the case, for instance, of the Inter-American Court of Human Rights (IACtHR), although most of the states who ratified the Inter-American Convention on Human Rights (IACHR) accepted the jurisdiction of the Court.[22] As for the

[18] Cesare PR Romano, 'The Shift from the Consensual to the Compulsory Paradigm in International Adjudication: Elements for a Theory of Consent' (2007) 39 New York University Journal of International Law & Politics 791, 792.

[19] ibid 795.

[20] At first, the jurisdiction of the ECtHR and the authorization to file individual complaints before the Commission were dependent on state consent. Protocol 11, which entered into force in 1998, merged the Commission and the Court and both made the jurisdiction of the Court compulsory and allowed individual complaints (Protocol No. 11 to the Convention for the Protection of Human Rights and Fundamental Freedoms, restructuring the control machinery established thereby 1994).

[21] Karen J Alter, *The New Terrain of International Law: Courts, Politics, Rights* (Princeton University Press 2014) 84.

[22] Out of twenty-five states that ratified the convention, only four did not accept the jurisdiction of the court: Dominica, Grenada, Jamaica, and Trinidad and Tobago. In addition, Venezuela denounced the Convention in September 2012 and formally withdrew from it one year later.

African Court on Human and Peoples' Rights (ACtHPR), its jurisdiction has only been accepted by slightly more than half of the member states, and very few (only eight) have accepted access to the court for NGOs and individuals.[23]

A trend from 'old-style' international courts—international courts that lack compulsory jurisdiction where access is limited to the States' parties—to the 'new-style' international courts, whose compulsory jurisdiction is far-reaching and where access by non-state actors is possible, has been documented by Alter.[24] The trend has come to the point where, currently, most international courts possess compulsory jurisdiction.[25]

With regard to domestic courts, Shapiro has drawn a link between judicial independence and the transition from arbitration to adjudication.[26] According to his argument, the arbitration model is premised upon the consent of the parties, which have a say in the choice of the law applied and the arbitrators who settle the dispute. The legitimacy of these tribunals is seen as stemming directly from the disputing parties' consent. As societies became more complex, Shapiro observes a shift from arbitration to adjudication, a process through which 'law and office' is substituted for consent. The parties lost their say in the choice of forum since both the law and the judge were provided by the state. It is largely because of this shift that institutional judicial independence became central to the legal regime's legitimacy.

There has also been a shift to an extent at the international level from arbitration to adjudication (or from consent to 'law and office') as a consequence of the creation of permanent courts with compulsory jurisdiction within multilateral regimes, such as the ECtHR, the CJEU, or the International Criminal Court (ICC). Moreover, individuals have gained access to several international courts, whose jurisdiction is therefore no longer limited to disputes between states. The independence of those international and regional courts thus becomes crucial for their claim to legitimate authority. As international courts evolve and mature institutionally, clarifying the applicable notion of judicial independence becomes increasingly central for their claim to legitimate authority and their perceived legitimacy.[27]

[23] Michael Rask Madsen, Pola Cebulak, and Micha Wiebusch, 'Backlash Against International Courts: Explaining the Forms and Patterns of Resistance to International Courts' (2018) 14 International Journal of Law in Context 197, 209.

[24] Alter (n 21) 81–85.

[25] Cesare Romano, Karen J Alter, and Yuval Shany, 'Illustrations: A Reader's Guide' in Cesare Romano, Karen J Alter, and Shany Y (eds), *The Oxford Handbook of International Adjudication* (Oxford University Press 2014).

[26] Martin M Shapiro, *Courts: A Comparative and Political Analysis* (University of Chicago Press 1981).

[27] ibid; Andreas Follesdal, 'The Legitimacy Deficits of the Human Rights Judiciary: Elements and Implications of a Normative Theory' (2013) 14 Theoretical Inquiries in Law 339; Daniel Bodansky,

2.3. Enforcement and compliance

Because international courts do not enjoy coercive powers to enforce their decisions, international courts depend on states for compliance.[28] The risk of backlash against or resistance to their decisions, which might take a variety of forms, such as non-compliance, treaty or legislative override, or even withdrawal from the regime, might constrain the action of international courts.[29]

Nonetheless, sometimes the enforceability difference between the domestic and the international judiciary is overstated. As such, domestic courts require collaboration from the executive branch to coercively enforce judgments. Shimon Shetreet is one scholar who has observed with concern the pre-emption of the enforcement of judicial decisions by the executive at the national level. Despite the executive's duty to enforce court decisions, in practice, it does not always comply with that expectation. Shetreet also notes that the failure to ensure compliance is not always intentional, and that practical or material limits for expeditious enforcement of judgments also exist.[30]

At the international level, although international courts' judgments are binding, international courts do not possess the means to coercively compel state authorities to comply with them or to directly annul legislation or overturn domestic court decisions. Nonetheless, several mechanisms enable national and international authorities to foster the enforcement of international courts' judgments. At the international level, supervisory bodies can improve compliance with court decisions through diplomatic and other means, such as the Committee of Ministers within the Council of Europe.[31] Moreover,

'Legitimacy in International Law and International Relations' in Jeffrey L Dunoff and Mark A Pollack (eds), *Interdisciplinary Perspectives on International Law and International Relations* (1st edn, Cambridge University Press 2012).

[28] Kanstantsin Dzehtsiarou and Donal K Coffey, 'Legitimacy and Independence of International Tribunals: An Analysis of the European Court of Human Rights' (2014) 37 Hastings International & Comparative Law Review 271, 279.

[29] Tom Ginsburg, 'Political Constraints on International Courts' in Cesare PR Romano, Karen J Alter, and Yuval Shany (eds), *The Oxford Handbook of International Adjudication* (Oxford University Press 2014); Clifford J Carrubba, Mathew Gabel, and Charles Hankla, 'Judicial Behavior Under Political Constraints: Evidence from the European Court of Justice' (2008) 102 American Political Science Review 435; Alec Stone Sweet and Thomas L Brunell, 'The European Court of Justice, State Noncompliance, and the Politics of Override' (2012) 106 American Political Science Review 204; Madsen, Cebulak, and Wiebusch (n 23).

[30] Shimon Shetreet, 'The Significance of the Independence of the Judiciary Creating a Culture of Judicial Independence: The Practical Challenge and the Conceptual and Constitutional Infrastructure' in Shimon Shetreet and Christopher Forsyth (eds), *The Culture of Judicial Independence* (Brill | Nijhoff 2012) 55–56.

[31] Protocol 14 has enhanced the role of the Committee of Ministers in that regard by providing for an action before the ECtHR in case of non-compliance (Article 46 ECHR) (Protocol no. 14 to the

international courts themselves sometimes oversee the enforcement of the respective judgments, the IACtHR being the main example.[32]

More and more, enforcement is also secured through the collaboration of various state authorities, such as domestic courts. The petition for preliminary reference in the European Union, for instance, has given the CJEU a means to foster the enforcement of its judgments through the action of state courts. National courts have also played relevant roles in other contexts for the enforcement or effectiveness of international court rulings, in particular involving the ECtHR.[33]

On balance, the relevance of state consent varies across international courts, and it is sometimes overestimated, while declining over time. As will be argued, the predominance of state governments in the international sphere requires, rather than isolation or higher standards of judicial independence, mechanisms to shield international courts from direct governmental pressure or control. At the same time, it will be argued that certain constraining mechanisms in the hands of state governments might be justified on normative grounds, but doing so would require identifying justificatory principles beyond sheer state sovereignty.

3. Between Common Standards and Institutional Diversity

The purpose of this work is not to argue for a single model of judicial independence that will fit all international courts, just as no single model for judicial independence exists at the domestic level. The principle of judicial independence is key in any well-functioning democracy, but the ways in which judicial independence is understood and implemented vary widely across countries and legal cultures. Beyond conceptual vagueness, the institutional arrangements to ensure judicial independence at the national level are diverse. Indeed, the way to conceive of judicial independence is very much linked to the domestic legal and political culture.[34] For instance, in terms of judicial selection,

convention for the protection of human rights and fundamental freedoms, amending the control system of the convention 2004).

[32] Alexandra Huneeus, 'Courts Resisting Courts: Lessons from the Inter-American Court's Struggle to Enforce Human Rights' (2011) 44 Cornell International Law Journal 493, 496.

[33] André Nollkaemper, 'Conversations Among Courts: Domestic and International Adjudicators' in Cesare PR Romano, Karen J Alter, and Yuval Shany (eds), *The Oxford Handbook of International Adjudication* (Oxford University Press 2014), regarding the role of national courts in implementing ICs' judgments. To the contrary, in the context of the IACtHR, see Huneeus (n 32).

[34] Shetreet (n 30).

there is a classic divide between the civil-continental bureaucratic model and the common law professional model. At the same time, neither of those models exists in pure form, and both have, as they evolve, been incorporating elements of the other. Moreover, identical legal arrangements might operate differently according to the broader sociopolitical and legal context.[35] For that reason, formulating the structural arrangements apt to adequately safeguard judicial independence in the abstract is difficult.

At the same time, the various features of the judicial career, such as selection, tenure, salaries, disciplinary regime, or administrative autonomy, among others, interact in such a way that in assessing judicial independence, focusing on individual features in isolation is insufficient.[36] For instance, a political appointment, which seems to compromise judicial independence, might be tempered by giving judges life tenure. Thus, the analysis of judicial independence demands a holistic and contextual approach.

In addition, the differing functions performed by certain courts within the same country might pose specific challenges for the notion of judicial independence, and, accordingly, diverse institutional arrangements might be put in place. For instance, constitutional courts, where they exist, perform the function of reviewing the constitutionality of legislation, and might also be vested with the function of solving disputes regarding the territorial allocation of powers and protecting fundamental rights. Given the politically charged issues under their jurisdiction, their independence from other political bodies becomes a matter of concern. Often the mechanism for constitutional judges' appointment differs from the selection of judges for the ordinary courts. In civil law countries, where ordinary judges tend to be recruited through merit-based bureaucratic methods, constitutional court judges are appointed by political bodies, such as parliament and government. While political appointment might undermine the perception of the court's independence, that might be justified in terms of the added democratic accountability that results, given the role that constitutional courts play in monitoring legislation.[37]

In any event, Seibert-Fohr, referring to the findings of a transnational research project on judicial independence, still argued that shared normative denominators regarding judicial independence do exist and identified common concerns and strategies which have become transnational, variations

[35] Jackson (n 5) 60.
[36] Jackson (n 5).
[37] Víctor Ferreres Comella, *Constitutional Courts and Democratic Values: A European Perspective* (Yale University Press 2009).

in implementation notwithstanding.[38] Indeed, several international organizations and associations have developed common standards for judicial independence, which have in turn made significant contributions to domestic rules.[39] Among these international sources, one finds the *New Delhi Minimum Standards on Judicial Independence*,[40] adopted by the International Bar Association in 1982; the *Montréal Universal Declaration on the Independence of Justice*,[41] adopted at the World Conference on the Independence of Justice in 1983; and the *UN Basic Principles of Judicial Independence*,[42] endorsed by the General Assembly in 1985. At the turn of the twenty-first century, the *Bangalore Principles of Judicial Conduct*[43] were enacted (2002). Then there is the *Mt. Scopus International Standards on Judicial Independence*,[44] approved by the International Association of Judicial Independence and World Peace in 2008 and revised in 2015. In addition, international human rights organizations, such as the Council of Europe, have made considerable efforts to formulate common standards, often through soft law instruments,[45] but also through the jurisprudence of the respective international or regional court. Moreover, in the context of what some call the rule of law backsliding crisis in Europe, many cases concerning judicial independence have reached the ECtHR and the CJEU,[46] the analysis of which falls outside the purposes of our analysis here.

While the independence of international courts has received less attention, efforts have also been made to identify common standards of judicial independence applicable to the international sphere. In fact, the *Montréal Universal Declaration on the Independence of Justice* included a first section on

[38] Anja Seibert-Fohr, 'Judicial Independence—The Normativity of an Evolving Transnational Principle' in Anja Seibert-Fohr (ed), *Judicial Independence in Transition*, vol 233 (Springer Berlin Heidelberg 2012) 1279–81, held that 'conceptualizing judicial independence as a functional principle which provides for an obligation of result rather than of means helps to identify it as an international norm which nevertheless gives room for diverse and context-specific implementation'.

[39] Shimon Shetreet, 'The Normative Cycle of Shaping Judicial Independence in Domestic and International Law: The Mutual Impact of National and International Jurisprudence and Contemporary Practical and Conceptual Challenges' (2009) 10 Chicago Journal of International Law 275, 275–76.

[40] International Bar Association, 'New Delhi Minimum Standards on Judicial Independence' (1982) <https://www.ibanet.org/MediaHandler?id=bb019013-52b1-427c-ad25-a6409b49fe29>.

[41] International Association of Judges, 'Montréal Universal Declaration on the Independence of Justice' (1983) <https://www.icj.org/wp-content/uploads/2016/02/Montreal-Declaration.pdf>.

[42] United Nations, 'UN Basic Principles on the Independence of the Judiciary' (1985) <https://www.ohchr.org/en/instruments-mechanisms/instruments/basic-principles-independence-judiciary>.

[43] Judicial Integrity Group, 'Bangalore Principles of Judicial Conduct' (2002) <https://www.unodc.org/pdf/crime/corruption/judicial_group/Bangalore_principles.pdf>.

[44] International Association of Judicial Independence and World Peace, 'Mt. Scopus Revised International Standards of Judicial Independence' (2008) <https://www.icj.org/wp-content/uploads/2016/02/Mt-Scopus-Standards.pdf>.

[45] Rafael Bustos Gisbert, 'La Influencia de Los Textos No Vinculantes Del Consejo de Europa Sobre Independencia Judicial En El TEDH y En La UE' [2021] Teoría y realidad constitucional 161.

[46] Rafael Bustos Gisbert, *Independencia judicial e integración Europea* (1ª edición, Tirant lo Blanch 2022).

the independence of international judges. In turn, the *Burgh House Principles on the Independence of the International Judiciary*[47] focused exclusively on the independence of international courts. The *Burg House Principles* were issued by the Study Group on the Practice and Procedure of International Courts and Tribunals of the International Law Association (ILA),[48] in collaboration with the Project on International Courts and Tribunals.[49] In 2015, those minimum standards for the independence of the international judiciary were incorporated, with minor amendments, into the *Mt. Scopus Revised International Standards on Judicial Independence*.[50]

The Preamble of the *Burgh House Principles* pointed out that each international court has its own characteristics and functions.[51] Indeed, in the international arena, the diversity of adjudicatory bodies, from arbitral panels to courts with compulsory jurisdiction, is great. In our query about international judicial independence, we therefore ought to be clear about the set of bodies under analysis. Following the definition by Romano, international courts must meet five criteria. International courts must be permanent, have been established by an international legal instrument, resort to international law in deciding the cases submitted to them, follow predetermined rules of procedure, and the outcome must be legally binding.[52] As a consequence, arbitral bodies are not included under the definition of international courts. This is not to mean that independence is not relevant in arbitration, but it might need to be understood differently, focusing instead on the lack of conflicts of interest, rather than on institutional considerations. Indeed, the main difference between international courts and international arbitral bodies is that arbitrators are selected and nominated by the parties to the dispute, and only after the dispute arises.[53]

[47] Study Group of the International Law Association (n 7).

[48] This Study Group was in place between 2002 and 2010. The Co-Chairs were Philippe Sands, Professor of Law, University College London; and Campbell McLachlan, Professor, Deputy Dean, School of Law, Victoria University of Wellington (https://www.ila-hq.org/en/study-groups/practice-and-procedure-of-international-tribunals).

[49] The Project on International Courts and Tribunals was co-directed by Philippe Sands and Cesare Romano (https://www.ucl.ac.uk/international-courts/).

[50] International Association of Judicial Independence and World Peace (n 44), under Part B.

[51] Mackenzie and Sands (n 1) 285, suggested that despite their diversity, 'it is both possible and desirable to identify certain common core guidelines for judicial independence applicable to all international judges, regardless of the tribunal on which they sit'.

[52] Cesare PR Romano, 'The Proliferation of International Judicial Bodies: The Pieces of the Puzzle' (1999) 31 New York University Journal of International Law & Politics 709.

[53] Cesare PR Romano, Karen J Alter, and Yuval Shany, 'Mapping International Adjudicative Bodies, the Issues, and Players' in Karen J Alter, Yuval Shany, and Cesare PR Romano (eds), *The Oxford Handbook of International Adjudication* (Oxford University Press 2014) 10; Victor Ferreres Comella, *The Constitution of Arbitration* (Cambridge University Press 2022) 54–58.

Regarding international judicial bodies, there is an important distinction in terms of standing. One can distinguish between courts for disputes arising between sovereign states and those other courts that enable individual access, including human rights courts, courts of regional economic/political integration, international criminal courts, and international administrative tribunals. Over time, individuals and other non-state parties have gained access to international and regional courts, and at present inter-state courts, such as the International Court of Justice (ICJ) and the WTO AB, are in the minority.[54] International adjudication has been removed from the exclusive domain of states, and hence the audiences and demands for judicial independence vary. Indeed, access to international courts is a relevant factor in determining the optimal degree of independence and the corresponding mechanisms to safeguard judicial independence.

At the same time, the mandates of international courts vary greatly, from maintaining world peace and security, protecting human rights, securing regimes of economic and political integration, or the demand for criminal responsibility. Moreover, international courts are also extremely diverse in terms of the functions performed.[55] The main function of international courts can be described as the application of the law to concrete cases.[56] As several authors have emphasized, however, the functions of international courts have diversified to the point that they are no longer limited to dispute settlement. In that regard, von Bogdandy and Venzke also include among the international courts' functions the stabilization of normative expectations, law-making, control, and legitimation of public authority exercised mainly at the national level but also internationally.[57] Shany refers to international norm advancement and the maintenance of cooperative international arrangements,[58] while Alter includes administrative review, law enforcement, and constitutional review.[59] Any single court, moreover, might fulfil a plurality of those functions. We can, however, basically distinguish three main types of functions: dispute settlement, maintaining cooperative regimes, and reviewing the exercise of (national and international) public authority. In order to exercise those functions, international courts need the capacity to adjudicate free from interference by

[54] ibid 12; Yuval Shany, 'No Longer a Weak Department of Power? Reflections on the Emergence of a New International Judiciary' (2009) 20 European Journal of International Law 73, 80.

[55] Romano, Alter, and Shany (n 53) 12–14.

[56] Armin von Bogdandy and Ingo Venzke, *In Whose Name? A Public Law Theory of International Adjudication* (Oxford University Press 2016) 67.

[57] ibid 9–17.

[58] Shany (n 54) 82–83.

[59] Alter (n 21).

the parties, (public and private) external actors, and the authorities they are expected to supervise.

In the end, the effort to establish common standards of judicial independence is certainly welcome. The elaboration of those standards fuels further debate on international judicial independence and promotes the development of a culture of judicial independence in the international sphere. At the same time, the diversity of international and regional courts needs to be taken into consideration when crafting and assessing the appropriate mechanisms for each. In that regard, independence, as a concept, is not monolithic,[60] but rather one of degree, and the desirable level of independence, as well as the adequate mechanisms to safeguard it, may well vary across courts. Besides, the same structural arrangements might work differently in different settings and political contexts. In any event, as a consequence of the growing institutionalization of international courts, individual access, and the performance of quasi-constitutional functions, judicial independence is becoming increasingly crucial for the claim to legitimate authority.

Taking into consideration the diversity and number of international courts, the analysis in this book will focus on selected courts. To avoid the risk of overgeneralization and to establish an adequate foundation for comparison, courts have been selected according to three main criteria: territorial scope, access, and mandate. The selection therefore includes regional permanent courts with jurisdiction over individuals, as opposed to courts whose jurisdiction is limited to inter-state disputes, with the main mandate of protecting human rights and fostering regional economic integration in Europe and America (see Table 1.1). Within each group, the selection has considered the salience and activity of the court, judged in terms of the average rulings on the merits and scope.[61]

Therefore, the human rights courts under analysis include the ECtHR and the IACtHR. The ECtHR was established by the European Convention on Human Rights (ECHR), signed in Rome in 1950, within the Council of Europe. The Council of Europe emerged after the end of World War II in 1949 with the main goal to promote democracy, human rights, and the rule of law across Europe. The ECHR entered into force in 1953, and the ECtHR held its first session in 1959. At present, the ECHR includes forty-six member states, after expelling Russia because of the invasion of Ukraïne. The jurisdiction of the ECtHR is compulsory for all state parties to the Convention.

[60] Burbank and Friedman (n 9) 16.
[61] Following Romano, Alter, and Shany (n 53).

The IACtHR was established by the Inter-American Convention on Human Rights signed in San José (Costa Rica) in 1969 under the umbrella of the Organization of American States (OAS).[62] Not until 1978 did the Convention enter into force, when it was ratified by eleven states.[63] Over time, out of the thirty-five member states of the OAS, twenty-five ratified the Convention.[64] The IACtHR began to function in 1979.[65] Most of those states that ratified the Convention also accepted the jurisdiction of the Court.[66]

In parallel, the selection includes the main courts for regional integration in Europe and America: the CJEU and the ATJ. The CJEU belongs to the European Union, which emerged in the fifties on the grounds of the foundational Treaties of the European Economic Community, the Coal and Steel Community, and the European Community of Atomic Energy. Currently, the EU is composed of twenty-seven member states, after the United Kingdom left the EU. The CJEU was established in 1952.

At present, the CJEU must be seen as the most successful regional integration court.[67] A wide array of courts of regional economic and/or political integration were created after the end of the Cold War, most of which tended to replicate the model of the CJEU, as opposed to other courts that followed the model of the WTO AB.[68] The ATJ explicitly modeled its design on the CJEU and has become one of the most active regional courts.[69] The Andean Community is a regional economic integration organization, created pursuant to the Cartagena Agreement of 26 May 1969, to promote regional economic development. At present, it includes four member states. The ATJ was created in 1979 and began operating in 1984.

[62] Sergio García Ramírez, 'Raíz, Actualidad y Perspectivas de La Jurisdicción Interamericana de Derechos Humanos' (2009) 1 Cuestiones constitucionales (Universidad Nacional Autónoma de México. Instituto de Investigaciones Jurídicas) 149.

[63] Colombia, Costa Rica, Ecuador, El Salvador, Grenada, Guatemala, Haiti, Honduras, Panama, Republica Dominicana, and Venezuela.

[64] Argentina, Barbados, Bolivia, Brazil, Chile, Colombia, Costa Rica, Dominican Republic, Ecuador, El Salvador, Grenada, Guatemala, Haití, Honduras, Jamaica, Mexico, Nicaragua, Panama, Paraguay, Peru, Suriname, Trinidad and Tobago, Uruguay, and Venezuela. Trinidad and Tobago and Venezuela denounced the Convention in 1988 and 2012 respectively. http://www.corteidh.or.cr/denuncias_consultas.cfm.

[65] Thomas Buergenthal, 'Recordando los inicios de la Corte Interamericana de Derechos Humanos' (2004) 39 Revista IIDH 11, very graphically, describes the difficulties faced by the Court at the beginning of its existence.

[66] Twenty states have recognized the jurisdiction of the Court: Argentina, Barbados, Bolivia, Brazil, Chile, Colombia, Costa Rica, Dominican Republic, Ecuador, El Salvador, Guatemala, Haití, Honduras, Mexico, Nicaragua, Panamá, Paraguay, Peru, Suriname, and Uruguay.

[67] In this work, the CJEU will be included within the group of international regional courts, although the EU is not a classic international organization, meaning the corresponding court is better conceived as a supranational court.

[68] Alter (n 21).

[69] Karen J Alter and Laurence R Helfer, 'Nature or Nurture? Judicial Lawmaking in the European Court of Justice and the Andean Tribunal of Justice' (2010) 64 International Organization 563.

Table 1.1 Selected regional courts under analysis

Regional courts \ Timeline	1950–69	1970–89
Human rights	European Court of Human Rights (ECtHR)	Inter-American Court of Human Rights (IACtHR)
Economic and political integration	Court of Justice of the European Union (CJEU)	Andean Tribunal of Justice (ATJ)

The goals of a comparative approach are developing a better understanding of the selected regional courts and the mechanisms that enhance or constrain independence, as well as assessing normatively preferable best practices.[70] The overall aim is better understanding the role of the diverse mechanisms and actors across courts so as to identify commonalities and differences of design and outcome. The comparative analysis offers an opportunity for greater insight into the functioning of the diverse mechanisms in place that in turn allows us to advance proposals for innovation.

Several scholars have developed comparative quantitative analyses examining the degree of independence of a significant number of domestic courts. Feld and Voigt[71] measured the independence of the highest courts of 57 countries, and the study was subsequently expanded to 104.[72] With regard to international courts, Squatrito developed a study mapping the formal independence, understood as the institutional safeguards for judicial independence, of twenty-four international courts.[73] There is also a more recent study on the selection and appointment of international courts from a political science perspective.[74] While these studies offer very valuable insights, our research employs a qualitative approach, since the aim is to assess the independence and power constraints on a relatively small number of courts. Furthermore,

[70] Vicki C Jackson 'Comparative Constitutional Law: Methodologies', in Michel Rosenfeld and András Sajó (eds) *The Oxford Handbook of Comparative Constitutional Law* (Oxford University Press 2012).

[71] Lars P Feld and Stefan Voigt, 'Economic Growth and Judicial Independence: Cross-Country Evidence Using a New Set of Indicators' (2003) 19 European Journal of Political Economy 497.

[72] Stefan Voigt, Jerg Gutmann, and Lars P Feld, 'Economic Growth and Judicial Independence, a Dozen Years on: Cross-Country Evidence Using an Updated Set of Indicators' CESifo Working Paper 5010 (2014) <https://www.ifo.de/DocDL/cesifo1_wp5010.pdf> accessed 19 March 2026; James Melton and Tom Ginsburg, 'Does De Jure Judicial Independence Really Matter?: A Reevaluation of Explanations for Judicial Independence' (2014) 2 Journal of Law and Courts 187.

[73] Theresa Squatrito, 'Conceptualizing, Measuring and Mapping the Formal Judicial Independence of International Courts' [2018] SSRN Electronic Journal.

[74] Olof Larsson and others, 'Selection and Appointment in International Adjudication: Insights from Political Science' (2023) 14 Journal of International Dispute Settlement 134.

statistical generalization is not conducive to understanding the impact of several actors and variables upon judicial independence in selected cases because of the diversity of regional courts. Also, not all factors necessarily count equally for assessing the prospects and degree of judicial independence.[75] The comparative analysis must be cautious and attentive to the institutional and political settings in which the regional courts operate. Indeed, qualitative approaches are characterized by their sensitivity to the heterogeneity and particularity of individual cases.[76]

4. The Principle of Judicial Independence as Instrumental and Relative

Judicial independence is not to be conceived as an end in itself, but rather as a means to an end.[77] If this is true, what ends does it serve in the international sphere? It is also important to avoid conceiving the principle of judicial independence in absolute terms, since this is neither feasible nor desirable. Absolutely unconstrained decision-making is a fallacy. There are multiple sources of constraints on regional courts. At the same time, some constraints might be necessary to prevent regional courts from overstepping their powers. Under what principles are constraints on courts justified?

4.1. The aims of international judicial independence

Since judicial independence is not a value in itself, we need to reflect upon the aims that it serves in the international sphere. First, independence is a necessary but insufficient condition for the legitimacy of the regional courts' adjudicative power.[78] Adjudication involves application of the law to the resolution of cases brought before the court following an established procedure. In that process, for the law to prevail, judges ought to be free from undue pressures or influences

[75] James Mahoney, Gary Goertz, and W Paul Vogt, 'A Tale of Two Cultures: Contrasting Quantitative and Qualitative Research', *Selecting Research Methods*, vol 4 (SAGE Publications 2008).
[76] Charles C Ragin and Charles C Ragin, *The Comparative Method: Moving Beyond Qualitative and Quantitative Strategies.* (First paperback edition, University of California Press 1989).
[77] ibid 11.
[78] Marc Bühlmann and Ruth Kunz, 'Confidence in the Judiciary: Comparing the Independence and Legitimacy of Judicial Systems' (2011) 34 West European Politics 317; Crawford and McIntyre (n 2); Harlan Grant Cohen and others, 'Legitimacy and International Courts—A Framework' in Nienke Grossman and others (eds), *Legitimacy and International Courts* (1st edn, Cambridge University Press 2018).

coming from external actors. In the context of the growing institutionalization of regional courts, judicial independence is central for the claim to legitimate authority.

The notion of legitimacy may be conceived from a normative and sociological perspective.[79] In a normative sense, legitimacy refers to the conditions or reasons that justify the claim of authoritativeness. Normative legitimacy aims to determine why the law or a particular institution should be obeyed. In a descriptive or sociological sense, following Weber,[80] legitimacy implies that a legal system or institution is perceived as legitimately binding by those under its jurisdiction. In this sense, legitimacy, as an empirical fact, solely reflects an attitude held by individuals.[81] The normative and sociological notions of legitimacy are not unrelated, since an institution that fulfils the conditions for normative legitimacy will improve the chances that it will enjoy social legitimacy.[82] This work will mainly focus on independence as a necessary condition for (normative) legitimacy, rather than inquiring into the dynamics governing the perceptions among the broader public of the legitimacy and independence of regional courts. Still, in order to gain support from key constituencies, courts not only need to meet normative strictures of independence; they must also be perceived as independent since, according to the oft-quoted aphorism, '[n]ot only must Justice be done; it must also be seen to be done'. In addition, both normative and sociological legitimacy are relevant for the authority of international courts and may well enhance compliance and effectiveness.

Second, judicial independence is inextricably linked to impartiality, for the very aim of judicial independence is promoting conditions for impartial decision-making. From this perspective, the goal of independence is to facilitate impartiality.[83] While the notions of independence and impartiality

[79] Daniel Bodansky, 'The Legitimacy of International Governance: A Coming Challenge for International Environmental Law?' (1999) 93 American Journal of International Law 596; Allen Buchanan and Robert O Keohane, 'The Legitimacy of Global Governance Institutions' (2006) 20 Ethics & International Affairs 405; Freya Baetens, 'Unseen Actors in International Courts and Tribunals: Challenging the Legitimacy of International Adjudication', in Freya Baetens (ed), *Legitimacy of Unseen Actors in International Adjudication* (Cambridge University Press 2019).

[80] Max Weber, *Economy and Society* (University of California Press 1968).

[81] Tom R Tyler, 'Psychological Perspectives on Legitimacy and Legitimation' (2006) 57 Annual Review of Psychology 375; Buchanan and Keohane (n 79).

[82] Follesdal (n 27); Mikael Rask Madsen, 'Sociological Approaches to International Courts', *The Oxford Handbook of International Adjudication* (Oxford University Press 2014); Bodansky (n 27).

[83] Mauro Cappelletti, '"Who Watches the Watchmen?" A Comparative Study on Judicial Responsibility' (1983) 31(1) The American Journal of Comparative Law 1, 15–16: 'independence, far from being an end in itself, is but an instrumental value, the goal of which is to safeguard another value-connected for sure, but different and much more "ultimate": the impartiality of the judge'; Eduardo Oteiza, 'El deber de respetar la independencia judicial. Esfuerzos y ambigüedades de los Estados en el plano internacional' in Jordi Nieva Fenoll and Eduardo Oteiza (eds), *La independencia judicial: un*

are certainly related and are sometimes used interchangeably, there is an important distinction that must be made.[84] Impartiality encapsulates the notion of the judge as a neutral third party. It is related to the specific case at hand and understood as the lack of interest or bias with regard to the parties or the object of the case.[85] Independence, for its part, refers to a set of institutional and other arrangements designed to ensure that judges take decisions free from undue influence or pressure from external actors.[86] The lack of a regional court's independence due to subordination to or cooptation by certain state governments may well undermine that regional court's impartiality when deciding cases in which those states are parties. It also bears remembering that independence does not in and of itself ensure impartiality, since a judge might be independent, meaning free from undue influence from external actors, but still be partial to her own personal interests, preferences, or biases.

Third, at the domestic level, judicial independence is paramount to the rule of law.[87] The rule of law is conceptually rooted in the emergence of liberal constitutionalism which fundamentally requires the submission of all public authorities and citizens to the law. Following Lord Bingham,[88] the core of the existing doctrine of the rule of law is that all public and private persons should be bound by and entitled to the benefit of laws publicly and prospectively issued and publicly administered by the courts. Although the exact content of the principles and standards stemming from the rule of law varies across national-constitutional legal systems, one of their common features is some guarantee of access to justice before independent and impartial courts.[89] For the rule of law to prevail, a legal system requires courts that will enforce that law and review the action of the public authorities solely against the law, without undue pressure or influence from the executive or other public or private actors. The end goal of judicial independence is upholding the rule of law.

In the international sphere, the very existence and the definition of some 'international rule of law' are contested. While some deny the existence of an international rule of law,[90] others argue that invoking the notion has merit, but

constante asedio (Marcial Pons 2019) 188; Pasquale Pasquino, 'Prolegomena to a Theory of Judicial Power' (2003) 2 The Law and Practice of International Courts and Tribunals 11.

[84] Pasquino (n 83).

[85] Crawford and McIntyre (n 2); Yuval Shany, *Assessing the Effectiveness of International Courts* (Oxford University Press 2014) 97–101.

[86] Voeten (n 8).

[87] Theodor Meron, 'Judicial Independence and Impartiality in International Criminal Tribunals' (2005) 99 American Journal of International Law 359.

[88] Lord Bingham, 'The Rule of Law' (2007) 66 The Cambridge Law Journal 67.

[89] European Commission for Democracy Through Law (Venice Commission), 'Report on the Rule of Law' (2011) <https://rm.coe.int/1680700a61>.

[90] Simon Chesterman, 'An International Rule of Law?' (2008) 56 The American Journal of Comparative Law 331.

only as long as an automatic transposition of the national understanding of the rule of law is avoided.[91] However rich, the conceptual debate on the international rule of law exceeds the scope of this work. Notwithstanding, a distinction can usually be made between a thin understanding of the international rule of law—a set of international rules that shall be complied with—and a thicker understanding that would include procedural and substantive elements: 'legal order and stability; equality of application of the law; protection of human rights; and the settlement of disputes before an independent legal body'.[92] From this thicker perspective, the independence of the international judiciary appears key for the realization of some international analogue of the rule of law. In particular, judicial independence enables regional courts to fulfil their functions of judicial review, which is key to the rule of law. As mentioned earlier, the functions of international and regional courts are no longer limited to dispute settlement. Regional courts are often granted functions of review of domestic legislation and more broadly monitoring the compliance of domestic public authorities with human rights norms or other international commitments. Were regional courts subordinate to the institutions they are expected to monitor, they could hardly fulfil their duty to provide oversight.

Finally, the principle of judicial independence is also instrumental for the realization of individuals' right to a fair trial.[93] To the extent that regional courts grant access to individuals, those courts must ensure the conditions for a fair trial as a fundamental right. Judicial independence has a dual institutional and individual dimension. From an institutional perspective, the principle of independence has structural implications for the conformation of courts, while from an individual perspective, the principle is key for the individual's right to a fair trial. International regional regimes for the protection of human rights, such as the ECHR (Article 6) and the IACHR (Article 8), enshrine the right to a fair trial before domestic courts. Also, the EU Charter of Fundamental Rights protects the right to a fair trial (Article 47). To what extent shall regional courts abide by those same standards? In the case of the CJEU, the court is expressly bound by the right to a fair trial enshrined in Article 47 of the Charter, since the Charter applies not only to the member states but also to the institutions of

[91] Robert McCorquodale, 'Defining the International Rule of Law: Defying Gravity?' (2016) 65 The International and Comparative Law Quarterly 277, 291; Ian Hurd, 'The International Rule of Law: Law and the Limit of Politics' (2014) 28 Ethics & International Affairs 39, 39.

[92] McCorquodale (n 91) 292.

[93] Mahoney (n 6) 313, 318, held that 'far from pointing to the inapplicability or reduced applicability of the ordinary principles of judicial independence, the international context rather highlights the need to immunize international judges against interference if the notions of justice, fair trial and the rule of law are to be maintained in relation to their work.'

the Union (Article 51 Charter).[94] However, this is not the case with the ECHR or the IACHR, which are addressed to the states' parties. In that regard, for instance, the ECtHR has held domestic courts liable for violating the right to a trial without unreasonable delay, but its own judgments might incur the same violation. From the perspective of the coherence and credibility of regional courts, in particular international human rights courts, the argument that different standards apply to the regional courts that monitor the observance of the right to a fair trial by domestic courts seems difficult to sustain.[95]

4.2. Constrained international judicial independence

Conceiving judicial independence in absolute terms is neither feasible nor desirable for several reasons. The indeterminacy of law, in particular international law, requires much interpretation. No one disputes that international and regional courts are often presented with cases that leave room for discretion in identifying and interpreting the law, and that their decisions often contribute to the creation or consolidation of legal norms through adjudication.[96] As Samantha Besson puts it, the problems of judicial discretion and law-making are magnified in the international sphere.[97]

In addition, as the functions of regional courts have diversified, they are increasingly granted functions of monitoring the action of democratic states, including the revision of domestic legislation against the yardstick of human rights norms, such as the ECtHR and the IACtHR. Political integration courts, such as the CJEU and the ATJ, are also granted powers to monitor state compliance with the founding treaties and ensuing legislation. Moreover, the institutional distance of regional courts from their constituencies and the lack of constitutional constraints greatly exacerbate the so-called counter-majoritarian difficulty.

Thus, just as any other body that exercises public power, regional courts shall operate under constraints to prevent them from overstepping their boundaries

[94] Sara Iglesias Sánchez, *La independencia judicial ante el Tribunal de Justicia de la UE* (Primera edición, Aranzadi Thomson Reuters 2023) 137–38.

[95] Dimitry V Kochenov and Graham Butler, 'Independence of the Court of Justice of the European Union: Unchecked Member States Power After the Sharpston Affair' (2021) 27 European Law Journal 262.

[96] Laurence R Helfer and Karen J Alter, 'Legitimacy and Lawmaking: A Tale of Three International Courts' (2013) 14 Theoretical Inquiries in Law 479.

[97] Samantha Besson, 'Legal Philosophical Issues of International Adjudication: Getting Over the Amour Impossible Between International Law and Adjudication', *The Oxford Handbook of International Adjudication* (Oxford University Press 2014) 413.

and also to respond to the demands of democratic accountability.[98] However, the risk that constraining mechanisms will be used in such a way as to subject regional courts to the arbitrary will of others must also be considered. Regional courts that are wholly independent are as problematic as courts that are overly dependent on outside actors.[99] In the end, the legitimacy of regional courts requires a balance between judicial independence and power constraints. A valuable conceptual legal analysis of international judicial independence was developed by Zimmermann, but it did not elaborate on checks to judicial power, focusing on the structural and personal dimensions of independence without sufficiently addressing power constraints.[100] Judicial independence does not demand that judges be free from any influence or constraint, but only from those influences or constraints that might distort the decision-making process by including considerations extraneous to adjudication or which might create an appearance of bias.[101]

However necessary, demarcating the line between proper and improper constraints is exceedingly difficult from a normative perspective.[102] It is thus a question of the principles that might justify forms of legal and political constraint. Here, the principles of accountability and checks and balances might be useful. Both are aimed at constraining power, while they are conceptually distinct. In that regard, Grant and Keohane describe checks and balances as 'mechanisms designed to *prevent* action that oversteps legitimate boundaries by requiring the cooperation of actors with different institutional interests to produce an authoritative decision'.[103] In contrast, they argued, accountability mechanisms operate *ex post*, as they enable an assessment of the actions of power-wielders against the corresponding standards and impose sanctions.

In any event, it is evident that judicial independence cannot be understood solely in terms of insularity, thus warranting that appropriate constraining mechanisms be put in place. What constraints on regional courts might be

[98] Andreas Follesdal, 'Law Making by Law Breaking? A Theory of Parliamentary Civil Disobedience Against International Human Rights Courts', *Cambridge University Press eBooks* (Cambridge University Press 2017) 329–31, held that 'there must therefore be ways to check and guide ICs' interpretations if their authority is to be legitimate' 'checks and balances should be developed in our multilevel legal order to alleviate these risks wrought by ICs' interpretation and law making' (331).

[99] Andreas Follesdal, 'Independent yet Accountable: Stress Test Lessons for the European Court of Human Rights' (2017) 24 Maastricht Journal of European and Comparative Law 484.

[100] Zimmermann (n 8).

[101] Aida Torres Pérez, 'Can Judicial Selection Secure Judicial Independence? Constraining State Governments in Selecting International Judges' in Michal Bobek (ed), *Selecting Europe's Judges* (Oxford University Press 2015) 184.

[102] John A Ferejohn and Larry D Kramer, 'Independent Judges, Dependent Judiciary: Institutionalizing Judicial Restraint' (2002) 77 New York University Law Review 962.

[103] Ruth W Grant and Robert O Keohane, 'Accountability and Abuses of Power in World Politics' (2005) 99 American Political Science Review 29, 30.

justified to prevent them from overstepping their powers? Chapters 2 and 3 will examine, respectively, accountability and checks and balances in the international sphere. It will be argued that, given the limits of the former from a legal perspective, the latter will be at the core of our inquiry regarding the need to provide a normative framework meant to ensure judicial independence while justifying constraining mechanisms from a multilevel perspective.[104]

In sum, although the domestic and international judiciaries differ in many respects, the differences between them are often overstated,[105] particularly when the spotlight is on multilateral courts with compulsory jurisdiction and individual access. Independence lies at the core of what defines a court. Nonetheless, the conceptualization of international judicial independence, and particularly its implementation, faces various distinct challenges: the dominance of state governments; diversity across courts in terms of institutional setting, mandate, and functions; and the normative quest regarding power constraints in a context of intimately intertwined politics and law.

[104] See Chapter 3 in this book.
[105] Ginsburg (n 29) 486.

PART 2

LEGAL AND POLITICAL CONSTRAINTS

2

Judicial Accountability in the International Sphere

1. Introduction

Accountability has become a buzzword in both national and international spheres. Broadly, the notion of accountability is associated with good governance and involves a relationship in which the power-wielders are evaluated by those who are affected by their actions or those who entrusted them with power.[1] In the global realm, given the democratic deficits of global institutions, scholars have turned their attention towards accountability as a source of legitimacy.[2] Decision-makers' accountability has been regarded as essential in securing the legitimacy of international lawmaking.[3] Referring to international organizations, Anne Peters has identified a shift in the scholarship from concern about the enabling function of the law (effectiveness) to the constraining function (accountability).[4] When we turn our attention to courts, we find tension between two potentially conflicting values: the independence of judges as adjudicators and their accountability as actors exercising discretionary power.[5] The interplay between independence and accountability is usually presented as a trade-off: more independence involves less accountability, and more accountability comes at the expense of independence.[6]

[1] Ruth Grant and Robert Keohane, 'Accountability and Abuses of Power in World Politics' (2005) 99 The American Political Science Review 29, 30–31, distinguished between a participation and a delegation model of accountability.

[2] John A Ferejohn, 'Accountability in Global Context' (2007) 5 International Law and Justice Working Papers.

[3] Anne-Marie Slaughter, 'The Accountability of Government Networks' (2001) 8 Indiana Journal of Global Legal Studies 347; Jost Delbruck, 'Exercising Public Authority Beyond the State: Transnational Democracy and/or Alternative Legitimation Strategies?' (2003) 10 Indiana Journal of Global Legal Studies 29; Benedict Kingsbury, Nico Krisch, and Richard B Stewart, 'The Emergence of Global Administrative Law' (2013) 27 Revue internationale de droit économique 37.

[4] Anne Peters, 'International Organizations: Effectiveness and Accountability' [2016] SSRN Electronic Journal 1.

[5] Martin M Shapiro, *Courts: A Comparative and Political Analysis* (University of Chicago Press 1981).

[6] Jeffrey L Dunoff and Mark A Pollack, 'The Judicial Trilemma' (2017) 111 The American Journal of International Law 225; Olof Larsson and others, 'Selection and Appointment in International Adjudication: Insights from Political Science' [2022] Journal of International Dispute Settlement 135.

Balancing International Judicial Independence. Aida Torres Pérez, Oxford University Press.
 DOI: 10.1093/oso/9780198852544.003.0002

In an effort to reconcile the tension between independence and accountability, these principles have been presented as the two sides of the same coin.[7] Indeed, independence and accountability are not in our view necessarily at odds with each other from a normative perspective.[8] The notion of independence does not require freedom from all constraints, but only from constraints that might unduly distort the decision-making process by including pressures, instructions, or considerations extraneous to adjudication, such as political allegiances or personal gain. However counterintuitive it might sound, moreover, accountability mechanisms may actually promote judicial independence. In Geyh's words, 'properly employed, accountability merely diminishes a judge's freedom to make herself dependant on inappropriate internal or external influences that could interfere with her capacity to follow the rule of law.'[9] After all, judicial independence does not allow judges to behave as they please, but rather the specific freedom to fulfil their adjudicative function. To put it bluntly, judges are not free to accept bribes. Therefore, holding judges to account does not necessarily reduce their independence from a normative perspective. At the same time, we must proceed with caution when implementing accountability mechanisms,[10] since those who have the power to hold judges accountable might use the power to influence or interfere with the judicial function. Judicial independence does not run counter to accountability, as long as the constraints imposed do not open a path to 'undue' influence or pressure. Hence, the design of accountability mechanisms needs to minimize to the greatest extent any opportunity for external or internal control or co-optation, political or otherwise.

While at the domestic level the literature regarding judicial accountability is extensive,[11] accountability has received less attention in the literature devoted to international and regional courts. Their authority and effectiveness have taken most of the attention; in fact, it is only in the last two decades that

[7] Stephen Burbank, 'The Architecture of Judicial Independence' (1999) 72 Southern California Law Review 315, 339; Stephen Burbank, 'Judicial Independence, Judicial Accountability and Interbranch Relations' (2007) 137(4) Georgetown Law Journal 16.

[8] David Kosař, 'Judicial Accountability in the (Post)Transitional Context: A Story of the Czech Republic and Slovakia' [2010] SSRN Electronic Journal, claims that 'judicial independence and judicial accountability are not necessarily competing values.'

[9] Charles Geyh, 'Rescuing Judicial Accountability from the Realm of Political Rhetoric' (2006) 56(4) Case Western Reserve Law Review 911, 916.

[10] ibid 912.

[11] John A Ferejohn and Larry D Kramer, 'Independent Judges, Dependent Judiciary: Institutionalizing Judicial Restraint' (2002) 77 New York University Law Review 962; Burbank (n 7); Daniela Piana, *Judicial Accountabilities in New Europe: From Rule of Law to Quality of Justice* (Routledge 2016); David Kosař, *Perils of Judicial Self-Government in Transitional Societies: Holding the Least Accountable Branch to Account* (Cambridge University Press 2016).

concern for their accountability picked up,[12] particularly once international and regional courts became firmly established.[13] The notion of accountability is particularly elusive when applied to courts and poses challenges from both conceptual and practical perspectives. What I seek to lay out here is a notion of accountability as a form of constraining the power of regional courts that bolsters the legitimacy of their authority.

Following the definition proffered by Grant and Keohane,[14] accountability implies that 'some actors have the right to hold other actors to a set of standards, to judge whether they have fulfilled their responsibilities in light of these standards, and to impose sanctions if they determine that these responsibilities have not been met'. A range of implications inherent to the notion of accountability, however, still need teasing out: To whom should regional judges be accountable and what specific supervisory or control procedures should be implemented? Similarly, what specific strictures of accountability should judges be expected to meet and what consequences should non-compliance entail?

Scholars have conceptualized accountability in several forms, most often regarding domestic courts.[15] For the purposes of our analysis, we will follow the basic distinction between legal, political, and societal accountability. Cappelletti[16] offered a taxonomy of judicial accountability in which the main criteria for distinction relied on the identity of the accountability holders and the standards to which judges may be held to account. Political accountability was to be scrutinized by representatives of the political branches on the basis of political criteria, societal or public accountability vis-à-vis the general public, and legal accountability[17] determined through processes and organs more juridical in nature on the basis of infringements of the law (rather than on

[12] Dinah Shelton, 'Legal Norms for Independence and Accountability of International Tribunals' (2003) 2 The Law and Practice of International Courts and Tribunals 27; Paul Mahoney, 'The International Judiciary—Independence and Accountability' (2008) 7 The Law and Practice of International Courts and Tribunals 313; Joe McIntyre and James Crawford, 'The Independence and Impartiality of the "International Judiciary"' in Christopher Forsyth and Shimon Shetreet (eds), *The Culture of Judicial Independence* (Brill 2011); Ronli Sifris, 'Weighing Judicial Independence Against Judicial Accountability: Do the Scales of the International Criminal Court Balance?' (2013) 8 Chicago-Kent Journal of International and Comparative Law 88.

[13] See Andreas Follesdal, 'Independent yet Accountable: Stress Test Lessons for the European Court of Human Rights' (2017) 24 Maastricht Journal of European and Comparative Law 484.

[14] Grant and Keohane (n 1) 29.

[15] Mauro Cappelletti, '"Who Watches the Watchmen?" A Comparative Study on Judicial Responsibility' (1983) 31 The American Journal of Comparative Law 1; Geyh (n 9); Kosař (n 11) 30–36.

[16] Cappelletti (n 15) 18.

[17] Mauro Cappelletti, '"Who Watches the Watchmen?" A Comparative Study on Judicial Responsibility' (1983) 31 The American Journal of Comparative Law 1, describing legal accountability, Cappelletti distinguished between the vicarious responsibility of the state and the personal responsibility of the individual judge.

politically or socially reproachable behaviour).[18] Regarding global institutions, Ferejohn distinguished between political and legal accountability with an emphasis on the type of reasons given to exercise control, a relevant distinction for our analysis. Political accountability is exercised directly by the principal and is 'fundamentally arbitrary in the sense that it is up to the principal at to whether to base its decisions on reasons, or not to offer any reasons at all'. In contrast, legal accountability 'is not arbitrary but is based on reasons, reasons connecting behaviour to the relevant law binding the agent' and tends to be imposed by a third party.[19]

In this chapter, we will focus on the legal accountability of the selected regional courts and the specific challenges for that form of accountability in the international sphere. As will be argued in the next chapter, we find political accountability or at least some forms of political accountability might be better conceived under the checks and balances principle. A deep analysis of societal accountability exceeds the scope of this work, but some reflections on this broader notion will be made in connection with the principle of transparency.

2. The Legal Accountability of Regional Judges

Legal accountability is understood in a narrow sense to distinguish it from related notions such as responsibility, responsiveness, or transparency. Legal accountability involves the set of legally defined standards to which regional judges are held and the capacity of the competent bodies to adopt the corresponding measures if those standards are not met in accordance with legal procedures.

Accountability mechanisms might target regional judges individually or the entire court from an institutional perspective. As will be shown, legal accountability instruments are usually individual. Moreover, from the perspective of the forms of judicial conduct that accountability mechanisms are meant to ensure, one can distinguish between individual judges' behavioural and decisional accountability.[20] Behavioural accountability focuses on the conduct of judges that is extraneous to the merits of their judicial decisions, which might include conduct on or off the bench. Decisional accountability focuses on judicial rulings themselves.[21] Holding judges

[18] ibid 33.
[19] Ferejohn (n 2) 3.
[20] Geyh (n 9) 919–24.
[21] ibid 917.

accountable for the content of their decisions is particularly risky from the perspective of judicial independence. At the domestic level, the main control mechanism for the content of judicial decisions is the appeal system, which is highly uncommon at the international level. Some courts, such as the European Court of Human Rights (ECtHR), establish internal processes of review. In the case of the ECtHR, the internal process makes it possible for the judgments of the Chamber, under certain conditions, to be appealed before the Grand Chamber.[22] In addition, judgments of the General Court in the European Union (EU) may be brought before the Court of Justice on points of law.[23]

Unpacking the notion of legal accountability[24] of regional judges involves reflection upon the standards of judicial conduct, the consequences or sanctions that may follow, the actors capable of holding regional judges to account and the corresponding oversight mechanisms. Those main features will be assessed from a critical perspective, considering not only the legal rules but also how they function in practice. The last part of the chapter takes up codes of conduct or ethics, which deserve particular attention as forms of soft law. The analysis of legal accountability regime will focus on a selection of courts, as explained in Chapter 1, that include permanent regional courts allowing for individual access in the fields of human rights and economic and political integration in Europe and Latin America: the ECtHR, the Inter-American Court of Human Rights (IACtHR), the Court of Justice of the European Union (CJEU), and the Andean Tribunal of Justice (ATJ).

2.1. Standards of judicial conduct

Legal accountability mechanisms tend to be established by the respective constitutive international treaty,[25] the statute of the court,[26] and/or the rules of

[22] Convention for the Protection of Human Rights and Fundamental Freedoms, Rome 1950 (ECHR), art 43.

[23] Consolidated version of the Treaty on the Functioning of the European Union Protocol (No 3), on the Statute of the Court of Justice of the European Union 2004 (CJEU Statute), art 56.

[24] Kosař (n 11) 40–58.

[25] ECHR; American Convention on Human Rights, San José, Costa Rica, 1969 (ACHR); Consolidated version of the Treaty on European Union OJ C 202, 7.6.2016 (TEU); Consolidated version of the Treaty on the Functioning of the European Union OJ C 202, 7.6.2016 (TFEU); Constitutive Treaty of the Andean Tribunal of Justice 1999 (ATJ Treaty).

[26] Statute of the Inter-American Court of Human Rights, adopted by the General Assembly of the OAS at its Ninth Regular Session, held in La Paz Bolivia, October 1979 (Resolution No 448) (IACtHR Statute); CJEU Statute; Statute of the Andean Tribunal of Justice, Codified by Decision 500 of the Andean Council of Ministers of Foreign Affairs, published in the Gaceta Oficial del Acuerdo de Cartagena N° 680, 28/6/2001 (ATJ Statute).

procedure.[27] Usually, those legal texts include norms meant to ensure the independence and impartiality of judges and avoid conduct that might impair the appearance of independence and impartiality.[28] Some examples are the prohibition on political or administrative activity or any professional activity that might compromise judges' independence or impartiality,[29] and the duty to disclose any additional activity.[30]

The case of the IACtHR poses specific challenges, since the position of judges is part-time, and thus they cannot be prevented from performing other remunerated activities. Article 18(1) of its Statute indicates that the position of judge is incompatible with the following positions and activities:

a. Members or high-ranking officials of the executive branch of government, except for those who hold positions that do not place them under the direct control of the executive branch and those of diplomatic agents who are not Chiefs of Missions to the OAS or to any of its member states;
b. Officials of international organizations;
c. Any others that might prevent the judges from discharging their duties, or that might affect their independence or impartiality, or the dignity and prestige of the office.

This regulation is not without risks. According to the exceptions in paragraph (a), judges could hold positions within the executive branch provided that they are not under the 'direct' control of the executive branch, without it being clear what should be understood by 'direct'. Also, judges may be diplomatic agents, as long as they are not Chiefs of Missions to the Organization of American States (OAS) or any of its member states. Nonetheless, as has been argued, diplomatic agents need to rely on the trust of the President, and judges may still be diplomats before the United Nations (UN) or other international organizations or countries.[31] As such, the appearance of independence would

[27] Rules of Court of the European Court of Human Rights 2013 (ECtHR Rules); Rules of Procedure of the Inter-American Court of Human Rights 2009 (IACtHR Rules); Consolidated version of the Rules of Procedure of the Court of Justice of 25 September 2012 (CJEU Rules); Rules of Procedure of the Andean Tribunal of Justice 2020 (ATJ Rules).

[28] ECHR art 21(4); ACHR art 71; IACtHR Statute art 18(1)(c); ATJ Statute art 11.

[29] ECtHR Rules art 4; CJEU Statute art 4; ATJ Statute art 11.

[30] ECtHR Rules art 4.

[31] Héctor Faúndez Ledesma, 'La independencia e imparcialidad de los miembros de la Comisión y de la Corte: paradojas y desafíos' in Juan E Méndez and Francisco Cox (eds), *El futuro del sistema Interamericano de los Derechos Humanos* (IIDH San José 1998) 200.

be put at risk, and thus the exercise of public power of any kind should be excluded.[32]

Those norms also might include standards for behaviour to ensure the proper functioning of the court and administration of justice, such as the secrecy of deliberations.[33] Nonetheless, provisions to promote diligence, competence, and efficiency are lacking in the legal instruments of the courts under examination,[34] even though that sort of standard might be included in the respective codes of conduct and ethics.[35] At the domestic level, standards concerning the organization of the judicial work or other professional standards have in fact recently been raised.[36] New public management theories have emphasized the relevance of effectiveness, efficiency, and a client-oriented approach of the judicial organization, but these kinds of managerial forms of accountability are much less developed at the international level.[37] In that regard, the qualifications and experience of regional judges are, according to several scholars, particularly relevant to the legitimacy of the courts on which they sit,[38] but instruments to evaluate judges' performance and competence once they are appointed are scarce. Bohlander has reported that 'one sometimes hears off-the-record comments from players in the system, mostly from defence counsel but occasionally also from judicial brethren, who are exasperated by what they perceive to be an unacceptable degree of incompetence or nonchalance in the handling of the proceedings',[39] but he is not the only analyst who has voiced concern about the qualifications and competence of international judges.[40]

[32] Aida Torres Pérez, 'La independencia de la Corte Interamericana de Derechos Humanos desde una perspectiva institucional' in Marisa Iglesias and others (eds), *Derechos humanos: posibilidades teóricas y desafíos prácticos* (Libraria 2014).

[33] IACtHR Rules art 15(2); CJEU Statute art 2; ATJ Rules art 2.

[34] Other international courts have included standards of conduct regarding diligence and efficiency, such as the Rules of Procedure and Evidence of the International Criminal Court 2002 art 24, which define a 'serious breach of duty' as gross negligence in the performance of one's duties or knowingly acting in contravention of those duties, such as where the judge '[r]epeatedly causes unwarranted delay in the initiation, prosecution or trial of cases, or in the exercise of judicial powers'.

[35] See section 4 below.

[36] Anja Seibert-Fohr, 'International Judicial Ethics' in Cesare PR Romano, Karen J Alter, and Yuval Shany (eds), *The Oxford Handbook of International Adjudication* (Oxford University Press 2014).

[37] Mahoney (n 12) 344.

[38] David Kosař, 'Selecting Strasbourg Judges' in Michal Bobek (ed), *Selecting Europe's Judges* (Oxford University Press 2015) 123–26; Andreas Follesdal, 'The Legitimacy of International Human Rights Review: The Case of the European Court of Human Rights' (2009) 40 Journal of Social Philosophy 595, 605.

[39] Michael Bohlander, 'Separation of Powers and the International Judiciary—A Vision of Institutional Judicial Independence in International Law' in Shimon Shetreet and Christopher Forsyth (eds), *The Culture of Judicial Independence* (Brill | Nijhoff 2012) 271.

[40] Regarding Strasbourg judges see: Follesdal (n 32) 605; Çalı Başak, Koch Anne, and Bruch Nicola, 'The Legitimacy of the European Court of Human Rights: The View from the Ground' (Department of Political Science, University College London 2011) <https://ecthrproject.wordpress.com/wp-cont

In general, standards of conduct are vaguely defined. The lack of certainty on how those standards of conduct might be interpreted in practice is concerning because, as Geyh has put it, 'the peril of leaving judicial accountability ill-defined is that it can be co-opted and misused more easily'.[41]

2.2. The consequences of failure to meet standards of conduct

Legal accountability involves verifying judges' compliance with the prescribed standards of conduct and, in case of infringement, imposing sanctions or other consequences.[42] In terms of the consequences that might follow, one can distinguish two regimes, that of recusal and disqualification and the disciplinary regime.

Some conducts or situations disqualify a judge from hearing a case.[43] All regional courts examined include a regime for recusal and disqualification. Usually, the rules exclude judges from situations in which they might have a personal interest in the case, whether because of previous involvement in the case as an agent or advisor or being in a parental, close family or personal relationship with the parties or their representatives, for in those situations, their impartiality may be compromised. The regime for recusal is mainly addressed to ensure the impartiality of judges.

In contrast, in terms of the disciplinary regime, the sanction typically available is the most extreme one from the perspective of judicial independence: removal from office. In the case of the ECtHR and the CJEU, judges may be removed, respectively, when 'the judge has ceased to fulfil the required conditions',[44] and when the judge 'no longer fulfils the requisite conditions or meets the obligations arising from his office'.[45] In the case of the IACtHR and the ATJ, a list of incompatibilities or serious misconducts that can justify removal is provided. For the IACtHR, the list of incompatibilities is provided in Article 18 of its Statute, as mentioned before. According to paragraph 3, 'incompatibilities may lead only to dismissal of the judge and the imposition

ent/uploads/2011/04/ecthrlegitimacyreport.pdf> accessed 19 March 2026; Yuval Shany, *Assessing the Effectiveness of International Courts* (Oxford University Press 2014).

[41] Geyh (n 9) 912.
[42] Kosař (n 11) 35–36.
[43] ECtHR Rules art 28; IACtHR Rules art 21; CJEU Statute art 18; ATJ Statute art 67; CJEU Statute art 18.
[44] ECHR art 23(2).
[45] CJEU Statute art 6.

of applicable liabilities, but shall not invalidate the acts and decisions in which the judge in question participated'. With regard to the ATJ, judges may be removed for incurring in serious misconduct. Article 6 of the Statute provides the list of serious misconducts, including notorious bad behaviour; any activity incompatible with the nature of the mandate; failure to fulfil the duties inherent to their function reiteratively; the development of remunerated activities, except for those of an academic nature; and violation of the oath taken in accordance with Article 4.

Less stringent sanctions for misconduct are much less clearly developed. In that regard, the CJEU Statute provides for the possibility of depriving judges of their pension or other benefits.[46] In the case of the IACtHR, Article 73 of the Convention refers to 'applicable sanctions' without further specificity. Nor does the IACtHR Statute specify the alternative sanctions that may be adopted.[47]

At the domestic level, removal from office is only contemplated in exceptional circumstances, given the potential interference with independence and the broad range of other disciplinary measures that can be adopted, such as suspension, pecuniary sanction, or reprimand. In the international sphere, however, the unlikelihood of dismissal and the relative lack of less intrusive measures hinder the practical functioning of the disciplinary regime, as will be discussed below.

2.3. The judges' accountability holders

A crucial question in the accountability regime is who can hold regional judges to account. The question is very sensitive since the accountability holder might act in a manner that undermines independence. Moreover, as indicated above, the standards against which judges may be held accountable afford a wide margin of interpretation.

With regard to the regime of disqualification in case of conflict of interests, judges have the obligation to recuse themselves in any of the barred situations.[48] The decision to disqualify a judge generally corresponds to the

[46] CJEU Statute art 6.

[47] In this context, the ICC stands out, since the Statute (arts 46–47) distinguishes several types of misconduct and designs a set of disciplinary measures according to their severity. Besides removal in cases of serious misconduct or breach of duty, the Rules of Procedure and Evidence (art 32) foresee other disciplinary measures for less serious misconduct, such as a reprimand or a pecuniary sanction.

[48] In the case of the IACtHR and the CJEU, the Court's President may take the initiative and then notify the judge. If the concerned judge contests the charge, then the Court will decide. See IACtHR Statute art 19(3); CJEU Statute art 18 (para 2).

Court's President and, if doubts or disagreement persist, to the corresponding Chamber or the Court as a whole.[49] In the case of the ATJ, the decision is attributed directly to the Court.[50]

The parties' prerogative to request the disqualification of judges is only explicitly stated in the ECtHR Rules of Procedure, after the amendment adopted by the Plenary of the Court in 2023, which entered into force in 2024. The updated Rule 28 strengthens the core procedural framework for the recusal of judges by expressly codifying the existing practice according to which the parties to the proceedings may request recusal of a judge.

Even if the parties' capacity to request a judge's disqualification is not explicitly stated, it can still, in some cases, be implicitly derived. In the case of the ATJ, for instance, a separate regulation governs the obligation of judges to recuse themselves and the procedure for requesting it, but does not explicitly indicate who may request recusal, making possible the interpretation that the initiative corresponds to the parties.[51] In the case of the CJEU, that possibility is implicitly derived from Article 18 of the CJEU Statute, which in paragraph 4 establishes that parties may not apply for a change in the composition of the Court on the grounds of the judge's nationality. It can therefore be interpreted *a contrario* that parties may request a change in the court's composition for other reasons related to the lack of impartiality. In practice, petitions from the parties have been considered.[52] Similarly, at the IACtHR, it can be inferred from the Rules of Court that regulate the moment at which the reasons for disqualification ought to be alleged before the Court that the capacity to make such a request corresponds to the parties.[53]

Regarding the disciplinary regime in case of misconduct, the judges themselves—whether represented by the court's President or the court as a collective body—are usually in charge of implementing accountability mechanisms, sometimes in combination with the political institutions of the corresponding regional organization. Three main models can be identified:

First is the *purely judicial model* in which the accountability holder is the court on which the judge sits. For instance, in the CJEU, decisions on removal or the deprivation of pension or other benefits require the unanimous opinion

[49] ECtHR Rules art 28; IACtHR Rules art 19; CJEU Statute art 18.

[50] ICC Rome Statute art 41; ATJ Statute arts 67–69.

[51] ATJ Statute art 69: 'La recusación se propondrá al Tribunal, en cualquier estado del proceso, mediante escrito en el que se expresarán los motivos de hecho en que se fundamenta y las pruebas que se pretenda aducir.'

[52] Sara Iglesias Sánchez, *La independencia judicial ante el Tribunal de Justicia de la UE* (Aranzadi Thomson Reuters 2023) 121–22.

[53] IACtHR Rules art 21(2).

of the judges and advocates general of the CJEU.[54] The Statute only stipulates that the decision be communicated to the Presidents of the European Parliament, the Commission, and the Council. In the ECtHR, the decision is also attributed to the Court, except that a two-thirds majority of the judges rather than unanimity is required for dismissal of a judge from office.[55] Article 7 of the Rules of Court offers no details on the procedure to be followed. The second model is *purely political*, in that the judges are held accountable to a political body of the corresponding international organization. For instance, in the ATJ, the decision to remove a judge requires a unanimous decision of the governmental representatives at the request of the government of a member state.[56] The third type is a *mixed model*, meaning both judicial and political actors participate in the decision-making. For instance, in the IACtHR, the OAS General Assembly holds disciplinary authority over the judges, but it may exercise that authority only at the request of the Court itself,[57] thus precluding unilateral action by the General Assembly.

A comparative analysis of the disciplinary regimes demonstrates that the standards of conduct tend to be defined in broad terms and that the sanctions are often unspecified or limited to removal. The main difference among the regional courts under analysis resides in the accountability holders, which is certainly a crucial aspect of the accountability regime from the perspective of safeguarding judicial independence (see Table 2.1). From a broader perspective, as a study covering twenty-four international courts corroborates, the purely political model is rare.[58] In terms of the accountability holders, the enforcement of standards and adoption of sanctions tend to be attributed to the judges themselves, or at least to the initiation of the investigation. Court Presidents play a central role, both in disqualification and disciplinary measures, sometimes in combination with a political body. From the perspective of the institutional design, the judicial nature of accountability holders might contribute to shielding judicial independence, but at the same time it might create a risk of corporate solidarity[59] and a threat to internal judicial independence.[60]

[54] Statute CJEU art 6.
[55] ECtHR Rules art 7.
[56] ATJ Statute art 10.
[57] IACtHR Statute art 20.
[58] Larsson and others (n 6) 147, focusing on the rules for removal.
[59] ibid 148, held that 'judges may be reluctant to remove one of their colleagues even if this would be called for as removal attempts might damage the reputation of the Court or undermine collegiality among the judges'.
[60] See section 3 below.

Table 2.1 Breakdown of disciplinary regimes

	Standards	Sanctions	Accountability holders
ECtHR ECHR art 23(3) Rules art 7	The judge has ceased to fulfil the required conditions.	Dismissal from office	Two-thirds of the plenary of the court
IACtHR ACHR art 73 Statute arts 18 and 20	Incompatibilities listed in Article 18 Statute	Applicable sanctions (ACHR art 73) Removal from office	The OAS General Assembly shall have disciplinary authority over the judges but may exercise that authority only at the request of the Court itself. Two-thirds majority vote of the States Parties to the Convention
CJEU Statute art 6	The judge no longer fulfils the requisite conditions or meets the obligations arising from his office.	Removal from office, loss of pension and other benefits	Unanimous opinion of judges and advocates general
ATJ Constitutive Treaty art 10 Statute art 11	Serious misconduct	Removal from office	Initiative at the request of a government. Governments of Member Countries shall appoint Plenipotentiary representatives who shall decide the case by unanimous vote

2.4. The disciplinary regime in practice

Beyond the analysis of the written legal norms, it is important to take into consideration their practical operationalization. In this regard, we immediately note that the removal of regional judges is very rare[61] and they are hardly ever sanctioned either. Judging on the basis of publicly available information, one can conclude that the disciplinary mechanisms have only been sparingly activated. The explanation might lie in the vagueness of the standards, the relative unavailability of sanctions less serious than removal, or some form of corporate solidarity, since the accountability holders largely tend to be judges themselves.

61 Larsson and others (n 6) 147.

Looking for cases that might exemplify the reluctance to make use of the disciplinary regime, we find the case of a judge at the IACtHR, García Sayán, who became the Peruvian government's candidate for the position of Secretary General to the OAS. For his candidacy to be successful, García Sayán needed the support of states' parties that could potentially become defendants before the IACtHR. He therefore requested to be 'disqualified' from all his activities on the Court for the duration of the campaign. The President of the Court at the time accepted his request,[62] but two other judges voiced their disagreement with the President's decision, arguing that the campaigning process involved political activities that were incompatible with his judicial office. In addition, they argued that the mechanism of disqualification was meant to apply to individual cases and could not be granted for an extended period of time. They held that García Sayán ought to have resigned or, at least, the plenary of the court should have been given an opportunity to assess whether candidacy for Secretary General of the OAS was compatible with holding judicial office within the meaning of Article 18(1) Statute.[63] Eventually, García Sayán's candidacy was withdrawn, but this case shows both the inherent difficulties of applying the disciplinary regime and the reluctance to do so. It is telling that the mechanism of disqualification was used instead.

Another example in the context of the IACtHR is the case of Argentine Judge Zaffaroni. A group of deputies from the Argentine Parliament submitted a request to the IACtHR for the initiation of disciplinary proceedings to remove Judge Zaffaroni from the Court. They claimed that several public statements he had made compromised his independence and impartiality. For instance, while a sitting judge on the IACtHR, he very visibly signed a petition (indeed, he was its first signatory) seeking pardon for a former Vice-President of Argentina, Amado Boudou, who had been convicted of corruption. The petition alleged that the judicial process against Amado Boudou represented a form of political persecution, a very serious charge,[64] and yet no disciplinary measure was taken.

[62] Corte Interamericana de Derechos Humanos, 'Comunicado de Prensa No. 14/14' <https://www.corteidh.or.cr/docs/comunicados/cp_14_14.pdf>: *Se acepta la excusa del juez Diego García-Sayán de participar de todas las actividades de la Corte mientras sea candidato a la Secretaría General de la OEA.*

[63] Manuel Ventura Robles, 'La Legitimidad de Los Jueces de La Corte Interamericana de Derechos Humanos' (2016) 145–46 Revista de derecho público 11, 19–20.

[64] Agustin Marcarian, 'Elisa Carrió y Un Grupo de Diputados Nacionales Pidió a La CIDH La Apertura de Un Proceso Disciplinario Contra Eugenio Zaffaroni' *Infobae* (9 January 2021) <https://www.infobae.com/politica/2021/01/09/elisa-carrio-y-un-grupo-de-diputados-nacionales-pidio-a-la-cidh-la-apertura-de-un-proceso-disciplinario-contra-eugenio-zaffaroni/>.

Moreover, Zaffaroni also provided legal representation for Evo Morales, the ex-president of Bolivia, while Evo Morales was in Argentina. In 2019, in response to a request from Colombia for a consultative opinion regarding the mechanism of indefinite presidential re-election, the Bolivian government requested Zaffaroni's disqualification on grounds of his relationship with Evo Morales, who had been re-elected four times even though the Bolivian Constitution only allowed presidents to be re-elected once. Although the President of the IACtHR duly noted Bolivia's concerns,[65] Zaffaroni was not disqualified. Eventually, the IACtHR issued Consultative Opinion 28/21, holding that indefinite presidential re-election is not an autonomous right protected by the Convention, that the prohibition of indefinite re-election was compatible with the Convention, and that indefinite presidential re-election clashed with the principles of representative democracy. The Opinion had the support of five judges against two dissenting judges, and, indeed, one of those two was Zaffaroni.

Notwithstanding, even if the disciplinary regime is hardly applied in practice, the deterrent effect of the norms for judicial conduct should not be neglected.[66] Informal practices for rebuke and reprimand are also often in place to communicate and enforce standards of conduct.[67] The reluctance or difficulties of applying formal accountability mechanisms might even enhance the relevance of informal sanctions, given the heavy weight that public disapproval or loss of prestige carries for judges.[68] That weight also enhances the relevance of analyses of inappropriate practices or behaviours for international judges from NGOs and legal experts. Çali and Cunningham have argued that individual judges are highly susceptible to naming and shaming tactics, citing a dissenting opinion from a Russian judge on the ECtHR, Dedov, in *Bayev and others v Russia*. A commentary published by Strasbourg Observers singled out 'outrageously homophobic statements that are unworthy of a judge at the European Court of Human Rights' in his dissent and called into question the judge's ability to meet the conditions for 'high moral character' laid down in Article 21 ECHR.[69]

[65] Opinión, 'Corte IDH: Bolivia Pide al Juez Zaffaroni Excusarse Por Ser Abogado de Evo Morales' (28 September 2020) <https://www.opinion.com.bo/articulo/pais/corte-idh-bolivia-pide-juez-zaffaroni-excusarse-ser-abogado-evo-morales/20200928130305788976.html>.

[66] Larsson (n 6) 147, claimed that 'although actual removal of IC judges is very rare, a perceived threat of removal may be expected to reduce judicial independence'.

[67] As conversations with international judges and personnel at the service of regional international courts have revealed.

[68] Kosař (n 11) 35.

[69] Başak Çalı and Stewart Cunningham, 'Judicial Self Government and the Sui Generis Case of the European Court of Human Rights' (2018) 19 German Law Journal 1977, 1997.

3. Trade-offs in Institutional Design: Internal and External Judicial Independence

At present, legal accountability mechanisms tend to rest in the hands of regional judges themselves, and in particular court Presidents. This model ensures external independence from political bodies, such as state governments or the respective regional bodies in which they are represented, but it also presents two main risks. First, the risk of exaggerated corporate solidarity. The fact that judges might tend to protect each other, or even if they are perceived as exceedingly collegial, may well undermine the effectiveness of accountability mechanisms, or the perception of their effectiveness, which in turn would jeopardize the credibility of the disciplinary regime and ultimately the court's public trust and social legitimacy. Second, a system in which judges are held to account to other judges might jeopardize internal judicial independence. While judges might tend to protect each other, the fact that the President holds disciplinary power, or has a prominent role in the process, could also generate internal dynamics that results in undue deference towards the accountability holder.

In order to reduce those risks, one might consider incorporating autonomous bodies as accountability holders. In that regard, Bohlander has expressed support for the creation of a General Council of the International Judiciary in order to foster judicial institutional independence. According to his proposal, the functions of the judicial council would include not only judicial discipline but also recruitment and promotion of judges, a system for continuing professional development, and budget administration.[70] The majority of the seats on the General Council would be composed of experienced senior judges and representatives of the international community[71] and it would be located within the UN institutional framework.[72]

While judicial councils are not found in the international sphere,[73] they became popular at the domestic level after the Second World War. Three main models of judicial (legal) accountability can be distinguished in terms of their accountability holders. The first is a governmental model in which judges are held accountable by the executive power, more specifically the Ministry of Justice, in countries such

[70] Bohlander (n 39) 275–76.

[71] ibid 276.

[72] ibid 275.

[73] Mahoney (n 12) 324, held that, as regards the removals of judges by judges, 'there is no alternative to direct self-regulation by each international court or tribunal, given the absence of an international "judicial council" of the kind found in many national legal systems'.

as Germany and Austria. In the second model, judges are held accountable by other judges, in particular court presidents, in several Eastern European countries.[74] The third model is a hybrid in that the accountability holder is more autonomous. In the judicial council model, accountability mechanisms are vested in an autonomous body that is partially composed of judges elected by their peers. Assigning oversight functions to judicial councils is meant to bolster external judicial independence and avoid the interference of the executive regarding judicial career and discipline. This model was born in Western Europe when the first councils were set up in Italy and France and then spread to Central and Eastern European countries after the fall of communism and to Latin America after the collapse of authoritarian regimes.[75]

Both the governmental and judicial models pose risks in terms of external political control, the former, and internal dependence and corporativism, the latter.[76] Judicial councils, for their part, might be somehow vulnerable to both risks, depending on their particular configuration. Politicization could arise through the appointment of judicial council members by political bodies, while corporativism might emerge when the judicial members of the council are elected by their peers. Moreover, as Kosař argued, in light of the judicial council experience of Eastern European countries after the fall of communism, the model promoted by the EU and the Council of Europe[77] might in the end empower court Presidents,[78] asserting that this model 'increases the independence of the judiciary, but does not—from an internal perspective—necessarily increase the independence of individual judges'.[79]

An interesting question, moving to the international sphere, might be the extent to which the adoption of judicial councils as institutions for the legal accountability of judges would be advisable from the perspective of the balance between institutional independence and accountability.

From this perspective, the International Criminal Court (ICC) stands out for having introduced an intermediate body, the Independent Oversight Mechanism (IOM).[80] The purpose of the IOM is 'effective and comprehensive

[74] Piana (n 11) 43–44, emphasized the role that court presidents play in holding judges to account in Czech Republic, Hungary, Poland, Bulgaria, and Romania.

[75] Kosař (n 11) 121–22.

[76] Cappelletti (n 15).

[77] Rafael Bustos Gisbert, 'Política, Independencia y Autogobierno Judicial: Cuatro Miradas' (2022) 198 Revista de estudios políticos 93; Kosař (n 11) 134, distinguishes between the Euro-model of judicial councils from other types of judicial councils.

[78] Kosař (n 11) 398–406.

[79] ibid 406.

[80] Assembly of States Parties to the Rome Statute, 'ICC-ASP/8/Res.1 Establishment of an Independent Oversight Mechanism'; Assembly of States Parties to the Rome Statute, 'ICC-ASP/12/Res.6. Adoption

oversight of the Court', a mandate it fulfils through 'inspections, evaluations and investigations',[81] as laid down by Article 112(4) of the Rome Statute. The IOM is defined as a subsidiary body of the Assembly of States Parties,[82] while the exercise of its competences is to be carried out with respect for the authority and independence of the Court.[83]

The IOM holds competences of investigation. All complaints are to be transmitted to the IOM, which may also initiate investigations on its own.[84] The IOM is to investigate all complaints and transmit the result of any investigation, together with its recommendations, to the Assembly of State Parties and other competent organs. The adoption of disciplinary measures corresponds to the Court's President.[85] In the event of a request for removal, however, the question will be put to vote at the Court's plenary session, and if removal is recommended (which requires a two-thirds majority), the Assembly of States Parties must also approve the decision by a two-thirds majority before it becomes final.[86] In sum, the IOM took the competence to conduct investigations of complaints over from the Court President,[87] but not the decision to adopt disciplinary measures. This competence remains with the Court President or, in the case of removal, with the Court's Plenary, whose recommendation must subsequently be ratified by the Assembly of State Parties to take effect. In sum, in this model, the investigative and punitive functions have been separated such that a new body is charged with the former. This institutional design aims to minimize the risk posed by improper corporate solidary, while at the same time avoiding placing the Court under direct political oversight.

of the Operational Mandate of the Independent Oversight Mechanism - Annex'; Assembly of States Parties to the Rome Statute, 'ICC-ASP/19/Res.6 Strengthening the International Criminal Court and the Assembly of States Parties - Annex II'.

81 Assembly of States Parties to the Rome Statute, 'ICC-ASP/12/Res.6' (n 74) para 5.

82 The Head of the IOM is selected by the Bureau of the Assembly of State Parties, and it is composed of four full-time staff members: the Head of IOM, a Senior Evaluation Specialist, an Associate Investigator, and a GS-OL staff member, Assembly of States Parties to the Rome Statute, 'ICC-ASP/12/Res.6' (n 74) paras 1 and 51.

83 ibid para 27.

84 Rules of Procedure and Evidence of the International Criminal Court, Official Records of the Assembly of States Parties to the Rome Statute of the International Criminal Court, First session, New York, 3–10 September 2002 (ICC-ASP/1/3 and Corr.1) (ICC Rules) art 26(2).

85 ibid art 30.

86 ibid art 29; ICC Rome Statute art 46(2).

87 ICC Rules art 26. Before the establishment of the IOM, the President possessed the competence to deal with complaints for misconduct with assistance from one or more judges appointed on a rotating basis.

Nonetheless, the current model has raised concerns. An *Independent Expert Review*[88] claimed that the current arrangement involving the IOM presents 'a series of principled, structural, and operational challenges and limitation' and that 'its suitability, in the eyes of the staff and other stakeholders, to investigate Judges effectively and credibly is questionable'.[89] The primary concerns raised by the *Review* as regards the IOM involve the assignment of investigative functions from a judicial organ to a subsidiary body of the Assembly of State Parties, which is a political body.[90]

The *Independent Expert Review* also included several recommendations. In the short term, the experts proposed creating an ad hoc Judicial Investigation Panel and a First Instance Panel, both of which would be three-judge, non-permanent, independent, impartial and external panels.[91] According to the *Review*, this model has the advantage of bringing in external judges to dissipate the perception of undue solidarity among the sitting judges, and at the same time relieve ICC judges from any involvement in a potentially adverse determination against a colleague. These panels 'would buttress the effectiveness of accountability measures and the integrity of the Judiciary' and 'enhance the credibility of the disciplinary mechanism against Judges'.[92] In the long term, the experts proposed creating a judicial council which would hold sole disciplinary authority for ICC judges.[93] According to the proposal, this council would be preferable to an ad hoc non-permanent panel of judges because the institutionalization of a quasi-judicial body would benefit from 'accumulating and building institutional memory and best practices'.[94] The *Independent Expert Review* suggested composing such a council from current or former national and international judges nominated jointly by the President of the Court and the President of the Assembly of State Parties.[95] In addition, they suggested that the judicial council could collaborate with other international courts and tribunals to ensure coherent standards and rationalise expenses.[96]

In the end, the main motives for creating a judicial council type of accountability mechanism should therefore address both corporate solidarity and foster internal judicial independence. At the same time, any institutional

[88] Independent Expert Review of the International Criminal Court and the Rome Statute System. Final Report (30 September 2020)https://asp.icc-cpi.int/sites/asp/files/asp_docs/ASP19/IER-Final-Report-ENG.pdf>.
[89] ibid para 304.
[90] ibid para 306.
[91] ibid paras 311–21 and Recommendation 125.
[92] ibid para 319.
[93] ibid para 324 and Recommendation 126.
[94] ibid para 325.
[95] ibid para 326.
[96] ibid para 327 and Recommendation 127.

change should be undertaken with caution, given the risk of external political control or co-optation. Might an international judicial council capable of responding to those needs be conceivable?

First of all, the appointment of its members and the institutional safeguards for the exercise of their responsibilities would be key in the institutional design. The appointment power should not exclusively correspond to the political body of the corresponding regional organization, in order to minimize the risk of politicization. A proposal for all or at least most of the members could come from the regional court itself. Preferably, the members should be former judges of the international judiciary or high domestic courts. From an operational perspective, autonomy in the exercise of their functions should be ensured and a high degree of transparency demanded, which might, for instance, be furthered by publishing an annual report on its activity.

A permanent body would be preferable over an ad hoc arrangement, given the relevance of the functions to be performed from the perspective of judicial independence. A permanent body, moreover, would promote the elaboration of coherent practices over time. Using a single judicial council for the oversight of several international courts, as suggested by Bohlander, might, however, raise difficulties in terms of institutional design, given the broad diversity of international courts.

Caution should also be taken, at the same time, to avoid overcomplicating the institutional design. In that regard, there is some relevant experience with autonomous panels that have already been created for the selection of judges in certain regional courts, such as the 255 Panel at the CJEU we might consider. Sauvé suggested that 'the Panel could perhaps be seen, [...] only as far as the appointment of judges is concerned, as a germ, of a council of judiciary within the Union'.[97] Actually, the IOM already intervenes in the process of selecting the ICC judges. The IOM carries out a so-called due diligence process for elected officials.[98] In the case of the Caribbean Court of Justice, both judicial selection

[97] Jean-Marc Sauvé, 'Selecting the European Union's Judges' in Michal Bobek (ed), *Selecting Europe's Judges* (Oxford University Press 2015) 84.

[98] The *Annual report of the Head of the Independent Oversight Mechanism*, ICC-ASP/22/21, 16 November 2023, 9–10, available at https://asp.icc-cpi.int/sites/default/files/asp_docs/ICC-ASP-22-21-ENG.pdf, explains that: 'The due diligence process was aimed at assisting the Assembly in determining whether the candidates for judicial elections at the Court in 2023 met the requirement of high moral character as set out in article 36(3)(a) of the Rome Statute. It was intended to complement the review of the Advisory Committee on Nominations of the qualifications and experience of nominated candidates to facilitate the election of the most qualified candidates as Judges.' The IOM 'carried out an in-depth background check of criminal, academic and employment records of nominated candidates, which included an open-source review and the interview of over 100 former and current employers, peers and staff of nominated candidates.' Not once did the IOM identify any concern regarding the moral character of any of the nominees.

and removal are allocated to an autonomous body, the Regional Judicial and Legal Services Commission, which is detached from state governments and the political bodies of the Caribbean Community.[99]

On balance, the dominance of state governments in the international and regional sphere recommends against placing legal accountability mechanisms in the hands of political bodies to avoid abuses and interferences with judicial independence, thus a judicial model of accountability is preferable to compensate for the asymmetry. To confront the risks of corporate solidarity and the threats to internal judicial independence, a body with enough autonomy to instruct proceedings and eventually even impose sanctions may be appropriate. The overall aim would be enhancing the credibility and effectiveness of the disciplinary regime for the sake of the court's legitimacy. In that regard, strengthening the transparency of accountability mechanisms in order to enable external oversight by the public at large is crucial.

Also, given the difficulties or reluctance to apply the disciplinary regime, the system of recusal and disqualifications should be strengthened. Indeed, the parties should explicitly be given the possibility to request the disqualification of a judge. Even if in practice they might be enabled to do so, given the relevance for the right to due process for individuals, regional courts' statutes should explicitly regulate the procedure to disqualify a judge.

4. International Codes of Judicial Conduct and Ethics

While codes of judicial ethics have proliferated at the national level,[100] they are still in the evolutionary stage at the international level.[101] All the regional

[99] Agreement Establishing the Caribbean Court of Justice, 14 February 2001, article V. The composition of the Regional Judicial and Legal Services Commission is very diverse, including the following persons: (a) the President who shall be the Chairman of the Commission; (b) two persons nominated jointly by the Organization of the Commonwealth Caribbean Bar Association (OCCBA) and the Organisation of Eastern Caribbean States (OECS) Bar Association; (c) one chairman of the Judicial Services Commission of a Contracting Party selected in rotation in the English alphabetical order for a period of three years; (d) the Chairman of a Public Service Commission of a Contracting Party selected in rotation in the reverse English alphabetical order for a period of three years; (e) two persons from civil society nominated jointly by the Secretary-General of the Community and the Director General of the OECS for a period of three years following consultations with regional non-governmental organizations; (f) two distinguished jurists nominated jointly by the Dean of the Faculty of Law of the University of the West Indies, the Deans of the Faculties of Law of any of the Contracting Parties, and the Chairman of the Council of Legal Education; and (g) two persons nominated jointly by the Bar or Law Associations of the Contracting Parties.

[100] Elaine Mak, 'Researching Judicial Ethical Codes, or: How to Eat a Mille-Feuille?' (2018) 9 International Journal for Court Administration 55.

[101] Seibert-Fohr (n 36) 758.

courts examined in this chapter, except for the ATJ, have enacted codes of conduct. Indeed, the respective codes of conduct have been adopted or amended in the last decade. The CJEU adopted a new *Code of Conduct for Members and Former Members of the Court of Justice of the European Union* (CJEU Code) in 2017, which replaced the Code of Conduct adopted in 2007.[102] The ECtHR adopted a *Resolution on Judicial Ethics* (ECtHR Resolution) on 21 June 2021,[103] replacing the pronouncement on principles of judicial ethics adopted in 2008. Moreover, the ECtHR Resolution was amended in December 2024 to set up an Ethics Council. The IACtHR adopted, for the first time, the *Code of Ethics for the Judges of the Inter-American Court of Human Rights* (IACtHR Code)[104] in October 2022. Indeed, it is also wise to consider the extent to which codes of conduct and judicial ethics actually enhance the accountability of regional courts, even though they are not legally binding. First, we will examine their main aims and contents, and next their legal nature and effectiveness in fostering the accountability and legitimacy of regional courts.

In the preambles of all the codes just mentioned, two main aims jump out. The first is an interest in providing guidance to judges regarding the requirements of holding judicial office (internal function) and the second is enhancing public confidence in the court by declaring the principles and standards they are committed to respect in carrying out their functions (external function).[105] For the latter, the codes seek to bring more transparency to the obligations imposed by judicial office and thereby enhance public confidence in adjudication.[106] For instance, the Preamble of the ECtHR Resolution affirms the positive effect that adherence to the principles set forth in the text has on public confidence in the Court.

Codes of conduct and ethics tend to specify the standards of conduct expected from holders of judicial office. In that regard, they can be seen as complementing the general provisions included in the respective Statutes or Rules of Procedure. The main goal is ensuring independence and impartiality and thereby exclude conducts liable for impairing a reasonable perception of independence. In terms of scope, the codes in force apply not only to current regional judges but also to former members of the court, meaning they specify the duties that former judges must continue to respect after ceasing to hold

[102] Code of Conduct for Members and Former Members of the Court of Justice of the European Union, OJ C 397, 30 September 2021.

[103] Resolution on Judicial Ethics (adopted by the Plenary Court on 21 June 2021, amended on 16 December 2024).

[104] Code of Ethics for the Judges of the Inter-American Court of Human Rights 10 October 2022.

[105] Mak (n 100) 59.

[106] Seibert-Fohr (n 36) 761.

office.[107] Additionally, the codes of conduct and ethics include standards referring to both the conduct of judges in professional and extra-professional capacities. Most of the codes address the personal conduct of judges in extra-judicial settings in specific terms, banning external or professional activities that may either impair their independence and impartiality.[108]

For instance, Article VII of the ECtHR Resolution establishes the obligation for judges to declare any activity outside their judgeship to the President of the Court,[109] and it further specifies that, among the additional activities, 'only teaching, research and publishing activities may give rise to remuneration'. The CJEU Code also includes the obligation to disclose financial interests upon taking up their duties, including every entity in which the judges have a direct financial interest that, because of the size of the stake, might be perceived as potentially giving rise to a conflict of interest.[110] In addition, the Code specifies that the external activities of the members of the Court of Justice shall be published on the Institution's website after the activity has taken place,[111] to comply with the transparency requirements.[112]

Furthermore, the codes include provisions on the exercise of freedom of expression, a particularly relevant issue since the widespread proliferation of social media.[113] In general, a measure of restraint is called for in order to avoid compromising the authority, independence and impartiality of the Court in the eyes of the public opinion. For instance, the ECtHR Resolution mandates:

> Judges shall exercise their freedom of expression in a manner compatible with the dignity of their office and their loyalty to the institution of the Court. They shall refrain from expressing themselves, in whatever form and medium, in a manner which may undermine the authority and reputation of the Court or give rise to reasonable doubt as to their independence or impartiality. This applies equally to the exercise of judicial function, representation of the Court, and to academic or other public or private activities outside of the Court. They shall proceed with the utmost care if using social media.[114]

[107] ECtHR Resolution art XI; CJEU Code arts 1 and 9.
[108] Art VII ECtHR Resolution; art 8 CJEU; art IX IACtHR Code.
[109] As provided for in Rule 4 of the ECtHR Rules of Court.
[110] CJEU Code art 5.
[111] CJEU Code art 8(3).
[112] Available at https://curia.europa.eu/jcms/jcms/p1_743290/en/.
[113] IACtHR Code art VII.
[114] ECtHR Resolution art VI.

The IACtHR Code also includes a specific reference to free speech in very similar terms to the ECtHR Resolution.[115]

Provisions regarding professional performance, diligence, and competence are also generally found in the codes of conduct or ethics. Although formulated in quite general language, they complement the respective Statutes and Rules of Procedure for the purpose of ensuring professional standards. For instance, the IACtHR Code sets forth the obligation of judges to perform their duties in a diligent manner and resolve the cases in a reasonable time.[116] The codes sometimes include references to the need to maintain a high level of competence and enhance their professional knowledge and skills.[117]

Having examined the content of international codes of conduct and judicial ethics, we might look more closely at their legal nature. Codes of conduct and judicial ethics are regarded as a form of soft law, since they are not enforceable in and of themselves, and they do not provide for any sanctions. With these factors in mind, the IACtHR Code clearly establishes that the ethical principles embodied in the Code are to serve as guidelines.[118] Some form of oversight, however, is, at best assigned to the Court's President. The CJEU Code stipulates that the President of the CJEU, assisted by a Consultative Committee, shall be responsible for ensuring the proper application of the Code.[119] The Consultative Committee shall be composed of the three longest-serving members of the CJEU and the Vice-President. Article 10(2) gives the Committee the competence to issue an opinion regarding a judge's compliance with the Code, after hearing the judge in question. For its part, the ECtHR Resolution indicates that, in case of doubt as to the application of the code in a given situation, a judge may seek advice from the President of the Court, and the President may consult the Bureau,[120] if needed. In December 2024, the ECtHR Resolution was amended to incorporate an Ethics Council to advise the Court's President on questions of judicial ethics, which has replaced the Bureau. The Ethics Council is composed of the most senior Vice-President of the Court, the most senior Section President, and three most senior sitting Judges. Its main role is to give guidance on ethical standards. Additionally, the President is to make an annual report to the Plenary Court concerning compliance with these principles.[121]

[115] IACtHR Code art VII.
[116] ibid VIII; ECtHR Resolution art IV.
[117] Art IV ECtHR Resolution.
[118] IACtHR Code *Observancia del Código y ámbito de aplicación* para 1.
[119] CJEU Code art 10.
[120] The Bureau is composed of the President of the Court, the Vice-Presidents of the Court, and the Section Presidents.
[121] ECtHR Resolution art XII.

Also, the IACtHR Ethics' Code lays down that judges may consult the Court's President in case of doubt.[122]

Although the effectiveness of codes of ethics, as a form of soft law, might, in sum, be questioned given the lack of sanctions, they may well be appropriate at the international level. For one, they are less intrusive from the perspective of the court's independence, because they avoid empowering external actors in a highly sensitive field. Indeed, internal independence may be of greater concern, since the President of the Court tends to be given a consultative role or even the competence to issue an opinion or report. Nonetheless, some form of internal oversight is advisable for the sake of enhancing the codes' motivating function.

Moreover, by enshrining the standards of conduct to which the judges must commit, these codes provide a frame of reference for a minimum of public accountability, meaning they at least offer a foothold for society to hold judges to account for their behaviour. This could lead to a virtuous circle, for to enhance public confidence,[123] the courts are incentivized to providing greater transparency regarding the standards of conduct and their fulfilment. In terms of standards of diligence and scrutiny, some courts already offer general statistics that enable some assessment of the court's efficiency, such as the length of procedures and the workload, yet much room for improvement remains in that field.

Finally, international codes of conduct and judicial ethics suffer from a particular difficulty because, in Mak's words, 'a code of ethics can only be fully understood within the legal culture and constitutional framework in which it functions'.[124] The international judiciary encompasses judges from very diverse backgrounds (including academics, judges, diplomats), who work in very different jurisdictions and are trained in distinct traditions with their own professional and cultural understandings. This makes it very difficult to speak of a common culture of independence among judges. Nonetheless, that inherent diversity is precisely why setting common standards is of utmost importance. The codes provide a frame of reference to individual judges capable of contributing in the long run to the emergence of common standards and a perceivable judicial culture of independence in international adjudication.

[122] IACtHR Code 'Observancia del Código y ámbito de aplicación' para 2.

[123] Mak (n 100) 56, regarding the codes' role in securing public trust.

[124] Elaine Mak, 'A Code of Judicial Ethics as a Signpost and a Beacon: On Virtuous Judgecraft and Dutch Climate Litigation' (2023) 26 Legal Ethics 97, 99, claimed that 'a code of judicial ethics can only serve as a signpost for an individual judge or as a beacon for a member of society if they are aware of this legal cultural background and constitutional framework in which the judiciary fulfils its role'.

Indeed, the examination has shown how the codes of different regional courts mirror each other and tend to contain similar provisions, which is some proof of their potential to arrive at converging standards.

To conclude, this chapter's analysis of legal accountability mechanisms as constraints on regional courts from the perspective of judicial independence has shown that the standards are loosely defined and oversight tends to rest in the hands of the judges themselves. The effectiveness of the current design of the disciplinary regimes seems susceptible to corporate solidarity, which in turn risks undermining the perceived legitimacy of the regional courts in the eyes of the public opinion. Furthermore, the emphasis on avoiding the empowerment of external actors to influence regional courts might make them vulnerable to undue pressure from internal forces. Given the context in which regional courts operate and particularly the dominance of national governments in the appointment of regional judges, however, prioritizing external judicial independence by denying political actors a protagonist or even a direct role in the disciplinary regime seems appropriate. This does not mean that the current design cannot be improved either. More clearly defined standards, the differentiation of tiers of sanction, and the creation of autonomous bodies with functions to investigate and impose sanctions may well all improve the admittedly limited forms of legal accountability currently available in the regional sphere.

3

A Checks and Balances Approach to Political Constraints on Regional Courts

1. Introduction

International adjudication poses a dual concern for independence and accountability. While in the previous chapter we discussed legal accountability mechanisms, this chapter will delve into the political constraints that other branches of power impose from an institutional perspective. Several scholars have examined the political constraints on international courts.[1] While those studies provide valuable insight, they tend to adopt a rather descriptive perspective and focus on the actions of state governments. Certainly, international and regional courts operate under multiple sources of constraints. Political constraints might be perceived as undermining judicial independence. Nonetheless, as any institution that exercises public power, the adjudicative power of international and regional courts needs to be counterbalanced to prevent those courts from overstepping their prerogatives and ensure their overall legitimacy. Our aim is to develop a normative account of the constraints on regional courts. One possible way to exert legitmate power constraints on courts might be found in applying the doctrine of checks and balances, which plays a central role at the domestic level in liberal democracies. Following Ferejohn and Kramer,[2] the principle of checks and balances helps to balance the concern for independence and the concern for (democratic) accountability. The extent to which this doctrine might be transposed to the international sphere as a regulative ideal for the interaction between regional courts and other authorities is open to question.

[1] Tom Ginsburg, 'Political Constraints on International Courts' in Cesare PR Romano, Karen J Alter, and Yuval Shany (eds), *The Oxford Handbook of International Adjudication* (1st edn, Oxford University Press 2014); Geir Ulfstein, 'International Courts and Judges: Independence, Interaction, and Legitimacy' (2014) 46 New York University Journal of International Law & Politics 849; Laurence Helfer and Anne-Marie Slaughter, 'Why States Create International Tribunals: A Response to Professors Posner and Yoo' (2005) 93 California Law Review 899.

[2] John A Ferejohn and Larry D Kramer, 'Independent Judges, Dependent Judiciary: Institutionalizing Judicial Restraint' (2002) 77 New York University Law Review 962.

Balancing International Judicial Independence. Aida Torres Pérez, Oxford University Press.
 DOI: 10.1093/oso/9780198852544.003.0003

In the first part of Chapter 3, judicial independence will be examined under the framework of the principles of separation of powers and checks and balances. Those two basic constitutional principles deeply influence the interaction of the several branches of powers from the perspective of limited government. Although the two principles tend to be blurred, following Waldron, the principle of separation of powers 'counsels a qualitative separation of the different functions of government—legislation, adjudication, and executive administration.'[3] In contrast, the principle of checks and balances holds that 'the exercise of power by any one power-holder needs to be balanced and checked by the exercise of power by other power-holders.'[4] A thorough theoretical account of the two principles would exceed the scope of this work, but there are elements to point out that are highly relevant for the conceptualization of judicial independence and the corresponding power constraints.

The second part, takes up the feasibility of transposing the principle of checks and balances to the international sphere as a guiding normative principle for the interaction of regional courts and other domestic and regional authorities. We will tackle the complexities that arise in such a multileveled context. Our analysis leads us to the claim that the principle of checks and balances does provide a regulative ideal for critical examination of current legal and political constraints and for framing new institutional design proposals to balance better the tension between the major values and interests in play.

2. Framing Judicial Independence: Functional Separation and Institutional Constraints

At the domestic level, the notion of judicial independence emerged and evolved hand in hand with the doctrine of separation of powers.[5] As Shetreet bluntly puts it, 'The culture of judicial independence can only exist in a system which is based on the doctrine of separation of powers.'[6] The classic formulation of

[3] Jeremy Waldron, 'Separation of Powers in Thought and Practice?' (2013) 54 Boston College Law Review 433, 434.

[4] ibid 433.

[5] Pasquale Pasquino, 'Prolegomena to a Theory of Judicial Power' (2003) 2 The Law and Practice of International Courts and Tribunals 11, 14–15; Dominik Zimmermann, *The Independence of International Courts: The Adherence of the International Judiciary to a Fundamental Value of the Administration of Justice* (1st edn, Nomos 2014) 55.

[6] Shimon Shetreet, 'The Significance of the Independence of the Judiciary Creating a Culture of Judicial Independence: The Practical Challenge and the Conceptual and Constitutional Infrastructure' in Shimon Shetreet and Christopher Forsyth (eds), *The Culture of Judicial Independence* (Brill | Nijhoff 2012).

the doctrine of separation of powers corresponds to Montesquieu, who argued for separating the judicial function from the legislative and the executive functions to protect liberty:

> There is no liberty, if the judiciary power be not separated from the legislative and executive. Were it joined with the legislative, the life and liberty of the subject would be exposed to arbitrary control; for the judge would then be the legislator. Were it joined to the executive power, the judge might behave with violence and oppression.[7]

In recent decades, however, the principle of separation of powers has been criticized as archaic and ill-suited to regulate the exercise of power in the modern state.[8] The current dynamics of governance and the emergence of distinct institutions have challenged the tripartite conception of the separation of powers. As such, we have seen constitutional courts perform a sort of quasi-legislative function, judicial councils set up for governance and oversight of the judiciary, and administrative agencies that combine rule-making and quasi-adjudicative functions.[9]

Analysts have also pointed out conceptual problems. Vile has asserted that the separation of powers 'represents an area of political thought in which there has been extraordinary confusion in the definition and use of terms'.[10] Carolan criticized its indeterminacy, stating it is 'too vague and imprecise to authoritatively regulate the institutional structures of the state' and concluding that it was ultimately outdated and ineffective.[11] Moreover, Kavanagh claimed that 'the purity of the "pure doctrine" is both descriptively inaccurate and normatively implausible'.[12] She argued that the correlation of 'one branch-one function' pertaining to a pure view of the principle is problematic since the several branches exercise multiple functions and suggested an approach based upon the idea of 'institutional roles', which might encompass multiple functions.[13]

[7] Charles Louis de Secondat de Montesquieu, *The Spirit of the Laws* (Anne M Cohler, Basia Carolyn Miller, and Harold Samuel Stone eds, Cambridge University Press 1989).

[8] Eoin Carolan, *The New Separation of Powers: A Theory for the Modern State* (Oxford University Press 2009) 19–45; Eric A Posner and Adrian Vermeule, *The Executive Unbound: After the Madisonian Republic* (1st edn, Oxford University Press 2010); MJC Vile, *Constitutionalism and the Separation of Powers* (2nd edn, Liberty Fund 1998) 6–8.

[9] Peter L Strauss, 'The Place of Agencies in Government: Separation of Powers and the Fourth Branch' (1984) 84 Columbia Law Review 573, 578.

[10] Vile (n 8) 2.

[11] Carolan (n 8) 22–28. He claimed that 'for the doctrine to function effectively, some external criterion or value is required capable of supplying the certainty lacking in its basic design', 27.

[12] Aileen Kavanagh, *The Collaborative Constitution* (Cambridge University Press 2024) 90.

[13] ibid 90–93.

Despite such criticism, the tripartite vision of the principle of separation of powers persists, although it is no longer understood (if it truly ever was) as a pure model of separation.[14] Notwithstanding, the principle of separation is relevant to the value of judicial independence and preservation of each function's integrity—'the dignity of legislation, the independence of courts, and the authority of the executive'[15]—to better rationalize and implement an articulated form of governance.[16]

The integrity of the judiciary can be approached from functional and institutional perspectives.[17] From a functional perspective, the main purpose of courts is adjudication, which consists of resolving the disputes brought before them through the application of the law following a formalized procedure.[18] The principle of separation warns us to guard against potential interference by the other powers, especially the executive. Indeed, the canonical definition of judicial independence requires freedom for courts from improper pressure or influence by external actors.

Another implication of separation of powers for the judicial function is a need to keep it separate from the legislative function, straightforwardly understood as the passing of generally applicable laws. Nonetheless, the law's indeterminacy forces courts to interpret the law, which necessarily leaves room for discretion. In exercising discretion, courts might effectively make law through interpretation. Moreover, some courts are granted the power of judicial review over legislation to ensure compatibility with the constitution. In decentralized systems of judicial review, in fact, all courts may exercise that function, such as in the United States following the famous *Marbury v Madison* decision of the Supreme Court. In centralized systems of judicial review, this power is limited to the Constitutional Court. Inevitably, the functions performed by courts sometimes go beyond the adjudication of cases and Montesquieu's conception of the role of judges as no more than the 'mouth that pronounces the words of the law'. Nonetheless, judicial law-making or judicial review of legislation does not necessitate altogether abandoning the principle of separation of powers. As Kavanagh has argued, a role-based approach to the principle of separation of powers may accommodate the multifunctionality of the branches of government such that 'the judicial role of adjudicating and resolving individual

[14] Vile (n 8) 13; Christoph Möllers, *The Three Branches: A Comparative Model of Separation of Powers* (1st edn, Oxford University Press 2013); Shetreet (n 6) 51–52; Kavanagh (n 12) 87–91.
[15] Waldron (n 3) 434.
[16] ibid 467.
[17] Cheryl Saunders, 'Separation of Powers and the Judicial Branch' (2006) 11 Judicial Review 337.
[18] Waldron (n 3) 462.

disputes can encompass the dual functions of applying and making new law'.[19] However true this argument may be, the principle of separation of powers alone does not account for the need to constrain judicial power. For an answer to those concerns, recourse must be made to the principle of checks and balances.

From the perspective of institutional design, separation of powers involves finding an arrangement that both differentiates the judiciary from the legislative and the executive and leaves the judiciary well-situated to perform the adjudicative function in terms of composition and decision-making procedures. From this perspective comes, for instance, the common understanding that judges are not to have roles or positions in the other branches, and that members of the other branches are not to sit on courts. Several other aspects of institutional design of the judiciary relevant to judicial independence include: the procedures for the appointment and removal of judges, the length of terms, salary protections, court administration, and disciplinary regime.[20] While institutional design should clearly incorporate measures to ensure judicial independence, this does not mean that courts should be wholly insulated, given their multifunctional bailiwick and the risk of jurisdictional overreach. As Saunders has usefully pointed out, there are several 'points of institutional interface between the judiciary and the other branches, representing checks on the judicial branch'.[21] For instance, federal judges in the United States are nominated by the executive and approved by the upper house of the legislature. Similarly, members of constitutional courts are usually appointed by parliament and/or government. As may now appear evident, the principle of separation of powers is highly relevant to institutional design in the interest of safeguarding judicial independence, yet also, from the perspective of the overall legitimacy of the judiciary, there is a need for mechanisms of constraint prescribed by the related principle of checks and balances.

In the constitutional tradition of the United States, the separation of powers has been dynamically understood in conjunction with the principle of checks and balances. Indeed, some critics have faulted the institutional design established by the 1787 US Constitution for not separating the powers clearly enough, pointing out areas where the divisions are blurred.[22] James Madison was perhaps the fiercest defender of the original institutional design. As he

[19] Kavanagh (n 12) 92.
[20] Saunders (n 17) 341.
[21] Saunders (n 17).
[22] Sam J Ervin, 'Separation of Powers: Judicial Independence' (1970) 35 Law and Contemporary Problems 108, 115.

argued in the *Federalist Papers*: 'Ambition must be made to counteract ambition.'[23] Madison went on to explain that the separation of powers 'does not require that the legislative, executive, and judiciary departments should be wholly unconnected with each other', holding that, 'unless these departments be so far connected and blended as to give to each a constitutional control over the others, the degree of separation (...) essential to a free government, can never in practice be duly maintained'.[24] According to the doctrine of checks and balances, each branch of government ought to exercise its assigned functions while mutually collaborating with and monitoring the others to prevent any of them from overreaching their powers.[25] The principle of checks and balances thus helps protect the separation of powers, blurred as they may be, by ensuring that no branch overreaches its role.[26]

With particular regard to courts, they have always been understood as political actors inasmuch as they do intervene in law-making and check both the legislative and the executive powers. Their independence must therefore be understood in light of the doctrine of checks and balances. Ferejohn's take on this dynamic is especially illuminating.[27] In 'Independent Judges, Dependent Judiciaries,' he makes an argument that combines the independence of judges from an individual perspective with constraining elements on the judiciary as a whole: 'The institutional structure established by the Constitution balances protections for individual judges with a judiciary that is rather thoroughly dependent on the other branches of government for the means to do its constitutional business.'[28] Following Ferejohn's argument, the dependence of the judiciary on the political branches is not a constitutional accident. The Constitution purposefully instituted a complex set of interdependencies among the major departments of government, rather than establishing a strict separation of powers.[29]

[23] Alexander Hamilton, James Madison, and John Jay, *The Federalist Papers* (New American Library 1961) 51.

[24] ibid 48.

[25] Shimon Shetreet, 'The Normative Cycle of Shaping Judicial Independence in Domestic and International Law: The Mutual Impact of National and International Jurisprudence and Contemporary Practical and Conceptual Challenges' (2009) 10 Chicago Journal of International Law 275, 302, argues that the doctrine of checks and balances is 'based on the concept that no function of one branch of government should be exercised by another branch and that each branch should function as a check on any improper use of power by the other branches'.

[26] Aileen Kavanagh, 'The Constitutional Separation of Powers' in David Dyzenhaus and Malcolm Thorburn (eds), *Philosophical Foundations of Constitutional Law* (Oxford University Press 2016) 233–34.

[27] John Ferejohn, 'Independent Judges, Dependent Judiciary: Explaining Judicial Independence' (1999) 72 University of Southern California 353, 362.

[28] ibid 365.

[29] ibid 362.

Ferejohn further elaborated this view in a subsequent article co-authored by Kramer that emphasized the need to search for balance between independence and accountability through complex institutional design: 'We mix and match various structural arrangements—some protecting the independence of judges, others making them accountable—in an effort to create a properly balanced judicial system.'[30] Doubtlessly, many models might achieve that balance, but 'what matters is to understand how a particular judicial system balances concerns for independence with concerns for accountability'.[31] One famous example of the separation and collaboration duality from the US Supreme Court jurisprudence is found in Justice Jackson's concurring opinion in *Youngstown Co v Sawyer*: 'While the Constitution diffuses power the better to secure liberty, it also contemplates that practice will integrate the dispersed powers into a workable government. It enjoins upon its branches separateness but interdependence, autonomy but reciprocity.'[32]

In the end, the principles of separation of powers and checks and balances emphasize different yet complementary aspects of the judiciary. First among these aspects is respect for the integrity of the main function attributed to courts and therefore the need to ensure the independence of courts in resolving disputes according to the law. At the domestic level, safeguards of the independence of individual judges often include life tenure and salary protections. Second, in terms of institutional design, to the extent that courts exercise public power, checks and balances as a principle recognizes the need for constraint mechanisms in the hands of the legislative and executive to curb potential abuses and ensure legal and political accountability. There is no single model to accomplish that goal, and the constraining mechanisms themselves also vary. For instance, Ferejohn and Kramer surveyed the many constraining attributes of the legislative and executive powers in the United States. For Congress, these include impeachment, control over the budget, the power to define the subject-matter jurisdiction of the federal courts, regulating deferral practice and procedure; for the President, the power of appointment and promotion; and for the executive more generally, non-enforcement.[33] We can therefore observe that judicial independence does not necessarily entail walling the judiciary off from the other branches.[34]

[30] Ferejohn and Kramer (n 2) 964.

[31] ibid 964.

[32] *Youngstown Sheet & Tube Co v Sawyer* [1952] US Supreme Court 343 U.S. 579 635.

[33] Ferejohn and Kramer (n 2) 976.

[34] John Thomas of Cwmgiedd, 'The Judiciary Within the State—the Relationship Between the Branches of the State' 7 <https://www.judiciary.uk/wp-content/uploads/2022/07/lcj-michael-ryle-memorial-lecture-20170616.pdf> accessed 19 March 2026.

Judges are required to decide free from undue pressures and thus adequate protections must be put in place, while the judiciary itself is enmeshed in a web of interdependency with the other branches of power under the checks and balances principle. Although apparently in tension, the complementarity between the principles of separation of powers and checks and balances needs to be emphasized because, ultimately, they serve the same values: preventing the abuse of power and ensuring the rule of law[35] for the benefit of individual liberty.[36]

3. A Checks and Balances Approach to International Judicial Independence

3.1. Global constitutionalism: pursuing the rule of law in the international sphere

The extent to which the principles of separation of powers and checks and balances might be transposed to the international sphere is worth exploring, in particular as regards the possible normative guiding principle to orient the interplay between regional courts and other political actors. Clearly, the political and institutional framework in which regional courts operate differs starkly from the domestic framework. The familiar tripartite separation of powers does not apply either. According to constitutional doctrine, all public power derives from the people and is distributed among the constituted powers by the constitution. At the international level, the sources of power are more diverse, and the institutions of each overlapping system are not regulated by a single superior norm. That the international sphere lacks any institutionalized system of checks and balances enshrined in an overarching constitutional structure is self-evident. Furthermore, while the domestic judiciary consists of a system of permanent courts hierarchically organized, the international judiciary is lacking in much integration, whether vertical or horizontal. The international judiciary resembles a motley collection of courts set up to address specific issues that pertain to a variety of legal systems where jurisdictions might partly

35 Waldron (n 3) 462.

36 Eric Barendt, 'Separation of Powers and Constitutional Government' (1995) Winter Public Law 599, 605–06, claims that the purpose of separation of powers is to protect the liberty of the individual by making tyrannical and arbitrary state action more difficult.

overlap.[37] This fragmented scenario might lead us to surmise that the principle of checks and balances cannot be applied to the international sphere.

I, nonetheless, would advise against discarding the principle of checks and balances as a regulative ideal so hastily, even though its application would clearly require great refinement and nuance in order to factor in the variety of interactions among national, supranational, and international institutions from a multilevel perspective. Moreover, we must remember that globalization has brought transformations at the national level as well.[38] Globalization, understood broadly as a set of developments that transcend national borders, has led to growing interdependence in fields ranging from economics to environmental protection, telecommunications, security, and public health, among others. On some occasions, these developments have prompted the creation of international regulatory regimes or other forms of collaboration through relatively informal transnational networks.[39] Sometimes typical state functions are even transferred to the international arena. In these situations, states retain coercive powers, although public power is fragmented because political decision-making takes place in a plurality of forums at inter-, supra-, and transnational spheres.[40]

In general, the creation of international regimes and the allocation of state functions at the international level have been justified with the argument that states' ability to effectively rule within their respective territories has been undermined as a consequence of mounting political and economic interdependence.[41] If states cannot perform their functions and attain goals, their legitimacy comes under threat. Hence, effective regulation in specific subject matters vindicates regional or international action.[42]

By consequence, state constitutions no longer regulate the exercise of power within the territory of the state in a comprehensive manner,[43] but rather state

[37] Joe McIntyre and James Crawford, 'The Independence and Impartiality of the "International Judiciary"' in Christopher Forsyth and Shimon Shetreet (eds), *The Culture of Judicial Independence* (Brill 2011) 190–91.

[38] Aida Torres Pérez, 'The Internationalization of Lawmaking Processes: Constraining or Empowering the Executive' (2006) 14 Tulsa Journal of Comparative & International Law 1.

[39] Anne-Marie Slaughter, *A New World Order* (Princeton University Press 2004).

[40] Jost Delbruck, 'Transnational Federalism: Problems and Prospects of Allocating Public Authority Beyond the State' 11 *Indiana Journal of Global Legal Studies* 30, 39.

[41] Robert O Keohane, 'Sovereignty, Interdependence, and International Institutions' in Michael Joseph Smith and Linda B Miller (eds), *Ideas and Ideals: Essays on Politics in Honor of Stanley Hoffmann* (1st edn, Routledge 1991) 92; Anne-Marie Slaughter, 'Sovereignty and Power in a Networked World Order' (2004) 40 Stanford Journal of International Law 283, 284.

[42] Benedict Kingsbury, Nico Krisch, and Richard B Stewart, 'The Emergence of Global Administrative Law' (2013) 27 Revue internationale de droit économique 37, 16.

[43] Anne Peters, 'The Merits of Global Constitutionalism' (2009) 16 Indiana Journal of Global Legal Studies 397, 405; Anne Peters, 'Compensatory Constitutionalism: The Function and Potential

constitutions must be complemented with norms deriving from other sources to complete an overall picture of the regulation of public power and its limits. The notion of constitutional pluralism has been developed in the scholarly literature to capture these transformations and offer a new theoretical framework for the organization of power beyond the state. This prolific field of research was initiated by Neil MacCormick.[44] Constitutional pluralism can be basically characterized as a compound in which several interacting legal systems, each with a functioning constitution, coexist without a hierarchical ordering of the foundational-constitutional norms of the respective legal systems.[45] The lack of hierarchy between the foundational norms of the interacting legal systems is not a shortcoming that needs to be overcome, but rather a defining element. The interplay among the national, supranational, and international systems has been reconstructed in non-hierarchical terms from several perspectives encompassing constitutional pluralism,[46] multilevel constitutionalism,[47] composite constitutionalism,[48] network constitutionalism,[49] and other theoretical constructs[50] that often not only aspire to provide a descriptive account, but a normative basis as well.

At the same time, a process of constitutionalization has been unfolding in the international sphere. This global constitutionalism 'advocates for the application of constitutional principles in the international sphere in order to improve the effectiveness and fairness of the international legal order'.[51] The goal of adopting applicable constitutional principles is bolstering the legitimacy of

of Fundamental International Norms and Structures' (2006) 19 Leiden Journal of International Law 579, 579.

[44] Neil MacCormick, *Questioning Sovereignty: Law, State, and Nation in the European Commonwealth* (Oxford University Press 1999).

[45] ibid 104. In MacCormick's words, 'Where there is a plurality of institutional normative orders, each with a functioning constitution (at least in the sense of a body of higher-order norms establishing and conditioning relevant governmental powers), it is possible that each acknowledge the legitimacy of every other within its own sphere, while none asserts or acknowledges constitutional superiority over another'.

[46] Neil Walker, 'The Idea of Constitutional Pluralism' (2002) 65 Modern Law Review 317, 317.

[47] Ingolf Pernice, 'Multilevel Constitutionalism and the Treaty of Amsterdam: European Constitution-Making Revisited?' (1999) 36 Common Market Law Review 703.

[48] LFM Besselink, *A Composite European Constitution: Een Samengestelde Europese Constitutie* (Europa Law Publishing 2008).

[49] Rafael Bustos Gisbert, *La Constitución Red: Un Estudio Sobre Supraestatalidad y Constitución* (Instituto Vasco de Administración Pública = Herri-Arduralaritzaren Euskal Erakundea 2005).

[50] Matej Avbelj and Jan Komárek, *Constitutional Pluralism in the European Union and Beyond* (Hart 2012); A von Bogdandy, 'Pluralism, Direct Effect, and the Ultimate Say: On the Relationship Between International and Domestic Constitutional Law' (2008) 6 International Journal of Constitutional Law 397; Nico Krisch, *Beyond Constitutionalism: The Pluralist Structure of Postnational Law* (Oxford University Press 2012).

[51] Peters, 'The Merits of Global Constitutionalism' (n 43).

the international legal order and institutions, albeit without calling for a world state or a world constitution.[52] The relevant legal rules and principles will not be found in a single document, but scattered in diverse legal texts and case law.

Constitutional principles cannot be automatically transposed to the international arena, nor should such an attempt be made. They will always require a degree of modification and adaptation, as will the modes of implementation. They might better be seen as parameters to include in planning strategies adequate for the international sphere.[53] We should also keep certain risks in mind. For instance, applying constitutional principles might implicitly confer the international order with unwarranted legitimacy.[54] Despite the risks, however, constitutionalism provides lenses through which the international order can be critically examined and principles for the assessment of current institutional arrangements and the elaboration of proposals for improvement. Indeed, the critical potential of global constitutionalism to identify areas where legitimacy is lacking and formulate remedies for them should be emphasized.[55]

Now we can turn to the extent to which the principle of checks and balances might serve as a guiding principle for the organization of power in this multilevel context. In our approach, the principle plays a key role in transcending the national-international divide and maintaining the focus on the exercise of public power by multiple actors in the context of increasingly intertwined national and international actors and authorities. As such, the action of state governments in the international sphere takes multiple forms: negotiating and enacting bilateral and multilateral treaties and agreements; participating in informal networks; and integrating intergovernmental bodies of international organizations. Replicating the principle of checks and balances from one level to the other is insufficient. It must be applied instead to the multiple interactions among multiple actors in multiple spheres.

In sum, the principle of checks and balances cannot and should not be automatically applied to discipline the interaction among institutions that exercise power in the international sphere, given the great difference in the institutional framework. Nonetheless, the basic objectives and methodologies are still relevant at the international level. As argued in the previous section, the main goal of the principle of checks and balances is preventing the abuse of power and ensuring the rule of law through the establishment of collaboration and

[52] Anne Peters, 'Global Constitutionalism' in Michael T Gibbons and Diana H Coole (eds), *The Encyclopedia of Political Thought*, vol 8 (Wiley-Blackwell 2014) 1–2.

[53] Ibid.

[54] Jan Klabbers, 'Constitutionalism Lite' (2004) 1 International Organizations Law Review 31, 48.

[55] Peters, 'The Merits of Global Constitutionalism' (n 43).

control mechanisms. As McCorquodale has succinctly puts it, 'The rule of law remains about values or meta-principles within a system, and constraints on the use of power, and not just about institutions per se.'[56] The realization of the rule of law at the international level does not depend on the replication of institutions or structures pertaining to the domestic legal system. The principle of checks and balances as such is not dependent on the canonical tripartite separation but it can embrace multilple actors. This is not to say that, in practice, power at the international level is attributed and organized according to this principle. Indeed, globalization has exacerbated imbalances in favour of the executive, which might be justified to some extent, but we must not neglect them. As argued elsewhere, the internationalization of law-making processes has constrained state sovereignty while empowering executive power.[57] The principle of checks and balances can be applied normatively in the assessment of current norms and practices to guide institutional design. The development of supranational and international legal frameworks offers an opportunity for instituting mechanisms that constrain the exercise of power in the international sphere.

3.2. From judicial independence to interdependence

The aim here is not to offer a general theory of checks and balances for the international order, but rather a normative framework to assess political constraints on regional courts, while preserving their independence. The principle of checks and balances may well provide a suitable lens to assess and guide institutional arrangements regarding regional courts, but several questions must be explored before such a determination can be made. Regional courts operate in a web of multiple constraints imposed by widely varying institutions. Do those constraints undermine the independence of regional courts, or might they be justified in light of the checks and balances principle? The goal here is to explore the checks and balances principle as a guiding regulative ideal.

The argument here is that judicial independence should not be sought through the insulation of regional courts (even if sufficiently insulating them were possible) and that constraints on regional courts can be justified in light of the checks and balances principle. Those constraints can be conceptualized

[56] Robert McCorquodale, 'Defining the International Rule of Law: Defying Gravity?' (2016) 65 The International and Comparative Law Quarterly 277, 292.

[57] Torres Pérez (n 38).

as forms of interdependence that enhance the overall legitimacy of regional courts. The principle of checks and balances helps to delimit the space for free judicial decision-making, which cannot nor should be unlimited. Justifiable forms of interdependence between regional courts and other institutions do exist. The notion of interdependence involves mechanisms of collaboration and control with other actors[58] without endangering the integrity of the adjudicative function.[59] The notion of interdependence incorporates the goal of protecting judicial independence while providing constraints on regional courts' power. It allows us to combine separation and constraint.[60] Indeed, following Ferejohn, interdependencies are leveraged to prevent each branch from overstepping its powers and to protect each branch against encroachment by the others.[61] From this perspective, the principle of checks and balances may well contribute to both constraining the judiciary and ensuring independent adjudication.

Whether those forms of institutional interdependence or constraining mechanisms curtail judicial independence will be determined by how those mechanisms are designed and used in practice.[62] Indeed, those mechanisms themselves, and here the appointment power comes to mind, might be liable to abuse out of self-interest. The appointment of regional judges tends to be assigned to state governments, which nominate the candidates and elect or appoint them in the corresponding intergovernmental body. The process of judicial selection tends to be highly politicized.[63] Judicial selection is regarded many times as an instrument in the hands of state governments that jeopardizes judicial independence. Nonetheless, there might be good reasons to attribute the power of judicial selection to state governments to enhance democratic accountability.[64] The key question is how the mechanism is designed and how this power is used in practice, since governments might be tempted to use this power to appoint loyal judges who will advance partisan interests. Sole governmental selection in the dark and behind closed doors may not deliver the expected value of democratic accountability. Moreover, to

[58] Zimmermann (n 5) 64: 'if [the judiciary] does have some real power, then its independence must be flanked by some degree of interdependence in order to prevent an abuse of isolated independence.'

[59] Aida Torres Pérez, 'From Judicial Independence to Interdependence in the International Sphere' (2017) 24 Maastricht Journal of European and Comparative Law 462, 472.

[60] Kavanagh (n 26).

[61] Ferejohn (n 27) 357: 'These interdependencies were aimed at providing the means for each branch of the federal government to protect itself against encroachments by the others.'

[62] Ferejohn (n 27).

[63] Ruth Mackenzie and others, *Selecting International Judges: Principle, Process, and Politics* (Oxford University Press 2010).

[64] Aida Torres Pérez, 'Can Judicial Selection Secure Judicial Independence?' in Michal Bobek (ed), *Selecting Europe's Judges* (Oxford University Press 2015) 188–90.

the extent that selection power is concentrated in the hands of the executive, it risks being abused. Therefore, participation of other bodies might be advisable to constrain executive action. Constraints on the executive might come from the national sphere, such as selection commissions with fair and transparent procedures for nominating the candidates, or the international one, such as advisory expert panels, or representative bodies. The participation of multiple actors in the process of selection potentially enhances judicial independence, since it creates incentives for mutual control.[65]

In the shift from the national to the international sphere, and in particular when the focus is on regional courts, the framing of the principle of checks and balances must comprehend and respond to several layers of complexity.

a) The multiplicity of spheres and actors

Conceptualizing checks and balances doctrine for application to international and regional courts requires a multidimensional approach that integrates multiple spheres in the analysis: national, supranational, and international. The diverse spheres themselves are better conceived of as a continuum rather than wholly separated levels of inquiry. Regional courts are created by the states and develop their functions in collaboration with the international organs of the respective international organizations as well as domestic institutions.

The multiplicity of institutional actors is another key characteristic that must be considered. Instead of conceiving states as indivisible actors in the international sphere, we need to disaggregate the state into its separate branches.[66] We also need to disaggregate the international organizations into the distinct bodies that exercise public power. The literature on the political constraints on international courts has usually focused on the checks on courts in the hands of state governments. Nonetheless, looking at international and regional courts through the prism of checks and balances reveals potential constraints from other institutional actors, such as the intergovernmental bodies of the international organizations in which they operate, legislative bodies, domestic and other international courts, as well as other institutions that do not fit nicely into the tripartite perspective, such as different types of commissions like the Inter-American Commission on Human Rights in the case of the Inter-American Court of Human Rights (IACtHR), or the Office of the Prosecutor of the International Criminal Court. We must therefore employ a

[65] James Melton and Tom Ginsburg, 'Does De Jure Judicial Independence Really Matter?: A Reevaluation of Explanations for Judicial Independence' (2014) 2 Journal of Law and Courts 187, 192.

[66] Slaughter (n 39).

disaggregated perspective of both the state[67] and the international organizations to which they belong.

As regards the institutional mechanisms of interdependence, these are not found in a single, solitary text, but are rooted in various legal sources that include diverse international and state norms. Moreover, while some of those mechanisms, such as judicial appointment, are explicitly established with formal processes others, such as voicing dissatisfaction with international courts' judgments, often follow more informal channels.[68] It is also important to understand how the formal mechanisms enshrined in written legal rules (*de iure*) are operationalized in practice (*de facto*).[69]

b) Dynamic perspective

The functioning of the principle of checks and balances cannot be understood from a static perspective, but rather must be considered as one that necessarily fluctuates over time. Note how the theoretical distinction between *ex ante* and *ex post* constraints tends to blur in practice.[70] Judicial appointment is usually understood as an *ex ante* control mechanism, but governments might consider a regional court's past judgments in order to decide whether to reappoint a judge. Similarly, treaty or legislative override is necessarily *ex post*, since the decision to amend a treaty or legislation is taken after a regional court passes judgment, but the possibility of treaty or legislative override might very well conceivably affect the regional court's behaviour in future cases, before issuing judgment. Indeed, the same mechanism can plausibly be regarded as both *ex ante* and *ex post*. For instance, in their analysis of the mechanisms for constrained independence, Helfer and Slaughter include among *ex ante* mechanisms the existence of precisely defined substantive rules, and then list the reinterpretation of substantive rules as an *ex post* mechanism.[71] For Ginsburg, the definition of jurisdiction would be an *ex ante* constraint, while any attempt at limiting the court's jurisdiction would be *ex post*.[72]

Moving on from the blurry theoretical distinctions among them, it is critical to keep in mind that mechanisms of collaboration and control are exercised

[67] Slaughter (n 39); Hinako Takata, 'Separation of Powers in a Globalized Democratic Society: Theorizing the Human Rights Treaty Organs' Interactions with Various State Organs' (2024) 13 Global Constitutionalism 458.

[68] Ulfstein (n 1).

[69] Lars P Feld and Stefan Voigt, 'Economic Growth and Judicial Independence: Cross-Country Evidence Using a New Set of Indicators' (2003) 19 European Journal of Political Economy 497.

[70] Several authors have distinguished between constraining mechanisms that operate *ex ante* and *ex post*: Helfer and Slaughter (n 1); Ginsburg (n 1).

[71] Helfer and Slaughter (n 1).

[72] Ginsburg (n 1).

over time and evolve in light of the course of action taken by other institutions. Whether constraining mechanisms are enforced or not, and the extent of their impact upon judicial behaviour, is an empirical matter. Indeed, the mere existence of those constraining mechanisms, even in the lack of enforcement, may well affect the regional courts' action, which might respond by developing forms of self-restraint. Ferejohn and Kramer, in their analysis of domestic courts in the United States, claim that institutional dependence has driven the judiciary to become a 'self-regulator, the creator of self-imposed institutional and doctrinal constraints',[73] and bring out several institutionalized forms of judicial restraint.[74] Analysing the evolution of mechanisms of interdependence over time shows that regional courts have also developed self-restraint mechanisms, doctrines of deference and other forms of resilience,[75] such as the margin of appreciation doctrine elaborated by the European Court of Human Rights (ECtHR).

c) Institutional mutual recognition and respect as precondition

At the domestic level, the duty of mutual respect among the interacting institutions underpins the accounts of the principle of separation and checks and balances.[76] Inter-institutional comity or respect is thus a precondition for the proper functioning of those principles. Kavanagh has identified two elements deriving from the duty of mutual respect: mutual self-restraint and mutual support.[77] The former requires that the institutions 'avoid interfering with the others' ability to carry out their respective roles',[78] while the latter requires them 'to actively support each other in various ways in order to realise the common goal of good government under the constitution'.[79] In turn, mutual respect is grounded on the deeper value of a coordinated approach to governance. The interacting branches of power are conceived as constituent parts of a constitutional system such that they mutually recognize each other as part of a common project of governance.[80] In that regard, Kavanagh posited that

[73] Ferejohn and Kramer (n 2) 964.

[74] ibid 964, the authors argued that as a result of this self-restraint, the political branches seldom need to exercise their constraining powers or even threaten to do so.

[75] Mikael Rask Madsen, Pola Cebulak, and Micha Wiebusch, 'Backlash Against International Courts: Explaining the Forms and Patterns of Resistance to International Courts' (2018) 14 International Journal of Law in Context 197.

[76] Dimitrios Kyritsis, *Where Our Protection Lies: Separation of Powers and Constitutional Review* (1st edn, Oxford University Press 2017) 45–47.

[77] Kavanagh (n 12) 98–101.

[78] ibid 98.

[79] ibid.

[80] Daniel Halberstam, 'Constitutional Heterarchy: The Centrality of Conflict in the European Union and the United States' in Jeffrey L Dunoff and Joel P Trachtman (eds), *Ruling the World?* (1st edn, Cambridge University Press 2009) 334.

'although the branches of government play distinct roles in the constitutional scheme, they nonetheless share the common goal of securing just government under the constitution.'[81]

In sum, the proper functioning of checks and balances through the co-ordinated action of different institutions requires, as a precondition, inter-institutional recognition and respect in pursuit of a common goal.[82] Mutual recognition involves the acknowledgement of the others as part of a common enterprise, while mutual respect conveys not only a duty of non-interference but also a positive duty to assist each other.[83] Without mutual recognition and respect, effective interdependence cannot be sustained.[84]

Given the need for mutual recognition and respect as part of a common enterprise for the principle of checks and balances to function properly at the domestic level, we might examine the prospects for this precondition in the international sphere. May regional courts be conceptualized as part of a broader institutional network composed of domestic and international institutions that mutually recognize and respect each other, and if so, to what extent?

At the domestic level, the common goal or joint enterprise is embodied in the constitution, understood as a common project of governance. In contrast, the mandates of international and regional courts are sectoral and vary according to the respective constitutive treaties. Nonetheless, the establishment of a regional court obeys the premise of a common goal, be it protecting human rights or fostering economic and political integration in the case of the regional courts under analysis, beyond the specific reasons why state governments create or accept the jurisdiction of those courts.[85] In practice, tension arises when regional courts are portrayed as external actors imposing their views on democratically legitimate institutions, such as the United Kingdom's reaction to *Hirst v the United Kingdom*,[86] or the Argentine Supreme Court's rebuke of the IACtHR in *Fontevecchia*.[87]

Not only do regional courts require recognition by domestic institutions as part of a joint enterprise in order to achieve those common goals, but also the interacting institutions owe each other mutual respect in terms of both mutual support and restraint. Mutual support is key for the well-functioning of

[81] Kavanagh (n 12) 101; Kavanagh (n 26) 235–36.
[82] Kyritsis (n 76) 45–46.
[83] ibid 46–47.
[84] Thomas of Cwmgiedd (n 34) 8.
[85] Andrew Moravcsik, 'The Origins of Human Rights Regimes: Democratic Delegation in Postwar Europe' (2000) 54(2) International Organization 217.
[86] ECtHR *Hirst v the United Kingdom* (No. 2), App no 74025/01 (ECtHR, 6 October 2005).
[87] IACtHR *Fontevecchia and D'amico vs Argentina*, 29 November 2011.

those regional regimes to the extent that regional courts do not possess coercive powers and need support from domestic authorities to enforce their judgments, and not only the cooperation of domestic governments, but also that of parliaments and judges. Actually, an alliance with domestic courts might promote effectiveness of regional courts' decisions and contribute to overcoming the resistance from state governments. For instance, given the specific nature of the preliminary reference procedure, the collaboration between domestic courts and the Court of Justice of the European Union or the Andean Tribunal of Justice, respectively, is fundamental. The action of those regional courts depends on domestic courts both in terms of submitting references and subsequent compliance with their judgments. Similarly, when international human rights courts such as the ECtHR or the IACtHR find a breach of a human right as a consequence of a legislative act, the violation's remedy commonly requires action by the domestic parliament. Another facet of the mutual support necessary for effective actions is the provision of funding for regional courts adequate for them to carry out their adjudicative function.

Mutual deference is also relevant at the international level, particularly from the perspective of the way regional courts exercise their authority. Discussions regarding judicial self-restraint, especially in terms of the deference owed by regional courts to domestic authorities, are increasingly common. In the context of the ECtHR, judicial deference is encapsulated in the margin of appreciation doctrine. The advisability of greater self-restraint by the IACtHR is also being voiced more frequently.[88] In turn, mutual deference also requires that political authorities show some deference towards regional courts and avoid interfering with their function. This duty partly overlaps with the demands of judicial independence, but it might sometimes go beyond that interest. For instance, political officials are expected certain self-restrain themselves from publicly criticizing judicial judgments or attacking judges for their decisions,[89] which may be conducive towards a political culture that respects the authority of regional courts' judgments.[90] The mechanisms of collaboration and control may fail or be subject to abuse when a regional court loses recognition and respect. Ultimately, mutual recognition and respect may well depend on extra-legal considerations.

[88] Roberto Gargarella, 'Tribunales Internacionales y Democracia: Enfoques Deferentes o de Interferencia' (2016) Revista Latinoamericana de Derecho Internacional 40.

[89] Thomas of Cwmgiedd (n 34) 18.

[90] Kavanagh (n 12) 100.

d) Coping with indeterminacy: how to justify the allocation of power constraints

The principle of checks and balances suffers from ingrained indeterminacy.[91] The principle calls for mechanisms of collaboration and control that protect judicial independence while counteracting the risk of judicial overreach, but it does not identify the institutions that should impose the constraints or even what the specific content of those constraints should consist of. Going back to the principle of separation of powers at the domestic level, several authors suggest that, from a constitutional perspective, separating power is not just about dispersing power;[92] they argue that we need positive justification for the allocation of any specific power to a particular branch that goes beyond the negative reason of curbing potential abuse. The justification might come from the interest in efficiency, which involves the determination of which institution is best placed to carry out whatever function.[93] Kyritsis put it this way: 'Different tasks call for different decision-making processes, so it is important to assign them to those state organs which by virtue of their composition and decision-making process are suited to perform them well.'[94] Nonetheless, efficiency on its own is not sufficient for the justification of allocating powers to certain institutions. If it were, investing all power in a king or a dictator might arguably be justified as more efficient than parliaments for the task of making laws. The values that institutions are specifically entrusted to uphold are key in justifying the powers allocated to them. In democratic systems, for instance, the enactment of general laws is entrusted to the body elected by the people according to the democratic principle. For this allocation of legislative power, Kyritsis argues, efficiency is neither the only criterion nor the most important one: 'At least equally important on many occasions is that a state institution exhibits virtues that are independent of any beneficial consequences that accrue from its carrying out a particular task.'[95] Along the same lines, Kavanagh argued that in allocating tasks to institutions 'we must also elicit the value these bodies instantiate given their various procedural features, because institutions only make sense in light of the purpose they are supposed to achieve and the value they are designed to embody'.[96] Indeed, the legitimate exercise of power by any given institution might ultimately hinge on a combined instrumental

[91] Waldron (n 3).
[92] Kyritsis (n 76) 39; Kavanagh (n 26) 230.
[93] Kavanagh (n 26); Kyritsis (n 76) 41; Vile (n 8) 334.
[94] Kyritsis (n 76) 39.
[95] ibid 41.
[96] Kavanagh (n 12) 91.

and value-based approach.[97] Good reasons exist to allocate functions to institutions that embody certain values, and whose composition and decision-making processes are designed to enable that institution to perform the function efficiently.[98]

Likewise, when the principle of checks and balances is our focus, we also need a positive justification for granting constraining mechanisms to specific actors that goes beyond the goal of avoiding the abuse of power. For the purposes of our analysis, then, we need to consider the institutions (international and/or national) that might provide appropriate checks on the power of regional courts, the interests and values those institutions might represent, and calibrate the mechanisms for implementing those power constraints accordingly. As will be further examined in Chapter 4, prominent among the values that might justify the allocation of constraining mechanisms to certain institutions is democratic accountability, given the concerns regarding the democratic legitimacy of regional courts. At the same time, constraining mechanisms might also respond to epistemic values, since interpretation is often a collaborative enterprise in search of the most appropriate interpretation for each community or regional system.

In this task, the distinction between the actual reasons for the adoption of any control mechanisms and their normative justification is important. Certainly, the international treaties setting up international regional courts were drafted by states understandably interested in retaining controlling mechanisms for their own benefit.[99] The principle of checks and balances facilitates not only critical examination of the constraining mechanisms already in place but also the formulation of proposals from the perspective of institutional design.

In the end, to assess the constraints on the action of regional courts that may be justified under the principle of checks and balances, it becomes paramount tracing the normative source of those constraints and identifying the risks of abuse or misuse that destabilize the balance. Here, as in so many contexts, institutional design involves trade-offs, for restrictions on judicial power might sometimes be justified in pursuit of certain values, such as democratic accountability or epistemic values.[100] Moreover, proper constraints on courts

[97] For a discussion of the feasibility of combining an instrumental and a value-based approach, see Kyritsis (n 76) 44–45. Regarding the difficulties in predicting the likely outcomes of different institutional arrangements, see Alon Harel, *Why Law Matters* (1st edn, Oxford University Press 2014) 200–01.

[98] Kavanagh (n 12) 91 stated that 'if an institution has epistemic or legitimacy-based strengths, it should be allocated tasks which speak to those strengths'.

[99] Helfer and Slaughter (n 1).

[100] Jeffrey L Dunoff and Mark A Pollack, 'The Judicial Trilemma' (2017) 111 The American Journal of International Law 225, 226.

do not undermine judicial independence, since judicial independence does not demand to be free of any constraint. The forms of appropriate constraints upon courts might be understood as sources of interdependence that advance the overall legitimacy of regional courts.[101] My ultimate objective is not a normative model applicable to every regional court, but rather a conceptual framework for evaluating institutional arrangements and the proper control mechanisms depending on the specific situation of the regional court in question. The remaining chapters will examine the relevant actors that provide constraints on regional courts and the values that they embody (Chapter 4), and assess selected constraining mechanisms as sources of interdependence from the normative perspective provided by the principle of checks and balances (Chapters 5 and 6).

[101] Aida Torres Pérez, 'In Nobody's Name: A Checks and Balances Approach to International Judicial Independence' in Hélène Ruiz Fabri and others (eds), *International Judicial Legitimacy* (Nomos Verlagsgesellschaft mbH & Co KG 2020) 48.

PART 3

CHECKS AND BALANCES: INSTITUTIONAL ACTORS AND MECHANISMS

4
Sources of Institutional Constraint

1. Introduction

In the international sphere, courts are potentially subject to constraint by a variety of institutional actors. The relevant actors and their level of influence, however, often vary depending on the court in question. Note that these institutional actors might exert influence or pressure that undermines independence, or rather provide adequate constraints under the principle of checks and balances. Potential influences and constraints on regional courts include a variety of national, supranational, and international institutions of diverse nature.[1] Different theoretical approaches to courts and international adjudication focus on different actors and sources of influence. From the perspective of realists and principal-agent theories, state governments pose the main threats to judicial independence in the international sphere,[2] while neofunctionalist and other sociological approaches emphasize the influence of other actors in the broader social environment and argue that courts might enhance their autonomy from governments by seeking the support of other actors, such as domestic courts or civil society organizations.[3] Such dialogue and collaboration between diverse sources can lead to interconnected networks that might actually establish independence from state governments through increased dependence on other actors.

Given the increasingly intertwined nature of the national and international spheres, our approach conceives the plurality of spheres along a continuum and also, importantly, disaggregates states so that the different positions of separate branches towards supranational judicial authorities can be considered.

[1] Dominik Zimmermann, *The Independence of International Courts: The Adherence of the International Judiciary to a Fundamental Value of the Administration of Justice* (1st edn, Nomos 2014).
[2] Erik Voeten, 'International Judicial Independence' in Jeffrey L Dunoff and Mark A Pollack (eds), *Interdisciplinary Perspectives on International Law and International Relations: The State of the Art* (Cambridge University Press 2012); Mark A Pollack, 'Political Science and International Adjudication' in Cesare Romano, Karen J Alter, and Yuval Shany (eds), *The Oxford Handbook of International Adjudication* (1st edn, Oxford University Press 2014).
[3] Voeten, 'International Judicial Independence' (n 2) 426.

Balancing International Judicial Independence. Aida Torres Pérez, Oxford University Press.
 DOI: 10.1093/oso/9780198852544.003.0004

Our approach similarly adopts a disaggregated perspective of the international organizations in which regional courts operate. Although the customary tripartite separation of powers cannot be automatically transposed to international organizations, the array of national and international actors can still be organized in three main categories: governmental, parliamentary, and judicial institutions. Moreover, other relevant institutions in the respective regional systems beyond the tripartite separation might also constrain regional courts, including the Inter-American Commission on Human Rights, a quasi-judicial body that determines which cases reach the Inter-American Court of Human Rights (IACtHR). Moreover, non-institutional actors that might also constrain the action of regional courts and contribute to shaping their authority include legal professionals, non-governmental organizations, business actors, and the public at large.[4] The analysis of non-institutional sources of constraint, however, exceeds the scope of this work.

Our inquiry into 'checks and balances' on regional courts requires careful study of the institutions that might constrain the power of regional courts and the values those institutions embody to justify the constraints they would impose. This reflection differs from the process by which, for various reasons, diverse actors were granted certain mechanisms in a certain political context involving the negotiation and ratification of treaties. Our approach starts not with a set of circumstances and positions but rather with a normative stance that requires investigation into the values that might justify the attribution of constraining mechanisms to certain institutions under the principle of checks and balances. Accordingly, each of the following sections will be structured in two parts. The first part explores from a descriptive perspective the sources of constraint coming from the diverse institutional actors: governments, parliaments, and courts. Thereafter, the second part will, from a normative perspective, critically examine the values that those institutions embody and the extent to which the attribution of constraining mechanisms is justified under those values.

2. Governmental Institutions

Regional courts are established by state governments through international treaties. Being responsible for their creation and design, it is unsurprising that

[4] Karen J Alter, Laurence R Helfer, and Mikael Rask Madsen, 'How Context Shapes the Authority of International Courts' (2016) 79 Law and Contemporary Problems 1, 34–36; Erik Voeten, 'Public Opinion and the Legitimacy of International Courts' (2013) 14 Theoretical Inquiries in Law 411, 415.

state governments often retain a degree of control over regional courts through different mechanisms that range from, at the most immediate level, the nomination of judges to be appointed to the court to, at a more indirect but just as relevant level, the provision of funds to finance the court's operation. State governments also reserve the power to amend the constitutive rules. Furthermore, states might defy courts' authority by refusing to comply with their judgments, criticizing their decisions, or when they threaten to withdraw from the court outright.[5]

A number of political scientists have employed principal-agent theory[6] to argue that the control mechanisms retained by state governments over international courts reduce the scope of the courts' independence, although these accounts have been challenged, and other scholars have argued that it would be more accurate to understand international courts as trustees than as agents.[7] Moving beyond the principal-agent dichotomy, we aim for a critical assessment of the justification for placing political constraints in the hands of state governments under a checks and balances principle. When moving beyond the principal-agent dichotomy, we also need to emphasize the possible allocation of constraining mechanisms to regional intergovernmental institutions instead of individual state governments.

2.1. Intergovernmental bodies and judicial governance

Intergovernmental institutions have generally been neglected in studies on the independence of international courts,[8] despite Blokker's observation that these institutions perform functions pertaining to judicial governance, including judicial selection, budgeting, and monitoring compliance. This is why Blokker conceptualized them as 'judicial governance institutions',[9] categorizing them in terms of three broad models: the first type of judicial governance

[5] Tom Ginsburg, 'Political Constraints on International Courts' in Cesare PR Romano, Karen J Alter, and Yuval Shany (eds), *The Oxford Handbook of International Adjudication* (1st edn, Oxford University Press 2014).

[6] Voeten, 'International Judicial Independence' (n 2); Pollack (n 2).

[7] K J Alter, 'Agents or Trustees? International Courts in Their Political Context', 35 European Journal of International Relations 135 (2008).

[8] Niels Blokker, 'The Governance of International Courts and Tribunals: Organizing and Guaranteeing Independence and Accountability' in Andreas Follesdal and Geir Ulfstein (eds), *The Judicialization of International Law* (Oxford University Press 2018) 27: 'It is true that sometimes importance is attached to the governance functions that states perform in relation to "their" international courts and tribunals, but it is largely neglected that such functions are almost always organized within collective institutions created by these states.'

[9] ibid.

institutions are organs of an international organization; the second type are judicial governance institutions created by a treaty, and as such are not part of an international organization, such as the Assembly of States Parties of the International Criminal Court (ICC); and the third type groups cases in which the cooperation between the states concerned is organized within a very loosely defined gathering of relevant states without a treaty mandate, a prominent example being the meetings of the States' parties of UN human rights treaty bodies.[10]

With regard to the specific regional courts under analysis in this work, the Committee of Ministers of the Council of Europe; the General Assembly of the Organization of American States (OAS); the European Council and the Council of Ministers of the European Union (EU); and the Andean Presidential Council of the Andean Community are intergovernmental bodies that fall into the first category. All of these institutions perform judicial governance functions, although the type of functions attributed to them varies greatly, as will be shown below. Moreover, they are usually granted functions that go beyond the respective court. For instance, the European Council of the EU, which is composed of the Heads of State or Government of the member states together with its President and the President of the Commission, is to 'provide the Union with the necessary impetus for its development and shall define the general political directions and priorities thereof'.[11] In turn, the Council of Ministers, which includes a representative of each member state at the ministerial level, exercises legislative and budgetary functions together with the European Parliament.[12] For its part, the Andean Presidential Council is not attributed any direct function regarding the Andean Tribunal of Justice (ATJ). Conceiving these institutions as judicial governance institutions might therefore be misleading, since the functions some of them perform in terms of the governance of the respective regional court are extremely limited. For this reason, taking a deeper look into the functions that the state governments or the corresponding intergovernmental institutions are allocated regarding the respective regional court seems worthwhile, particularly in terms of the constraining mechanisms they are granted.

The functions attributed to the respective intergovernmental institutions differ greatly across the regional courts under analysis. The functions also vary across regional courts with the same mandate. In the case of human

[10] ibid 34.
[11] Treaty on European Union 2016 art 15(1).
[12] ibid 16(1).

rights courts, the functions attributed to the Council of Europe's Committee of Ministers and the OAS General Assembly are quite different. Judicial selection corresponds to the General Assembly for the IACtHR, while judicial selection is attributed to the regional parliamentary body in the case of the European Court of Human Rights (ECtHR), based on lists of three candidates provided by each state government. Also, whereas the Committee of Ministers of the Council of Europe is attributed the function of supervising the execution of ECtHR judgments,[13] in the case of the IACtHR, the Court itself is in charge of monitoring compliance. The American Convention establishes that the IACtHR submit an annual report to the General Assembly on its work and non-compliance,[14] yet the OAS rarely responds to the reports.[15] Finally, both the OAS General Assembly and the Committee of Ministers of the Council of Europe are to approve the respective court's budget, but important differences arise here too. At present, the ECtHR does not have a separate budget apart from the general budget of the Council of Europe. As such, its budget is subject to approval by the Committee of Ministers in the course of their examination of the overall Council budget.[16] This contrasts starkly with Article 72 of the American Convention on Human Rights, which establishes that the IACtHR draw up its own budget for submission to the General Assembly, which is not granted the power to introduce any changes.

Moving to integration courts, one might expect more similarity, especially because the ATJ's institutional design was modelled after the Court of Justice of the European Union (CJEU). In both, judicial selection is directly attributed to state governments, but the similarities stop there. In the EU, for example, budget approval corresponds to the Council and Parliament, while in the Andean Community, the budget of the ATJ is drawn up by the court itself and approved by the Commission.[17]

In the end, individual state governments are only granted the power to make judicial appointments in the case of the CJEU and the ATJ, though they do play a significant role in selecting and proposing the candidates to serve on the ECtHR and the IACtHR. For the latter, the representatives of state governments in the General Assembly elect the judges. Moreover, regardless of

[13] European Convention on Human Rights 1950 art 46(2).

[14] American Convention on Human Rights 1969 art 65.

[15] Alexandra Huneeus, 'Courts Resisting Courts: Lessons from the Inter-American Court's Struggle to Enforce Human Rights' (2011) 44 Cornell International Law Journal 493, fn 134; Viviana Krsticevic, 'El papel de las ONG en el Sistema Interamericano de Protección de los Derechos Humanos' in *El sistema interamericano de protección de los derechos humanos en el umbral del siglo XXI* Tomo I (Corte IDH 2003) 37.

[16] https://www.echr.coe.int/documents/d/echr/Budget_ENG.

[17] Constitutive Treaty on the Andean Tribunal of Justice art 16.

the institution in charge of monitoring compliance with court judgments, state governments play a significant role in the actual enforcement of regional courts' judgments. Despite the important role played by state governments, however, it should be remembered that enforcement is not solely the responsibility of the state government in power. Here again, the importance of maintaining a disaggregated perspective of the state is evident, for national parliaments and courts are also called upon to enforce regional court judgments, depending on the type of remedies mandated by the regional courts.

2.2. Between state sovereignty and democratic legitimacy

From the perspective of the principle of checks and balances, placing constraining mechanisms in the hands of state governments or the corresponding intergovernmental institutions can be justified in terms of democratic legitimacy. As argued in prior chapters, international adjudication poses concerns from a democratic perspective because interpretation necessarily leaves a margin of discretion to international judges, whose interpretation of open-ended international provisions may effectively result in law-making. Moreover, the functions of regional courts tend to include monitoring state (democratic) action against the yardstick of human rights norms or rules for economic and political integration. In that respect, Kelemen has argued that the selection of international judges by democratically elected officials contributes to their legitimacy,[18] affirming that 'insofar as judges are appointed by democratically elected officials, courts have a 'democratic pedigree'.'[19]

Nonetheless, we must question the argument according to which placing countervailing mechanisms in the hands of state governments promotes democratic legitimacy. First of all, to state the obvious, the participation of state governments can only bestow democratic legitimacy when they represent democratic systems wherein the state governments are directly or indirectly democratically elected by the people.[20] Even in the case of democratic states, however, the participation of state governments in judicial selection or

[18] R Daniel Kelemen, 'Selection, Appointment, and Legitimacy' in Michal Bobek (ed), *Selecting Europe's Judges* (Oxford University Press 2015) 245–46: 'in order for courts, including the ECJ, to maintain their legitimacy in the eyes of the public and their legitimacy in the eyes of countervailing political branches of government, democratically elected officials must continue to play a central role in the process of judicial selection and appointment.'

[19] ibid 252.

[20] Allen Buchanan and Robert O Keohane, 'The Legitimacy of Global Governance Institutions' (2006) 20 Ethics & International Affairs 405, 413.

budget approval does not in and of itself provide the international judiciary with robust democratic legitimacy. Democratic legitimacy involves both an institutional and a procedural dimension. Accordingly, democratic legitimacy requires that decisions be taken by popularly elected institutions and that those decisions be arrived at through fair, transparent, and deliberative processes.[21] In this regard, judicial appointments by an intergovernmental institution do not fully benefit from democratic legitimacy if the selection process takes place in the dark without any sort of public scrutiny or transparency. Likewise, when the appointment or proposal of judicial candidates corresponds to state governments, their sole participation, without public criteria and open procedures, may only partially bestow democratic legitimacy. Buchanan and Keohane highlighted the difficulty of reconciling democratic values and unavoidable 'bureaucratic discretion' in the international sphere.[22] From this perspective, the weakness of the 'democratic pedigree' of governmental decisions in the international sphere is compounded by the relative isolation of the decision-making from the popular will. This is not to deny the margin of discretion afforded to state governments, but to highlight that robust democratic legitimacy requires more than mere allowance of governmental action.

In addition, putting constraining mechanisms in the hands of state governments has been defended from the perspective of state consent. In exchange for their acceptance of regional courts' jurisdiction, state governments are entrusted with a measure of control over regional courts. This position is grounded on the view that state consent represents the source of legitimacy of the constraining mechanisms on regional courts.[23] However, what makes state consent a source of legitimacy is precisely its grounding in the popular will. If state consent is not derived from the popular will, it only expresses the state's right to non-intervention as a matter of sheer sovereignty, rather than conveying any democratic legitimacy to the regional court's jurisdiction. State consent makes all the difference in terms of joining as a full member of a certain international regime and the corresponding regional court. As was discussed in Chapter 1, the institutional design will subsequently often include control mechanisms. However, the states' interest in constraining regional

[21] Armin Von Bogdandy and Christoph Krenn, 'On the Democratic Legitimacy of Europe's Judges' in Michal Bobek (ed), *Selecting Europe's Judges* (Oxford University Press 2015) 168–69.

[22] Buchanan and Keohane (n 20) 414 claimed that 'The problem is that for a modern state to function, much of what state agents do will not be subject to democratic decisions, and saying that the public has consented in some highly general way to whatever it is that state agents do is clearly inadequate. The difficulty is not in identifying chains of delegation stretching from the individual citizen to state agents, but rather that at some point the impact of the popular will on how political power is used becomes so attenuated as to be merely nominal.'

[23] Kelemen (n 18) 256–57.

courts does not justify in itself normative controls. Moreover, any constraining mechanisms that might undermine the court's independence must be justified on stronger grounds than solely the state's will. In the international sphere, it turns out that conceptualizing sovereignty claims on democratic grounds is not uncommon. Under international law, von Bogdandy explains:

> [S]overeignty protects the state against foreign interference. Under municipal law, sovereignty expresses the state's supreme power and therefore its supremacy over all other societal spheres. Under a democratic constitution, popular sovereignty is nothing but the realization of democracy upon which the legitimacy of all public power rests. On this basis the symbiosis of the nation-state and democracy was formed; it has determined most theories of democracy, and continues to do so.[24]

The symbiotic relationship between the nation-state and democracy, however, has been challenged by the development of trans- and supranational law-making processes during the surge of globalization that began with the end of the Cold War. As a consequence, questions have opened up about the democratic deficits both in the national and international spheres. Moreover, state sovereignty could never be conflated with democratic legitimacy, since many sovereign states are not democratic and even ones that are vary in terms of the democratic robustness of their elected institutions, which must be complemented by procedures that enable participation, deliberation, and public scrutiny to ensure democratic legitimacy. While we do not advocate removing mechanisms for constraint from the hands of state governments, it is important to emphasize that state government-controlled constraints on their own may only confer limited democratic legitimacy to regional courts.

It is also important to note, along with the reasons from a democratic perspective for giving state governments the power to wield constraining mechanisms, the risks those mechanisms pose for judicial independence if used to pursue self-interest. As Kelemen has stated, 'the line between democratic input that can enhance judicial legitimacy and political manipulation that can undermine it may be a fine one'.[25] Some design arrangements might be inherently problematic, while others might be liable to abuse in practice. The solution, however, need not necessarily be depoliticization (which might not even

[24] Armin von Bogdandy, 'Globalization and Europe: How to Square Democracy, Globalization, and International Law' (2004) 15 European Journal of International Law 885, 887.

[25] Kelemen (n 18) 252.

be feasible), but rather should incorporate mechanisms to curb potential abuse by state governments. To this effect, the institutional design could bring in the participation of other institutions to constrain executive power and reinforce the democratic legitimacy or represent other values.[26] For instance, parliamentary institutions at the national or international level, depending on the case, may provide appropriate checks on the executive power, as will be argued below. The shared budget approval competence between the Council and the Parliament in the EU is an apt example. In the end, increasing the number of actors that have a role in the constraint mechanisms could reinforce the international courts' democratic legitimacy while keeping the risk of abuse by the executive power of member states in check at the same time.

A final observation can be made of the potential advantages of involving the intergovernmental institutions of the corresponding regional or supranational organizations instead of state governments acting individually at their discretion. By attributing constraining mechanisms to such intergovernmental bodies instead of uniquely allocating them to the state governments acting individually, a need for coordinated action and consensus building is created, processes in which the individual action by state governments faces constraints from other governments.[27] This is especially evident when the adoption of decisions requires qualified majorities or unanimity. As Blokker has argued, 'While sovereign states play an essential role in these governance institutions, they do not act as individual states, but within a collective body that is functioning on the basis of predetermined rules and established practices. This also raises the question how such a body should best be structured.'[28] In any event, to the extent that decision-making procedures remain obscure, involving closed-door negotiations, improving mechanisms to increase transparency within those bodies through open deliberation becomes necessary from a democratic perspective.

[26] James Melton and Tom Ginsburg, 'Does De Jure Judicial Independence Really Matter?: A Reevaluation of Explanations for Judicial Independence' (2014) 2 Journal of Law and Courts 187, 192; Kelemen (n 18) 246:

> even in a context where the appointment of judges becomes more politicized, this politicization need not undermine the reputation of the courts as independent and impartial arbiters of the law. Political influence over judicial appointments is a threat to independence only where that influence is concentrated in a narrow set of hands or in one period of time.

[27] Eyal Benvenisti and George W Downs, 'Prospects for the Increased Independence of International Tribunals' (2011) 12 German Law Journal 1057 emphasized the role of inter-state competition, understood as the political division between the state parties, in facilitating independence and legitimacy of international courts.

[28] Blokker (n 8) 37.

3. Parliamentary Institutions

The role of parliamentary bodies is often overlooked in the analysis of the independence of and constraints on regional courts. Yet regional and domestic parliamentary institutions could play a relevant role in the oversight of the international judiciary that warrants serious study in the interest of reinforcing institutional interdependence. Parliaments could conceivably play a relevant role in constraint mechanisms for regional courts, or they might be called on to discipline the action of state governments in the field.

3.1. The role of regional and domestic parliaments

The regional organizations in which regional courts operate sometimes include a parliamentary body. This is the case of three of the four regional courts selected for this study, namely, the Parliamentary Assembly of the Council of Europe (PACE), the European Parliament, and the Andean Parliament. The members of the European Parliament[29] and the Andean Parliament[30] are elected by popular vote, while the members of the PACE are elected by the respective national parliaments of the state parties among the national deputies.[31] In the international regional sphere, we find bodies called parliaments and elected by popular vote that lack a legislative mandate, such as the Andean Parliament.[32] The PACE also lacks legislative power. Despite the conceptual looseness of regional parliaments, constraining mechanisms on the action of regional courts may well be productively attributed to such organs. To defend this assertion, we might look more closely at the functions allocated to the PACE, the European Parliament, and the Andean Parliament with regard to the respective regional courts.

Significantly, the PACE is charged with judicial selection. Each state party nominates three candidates from which the PACE elects the one who will serve on the ECtHR.[33] Within the PACE, the Committee on the Election of Judges to the ECtHR interviews and assesses the candidates. The committee issues a

[29] Article 14(3) Treaty on European Union.
[30] Aricle 42 Acuerdo de Cartagena.
[31] Statute of the Council of Europe 1949 art 25.
[32] Luis Felipe Aguilar Feijoó, El Parlamento Andino, un órgano del Sistema Andino de Integración moldeado por el Tribunal de Justicia de la Comunidad Andina, in Hugo R Gómez Apac and others (eds), *Tribunal de Justicia de la Comunidad Andinda 1979-2024: 45 años de creación y 40 años al servicio del derecho y de la integración* (Tribunal de Justicia de la Comunidad Andina 2024) 260–61.
[33] ECHR art 22.

recommendation for the PACE, indicating which candidate or candidates it believes are the strongest. An absolute majority of votes cast in the PACE is required for appointment in a first round. If an absolute majority is not achieved, a second round of voting is held, and the candidate who gathers the most votes is duly elected to serve on the ECtHR.[34] For its part, the European Parliament plays no significant role in judicial selection despite demands for some part in the process. At the same time, however, it is charged with approving the CJEU's budget. More specifically, approval of the EU's annual budget is allocated to the European Parliament and the Council together by Article 314 of the Treaty on the Functioning of the European Union. Like the other EU institutions, the CJEU is expected to submit estimates of its expenditures for the subsequent financial year (Art 314(1)). The Parliament and the Council may then review the budget and propose amendments before a final agreement is reached.[35] As for the Andean Parliament, it is attributed no specific function regarding the ATJ. The systems under analysis thus vary greatly in terms of the constraining mechanisms attributed to the respective regional parliaments vis-à-vis the regional courts.

Turning to the role of domestic parliaments in the international sphere, their participation tends to be limited, to the benefit of the national executive power. Depending on the respective domestic constitution, parliaments play a greater or lesser role in the conclusion of international treaties, so treaties establishing regional courts might require parliamentary authorization. Usually, however, parliaments do not enjoy any capacity to make substantive changes to the respective international treaties and must instead content themselves with an 'all or nothing' choice.[36] Still, domestic parliaments interact with regional courts in other ways.[37] In particular, the interaction of national parliaments with regional human rights courts has been underscored as important for both the legitimacy and effectiveness of the international judiciary.[38] In terms of potential checks on the action of regional courts, domestic parliaments sometimes play

[34] Parliamentary Assembly, *Procedure for the election of judges to the European Court of Human Rights*, SG-AS (2025) 1 at https://rm.coe.int/procedure-for-the-election-of-judges-to-the-european-court-of-human-ri/1680aa8ddf.

[35] Christoph Krenn, 'The European Court of Justice's Financial Accountability' (2017) 13 European Constitutional Law Review 453, 461.

[36] Aida Torres Pérez, 'The Internationalization of Lawmaking Processes: Constraining or Empowering the Executive' (2006) 14 Tulsa Journal of Comparative & International Law 1.

[37] Saul Matthew, Andreas Follesdal, and Geir Ulfstein (eds), *The International Human Rights Judiciary and National Parliaments: Europe and Beyond* (Cambridge University Press 2017).

[38] Matthew Saul, 'Conclusion: How Does, Could and Should the International Human Rights Judiciary Interact with National Parliaments?' in Matthew Saul, Andreas Follesdal, and Geir Ulfstein (eds), *The International Human Rights Judiciary and National Parliaments* (Cambridge University Press 2017) 353.

a role, however limited, in the process of judicial selection. In some countries, for example, parliamentary commissions assess and select the candidates to be nominated to regional courts,[39] and in other instances, the selecting commissions at least include some members of parliament (MPs).[40] In addition, the enforcement of regional court judgments sometimes requires amending domestic legislation. Indeed, since regional courts do not have the power to declare domestic legislation null and void in order to put an end to a declared breach of international norms, the task falls to domestic parliaments to repeal or amend the piece of legislation in question. In this respect, domestic parliaments exercise a relevant constraint on the action of regional courts. Follesdal has observed that 'some such acts of non-compliance may be understood as checks on the IC "ex post" for example by finding their judgments ultra vires'.[41] Refusal to comply reflexively with regional court judgments clearly undermines the court's authority and might potentially undermine judicial independence by pressuring the regional courts to consider carefully domestic factors that may affect compliance.

3.2. Democratic legitimacy, deliberation, and transparency

Despite the risk of compromised judicial independence, granting constraining mechanisms to domestic or regional parliaments may well enhance the values of democratic legitimacy, and in particular deliberation, and transparency. The composition of parliaments is diverse, following the preferences of the electorate, and they are expected to follow fair, transparent, and deliberative processes, in which the plurality of ideological positions is openly discussed before decisions are reached. Nonetheless, we should be wary of any ideal conception of parliamentary action in order to keep sight of the conditions under which constraining mechanisms in the hands of parliaments actually promote

[39] Bogdandy and Krenn (n 21) footnote 104, indicate that according to the Austrian Constitution (art 23c paras 1 and 2), the federal government has to reach an agreement with the parliament's main committee in nominating candidates for the ECtHR, but that, in practice 'the main committee does not discuss several applications but merely rubber-stamps the candidates proposed by the government'.

[40] Koen Lemmens, 'Selecting Judges for Strasbourg: A (Dis)appointing Process?', in Michal Bobek (ed), *Selecting Europe's Judges* (Oxford University Press 2015), explains that the Belgium selection panel for ECtHR judges comprises six members: a member of the judicial service, two parliamentarians, a member of the High Council for Justice, and two members of the office of the government agent before the Court.

[41] Andreas Follesdal, 'Law Making by Law Breaking? A Theory of Parliamentary Civil Disobedience Against International Human Rights Courts' in Matthew Saul, Andreas Follesdal, and Geir Ulfstein (eds), *The International Human Rights Judiciary and National Parliaments* (Cambridge University Press 2017) 334.

democratic legitimacy. First, regarding regional parliaments, without entering into discussion over the democratic deficit of international governance, the lack of either a regional demos or full-fledged democratic systems at the regional level weakens the capacity of regional parliamentary institutions to provide robust democratic legitimacy.[42] In addition, a second highly relevant factor from the perspective of providing democratic legitimacy is the robustness of the deliberations conducted within the parliamentary institution, and the effective participation of all the pertinent political forces. Third, transparency of the decision-making process is particularly relevant for the perception of civil society organizations such as trade unions and interest groups, and the public opinion at large. A final motive for caution with regard to parliamentary constraints on judicial power involves the risk that constraining mechanisms exercised by parliaments be hijacked by state governments, since state governments often enjoy an advantageous position to lobby parliamentarians. This advantage increases. Moreover, the formal and informal channels for executive influence over parliaments also limit the potential of parliaments to check the action of state governments.

These normative observations allow a critical assessment of the role regional parliaments currently play with regard to the selected regional courts. The PACE is granted an important mechanism of constraint on the ECtHR, consisting of the selection of judges. Placing this mechanism in the PACE can certainly be justified on grounds of democratic legitimacy. The key for assessment is then the process of judicial selection in terms of both design and practice. It seems appropriate to note the harsh criticism levelled against the process for appointing judges to the ECtHR in the past, in particular by the Limbach Report, which qualified the overall process for selecting judges as 'fundamentally flawed'. The Report noted that the late Sub-Committee on the Election of Judges:

> consists of parliamentarians, most of whom lack human rights or international expertise [. . .] There have been cases where its ranking of candidates has appeared to be based on or influenced by party politics rather than the merits of the prospective judges.[43]

[42] Kelemen (n 18) 256–57 is critical about the effectiveness of the Parliamentary Assembly of the Council of Europe as check on the state governments, and the capacity of the Parliamentary Assembly to provide legitimacy.

[43] Jutta Limbach and others, 'Judicial Independence: Law and Practice of Appointments to the European Court of Human Rights' (2003) 9 <https://www.corteidh.or.cr/tablas/32795.pdf> accessed 19 March 2026.

The Limbach Report also questioned the ability of members of the Sub-Committee to assess the judicial candidates, the way the interviews were carried out, the lack of transparency and the influence of party politics. The Report criticized the limited information on the candidates provided to the PACE, as well as lobbying by state governments, and even, on occasion, by the candidates themselves, which 'jeopardizes the future independence (actual and apparent) of judges'.[44] Kelemen argued that governments manage to signal which is their preferred candidate, who is usually then selected.[45] Admittedly, the process has improved since then. The current Committee on the Election of Judges to the ECtHR is composed of twenty-two members who are nominated by the political groups in proportion to their strength in the Assembly, and the nominees must meet requirements pertaining to legal expertise and experience. This is the only Assembly committee to which such requirements apply.[46] Yet the meetings are still held *in camera*, and strict confidentiality is demanded.[47] Neither the interviews nor the minutes of the meetings held are publicly available.[48]

Notwithstanding, the PACE has contributed from a democratic perspective to the formulation of selection standards regarding both the quality of the candidates and the national procedures for nomination.[49] The PACE has played a particularly significant role in promoting open and transparent processes at the national level. It required that, when submitting candidates, the state governments describe their selection process and that 'the process of nominating candidates to the Court must reflect the principles of democratic procedure, transparency and non-discrimination'.[50] Moreover, it has claimed the prerogative of the Assembly to reject lists submitted 'in the absence of a fair, transparent and consistent national selection procedure'.[51] The Committee on the Election of judges first decides whether any procedural or substantive grounds might justify rejecting the list without interviewing the candidates. The procedural grounds refer to the minimum requirements of fairness and transparency that the national selection procedure must satisfy; for example, a public call for candidatures must be issued, and interviews must be held.[52] In practice,

[44] ibid 9.
[45] Kelemen (n 18) 256–57.
[46] *Procedure for the election of judges to the European Court of Human Rights* (n 34) para 15.
[47] ibid para 16.
[48] ibid para 29.
[49] Bogdandy and Krenn (n 21) 170.
[50] Resolution 1646 (2009) on *Nomination of candidates and election of judges to the European Court of Human Rights* 2009 para 2.
[51] ibid para 2. In 2012, the Committee of Ministers adopted 'Guidelines on the selection of candidates for the post of judge at the European Court of Human Rights' CM (2012) 40 final (29 March 2012).
[52] *Procedure for the election of judges to the European Court of Human Rights*, para 19.

those standards have been effectively enforced. For instance, in 2016, a list was rejected on purely procedural grounds because no meaningful national selection procedure was carried out. In 2019, the committee decided that it would no longer consider lists of candidates when no interviews had been carried out during the national selection procedure. The committee also rejected a list on procedural grounds in 2021, considering that the national selection procedure was disproportionately dominated by government representatives.[53] Also, the PACE adopted several resolutions and recommendations to ensure gender balance in the lists submitted by the state governments, spurring heated debate.[54] On balance, while transparency of the process within the PACE could stand further improvement, the PACE has promoted procedures for greater transparency and openness at the national level by elaborating and issuing recommendations on standards and procedures to be followed. Moreover, although state governments retain the initiative in nominating the candidates, the PACE, by not only assessing the candidates but also the procedures at the national level, provides a relevant check on executive action. Even though this form of check is political in nature, it potentially bolsters judicial independence.

To enhance constraints on the executive and bolster judicial independence even further, the role of other regional parliaments in the process of judicial selection could be expanded. In the case of the European Parliament, proposals for greater participation have been made, such as giving it the responsibility to nominate half of the judges, making parliamentary consent a condition for appointment, or at least having candidates appear before Parliament in public hearings.[55] In order to improve the democratic legitimacy in the selection of judges for the CJEU and the ECtHR, von Bogdandy and Krenn called for, 'first, that representative institutions develop the criteria and procedures for becoming a judge in an open and co-operative fashion; and second, that these criteria are applied in a transparent and deliberative manner in concrete selection cases'.[56] Again, the focus is on establishing criteria and transparent, deliberative procedures.

With regard to the role of the European Parliament in the approval of the CJEU's budget, Krenn has argued that the budgetary control exercised by the European Parliament has become a powerful accountability mechanism that can contribute to 'framing the Court's power and enhancing its democratic

[53] ibid para 8.

[54] Bogdandy and Krenn (n 21) 171–72.

[55] Sally J Kenney, 'Breaking the Silence: Gender Mainstreaming and the Composition of the European Court of Justice' (2002) 10 Feminist Legal Studies 257, 262.

[56] Bogdandy and Krenn (n 21) 165.

legitimacy'.[57] Also, the author maintains that this control does not compromise judicial independence, 'due to the specific focus the Parliament has chosen and the dialogical relationship that has evolved'. Krenn goes on to explain:

> The Parliament does not employ the budgetary process for debating and reacting to the Court's judicial decisions, which would be problematic from the perspective of judicial independence. Rather, it lays the focus on how justice is done, i.e. on how the Court organises the institution and conducts its procedures.[58]

In this way, the Parliament is able to offer a political critique of the CJEU's performance without interfering with the Court's case law. In addition, the European Parliament might serve as a check on the Council. Krenn points out that 'the Parliament generally acts vis-à-vis the Council as a guardian for the Court's adequate financing, while at the same time critically supervising the Court's institutional and procedural development'.[59] The European Parliament is thus able to insulate the CJEU from Council interference, which in turn gives it some informal constraining power over the CJEU.

For their part, although domestic parliaments are not as vulnerable to the democratic deficit critique as regional parliaments, their behaviour, assessed in terms of deliberative quality and transparency, is still relevant for their capacity to confer democratic legitimacy through constraints on regional courts. As mentioned, domestic parliaments hold an important check on regional courts that rely on them for the enforcement of their judgments. A salient case in point is the *Hirst* controversy over prisoners' voting rights in the United Kingdom. In *Hirst*,[60] the ECtHR declared that a blanket ban on the right to vote of convicted people was in breach of Article 3 of Protocol 1. In light of the failure to comply with that ruling, in November 2010, in a pilot procedure, the ECtHR ordered the United Kingdom to bring forward legislative proposals to amend the current legislation.[61] Yet the UK Parliament continuously resisted implementing the ECtHR rulings.[62] In February 2011, the British MPs (by 234

[57] Krenn (n 34) 456.
[58] ibid.
[59] ibid 462.
[60] *Hirst v The United Kingdom (no 2)* [2005] The European Court of Human Rights (Grand Chamber) 74025/01.
[61] *Greens and MT v The United Kingdom* [2010] The European Court of Human Rights 60041/08 and 60054/08 [6 of the ruling].
[62] Mikael Rask Madsen, 'The Challenging Authority of the European Court of Human Rights: From Cold War Legal Diplomacy to the Brighton Declaration and Backlash' (2016) 79 Law and Contemporary Problems 141.

to 22) backed a motion stating that 'legislative decisions of this nature should be a matter for democratically elected lawmakers; and supports the current situation in which no prisoner is able to vote except those imprisoned for contempt, default or on remand'.[63] The MPs justified their disobedience on democratic grounds, arguing that the key issue was ECtHR overreach and the role and function of the ECtHR in the United Kingdom.[64] An open debate continues on the extent to which non-compliance by national parliaments might, and under which circumstances, be justified in terms of 'democratic rejection' or 'democratic override'.[65] Follesdal has claimed that parliaments, rather than state governments, 'are often suited to such attempts at changing an IC's interpretation: their law making may enjoy legitimacy by being democratically accountable, and they engage in extensive public deliberation and justification'.[66] Still, non-compliance by parliaments would only be justified in exceptional cases and under certain conditions, which will be discussed in Chapter 6.

To conclude this section, attributing constraining mechanisms with regard to judicial selection, budget control, and enforcement to parliamentary bodies might potentially be justified from a democratic perspective. Still, merely involving parliaments is not enough to justify constraint mechanisms on grounds of democratic legitimacy, for the procedures that discipline parliamentary involvement must themselves be sufficiently deliberative, open, and transparent. In any event, the capacity of parliaments to check the action of regional courts remains limited in practice. Still, there might be reasons to establish forms of interdependence with regional courts that might help countervail the dominant role currently played by state governments. To mitigate the influence of state governments and enhance the effectiveness of parliamentary checks, greater transparency appears to be crucial.[67]

4. Domestic and International Judiciary

International, regional, and domestic courts are also capable of influencing the action of regional courts in several ways and thus act as counterweights.

[63] Ed Bates, 'Democratic Override (or Rejection) and the Authority of the Strasbourg Court: The UK Parliament and Prisoner Voting' in Matthew Saul, Andreas Follesdal, and Geir Ulfstein (eds), *The International Human Rights Judiciary and National Parliaments* (Cambridge University Press 2017) 287.

[64] ibid 286.

[65] Bates (n 63).

[66] Follesdal (n 41) 335.

[67] Bogdandy and Krenn (n 21) 179–80.

Studies on judicial independence, however, have rarely focused on the role of courts as sources of constraint on regional courts. In this section, we will explore the role of domestic and international courts in their interaction with the selected regional courts under the checks and balances principle. The examination of the interaction between domestic and regional courts reveals patterns of collaboration and resistance. I will provide a general overview of the forms of constraint on the regional courts under analysis coming from other courts and then offer some reflection upon those sources of constraint from a normative perspective.

4.1. Patterns of collaboration and resistance

Sociological and neofunctionalist approaches have emphasized the importance of domestic courts in the enforcement of international judgments and maintaining the effectiveness of international regimes.[68] Collaboration and alliances with domestic courts might help shield regional courts from undue or improper governmental influence, while also creating new sources of (inter) dependence. Contrariwise, resistance to the judgments of regional courts, whether in the form of explicit or implicit lack of compliance with an order to take judicial action or merely through the threat of non-compliance, might serve to constrain the action of regional courts. Courts might thus become sources of constraint, as well as sources of collaboration to promote the authority of regional courts. We will examine the interaction between domestic and regional courts to identify the constraining mechanisms allocated to domestic courts that might contribute to counterbalancing the power of regional courts.

Domestic courts play an important role in the enforcement of regional court judgments.[69] From the perspective of international law, states themselves are to determine the institution responsible for implementing regional courts' judgments, but often domestic courts are needed to ensure the enforcement and broader effectiveness of regional court decisions. As such, beyond the enforcement of specific rulings, in truth, the incorporation of the regional courts' case law more broadly, and the direct application of international regional law, are

[68] Voeten, 'International Judicial Independence' (n 2) 426.

[69] André Nollkaemper, 'Conversations Among Courts: Domestic and International Adjudicators' in Cesare PR Romano, Karen J Alter, and Yuval Shany (eds), *The Oxford Handbook of International Adjudication* (1st edn, Oxford University Press 2014) 524 emphasized the 'powerful role of national courts in relation to the implementation of international decisions'.

crucial for the effectiveness of regional integration regimes or the protection of human rights at the domestic level. Moreover, by collaborating with regional courts, domestic courts provide valuable input regarding the interpretation of regional norms.

At the same time, domestic courts are also able to contest international courts decisions by refusing or threatening to refuse to enforce them. Nollkaemper has argued that such contestation might serve critical functions in relation to national and international law.[70] The reasons for the failure to implement international courts decisions or contestation vary in nature. Legal or procedural obstacles, such as ramifications of *res judicata* at the domestic level, often present, comprise one category. Many judgments of the ECtHR immediately confronted that difficulty in several states since domestic courts did not have the power to annul a prior ruling deemed *res judicata*. A second large category groups instances when domestic courts contest the decision of an international court on constitutional grounds, usually alleging that the international court ruling violates the substantive national fundamental constitutional principles or rights. A third category groups instances of contestation grounded on institutional concerns regarding the scope of the international court's jurisdiction and the extent of its legitimacy. In that regard, judicial politics and power struggles over authority, particularly between domestic apex courts and international courts, often come to a head.

In that regard, focusing on the human rights regional courts under analysis, Huneeus has identified patterns of resistance from domestic courts towards the rulings of the IACtHR. In a 2011 article,[71] Huneeus observed the failure of domestic courts to enforce a vast number of IACtHR judgments following a clear paradigm: 'While states implement the majority of orders that primarily require executive action, they implement only one in ten orders that invoke action by justice systems.'[72] Huneeus argued that the explanation involved both the institutional setting and political will. Among the institutional factors, the author listed the exclusion of domestic courts' involvement in foreign affairs, the lack of any formal relationship between national courts and the IACtHR, the unclear position that predominates in many states regarding the position of the IACtHR judgments in national law, resentment from national courts to the intrusion of the IACtHR into their jurisdiction and the perception that the IACtHR has 'usurped' the status of higher courts 'as final instance'.[73]

[70] ibid 535.

[71] Alexandra Huneeus, 'Courts Resisting Courts: Lessons from the Inter-American Court's Struggle to Enforce Human Rights' (2011) 44 Cornell International Law Journal 493.

[72] ibid 494–95.

[73] ibid 514–15.

In contrast, Keller and Stone Sweet, looking at the relationship between domestic courts and the ECtHR, found that the former played an important role in the reception of the European Convention on Human Rights (ECHR), so much so that 'in many States, the courts have taken the lead in incorporating the Convention, and in strengthening other quasi-constitutional mechanisms of reception'.[74] The explanation they offer focuses on the empowerment of domestic courts, since 'in most States, the incorporation of the ECHR has enhanced the overall authority of the ordinary courts vis-à-vis all other non-judicial officials'.[75] At the same time, the ECHR has arguably weakened the authority of national constitutional courts as the ultimate interpreters of constitutional rights.[76] In response, we see instances of resistance and contestation by domestic courts on constitutional grounds, such as the *von Hannover* saga,[77] which pitted German courts against the ECtHR over the right to freedom of information and the right to privacy following the publication of private images of Princess Caroline of Monaco.[78]

Here it is worth noting that the selected regional integration courts, the CJEU and the ATJ, enjoy an institutionalized mechanism for direct interaction between domestic and regional courts through the instrument of preliminary reference. The instrument allows domestic courts to seek guidance from the regional court when they are directly called to enforce supranational legislation. The instrument not only facilitates collaboration between domestic and regional courts but also bestows domestic courts with added responsibility for the effectiveness of the supranational legal order. At the same time, once the regional court decision is implemented through a domestic court decision, it becomes more difficult for state governments to ignore it.

In the EU, collaboration between the CJEU and domestic courts through the preliminary reference has been key in fostering the authority and effectiveness of the CJEU judgments. Important principles were crafted in response to preliminary references, such as the primacy and direct effect of EU law and of fundamental rights as general principles of EU law. Even more importantly, the collaboration between domestic courts and the CJEU has helped shield the latter from pressure from national governments and in the process

[74] Helen Keller and Alec Stone Sweet (eds), *A Europe of Rights: The Impact of the ECHR on National Legal Systems* (1st edn, Oxford University Press 2008) 687: 'In many states, the courts have taken the lead in incorporating the Convention, and in strengthening other quasi-constitutional mechanisms of reception.'

[75] ibid 687–88.

[76] ibid 688.

[77] *Von Hannover v Germany* [2004] European Court of Human Rights 59320/00.

[78] Nico Krisch, 'The Open Architecture of European Human Rights Law' (2008) 71 The Modern Law Review 183.

reinforcing judicial independence.[79] In addition, collaboration through the preliminary references has fostered compliance by encapsulating the content of CJEU judgments in domestic court decisions such that 'governments could not defy the ECJ without also calling into question the independence and authority of their own courts'.[80] A convincing argument can thus be made that domestic courts have empowered the CJEU by backing its authority and independence, and that the predominant explanations for the domestic courts' willingness to collaborate with the CJEU precisely involve the empowerment that the collaboration has afforded them.[81] According to the accounts of judicial empowerment, cooperation with the CJEU was seen by domestic courts as a means to reinforce their power vis-à-vis other branches of government, as well as with regard to superior national courts.[82]

At the same time, resistance from higher courts, in particular from constitutional courts, often seems to follow certain patterns. The revolt of the German and Italian constitutional courts is well-documented.[83] Both constitutional courts challenged the CJEU, threatening to review compliance with fundamental rights of state authorities in implementing EU law (which would require them to reject compliance with EU law if in breach of constitutional rights), unless fundamental rights were protected to an equivalent level in the EU. The CJEU bowed in its case law by extending the protection of fundamental rights as general principles of EU law. The 'threat' thus had a significant influence on the regional court's interpretation.

Nonetheless, a direct mechanism for interaction such as the preliminary reference does not, if we look at the other regional court under study, ensure

[79] Kelemen (n 18); Alec Stone Sweet and Thomas Brunell, 'The European Court of Justice, State Noncompliance, and the Politics of Override' (2012) 106 The American Political Science Review 204.

[80] Laurence R Helfer and Karen J Alter, 'The Andean Tribunal of Justice and Its Interlocutors: Understanding Preliminary Reference Patterns in the Andean Community' (2009) 41 NYU Journal of International Law and Politics 871.

[81] Joseph HH Weiler, 'A Quiet Revolution: The European Court of Justice and Its Interlocutors' (1994) 26 Comparative Political Studies 510, 523; Anne-Marie Burley and Walter Mattli, 'Europe Before the Court: A Political Theory of Legal Integration' (1993) 47 International Organization 41; Karen J Alter, 'Explaining National Court Acceptance of European Court Jurisprudence: A Critical Evaluation of Theories of Legal Integration' in Anne-Marie Slaughter, Alec Stone Sweet, and Joseph Weiler (eds), The European Court and National Courts—Doctrine and Jurisprudence: Legal Change in Its Social Context (Hart Pub 1998) 227, 241–46.

[82] Weiler (n 81) 510; Karen J Alter, *Establishing the Supremacy of European Law: The Making of an International Rule of Law in Europe* (Oxford University Press 2003).

[83] Juliane Kokott, 'Report on Germany' in Anne-Marie Slaughter, Alec Stone Sweet, and Joseph Weiler (eds), *The European Court and National Courts—Doctrine and Jurisprudence: Legal Change in Its Social Context* (Hart Pub; Distributed in the United States by Northwestern University Press 1998); Marta Cartabia, 'The Italian Constitutional Court and the Relationship Between the Italian Legal System and the European Union' in Anne-Marie Slaughter, Alec Stone Sweet, and Joseph Weiler (eds), *The European Court and National Courts—Doctrine and Jurisprudence: Legal Change in Its Social Context* (Hart Pub; Distributed in the United States by Northwestern University Press 1998).

forthright and robust cooperation. Despite the—purposeful—similarities in terms of design, the divergences between the CJEU and the ATJ in practice are significant. In the Andean Community, domestic courts have been much less eager to engage with the ATJ. According to Helfer and Alter, domestic courts in the Andean Community 'have a limited conception of their relationship with the ATJ and have generally refrained from using the Andean legal system as a tool of judicial empowerment'.[84] Interestingly enough, Helfer and Alter found other actors that have had more success fostering judicial collaboration, in particular administrative agencies charged with protecting intellectual property. In practice, domestic judges in the Andean Community mainly remain 'passive intermediaries'[85] while the principal interlocutors for the ATJ are intellectual property agencies.[86]

Shifting our attention now to the extent to which international and regional courts might influence or constrain the power of other regional tribunals, we can, at present, observe multiple forms of transjudicial communication or at least cross-reference and citation. Indeed, Voeten has claimed that 'There are complaints aplenty that international courts rely either too much or too little on each other's decisions.'[87] In general, cross-citation might promote coherence and contribute to counteract fragmentation in the international sphere. Citing the case law of other international and regional courts might sometimes mutually reinforce regional courts' authority vis-à-vis state governments and boost the other court's legitimacy. At the same time, however, routine references to other international or regional courts could lead to a sort of epistemic dependence that actually undermines their authority.[88] The variation in the patterns of cross-citation among international and regional courts and over time does indeed vary greatly. The overall pattern indicates that international courts tend to strategically cite other prominent courts for the sake of reinforcing persuasiveness.

In human rights law, cross-citation is quite common, though the patterns vary. When the CJEU started to protect fundamental rights as general principles of EU law, its reasoning was based in large part on the ECHR.

[84] Helfer and Alter (n 80) 878.

[85] ibid 875.

[86] ibid 912.

[87] Erik Voeten, 'Borrowing and Nonborrowing Among International Courts' (2010) 39 The Journal of Legal Studies 547, 548.

[88] Laurence R Helfer and Anne-Marie Slaughter, 'Toward a Theory of Effective Supranational Adjudication' (1997) 107 The Yale Law Journal 273; Osvaldo Saldías, '¿Refugiándose En Redes Epistémicas? El Tribunal de La Comunidad Andina y La Independencia Judicial' in Santiago Deluca and others (eds), *Tribunales en organizaciones de integración: Mercosur, Comunidad Andina y Unión Europea* (Primera edición, Thomson Reuters/Aranzadi 2012).

Subsequently, the CJEU went on to quote the ECHR and ECtHR case law in an effort to confer legitimacy to the heightened status of fundamental rights by the Court. All EU member states were already parties to the ECHR, so the ECHR provided particularly strong ground for the CJEU rulings. In fact, as de Búrca observed, once the EU Charter of fundamental rights became legally binding, the number of references to the ECHR decreased,[89] since the Charter became the main source of fundamental rights in the EU. In turn, the ECtHR often refers to the EU Charter, CJEU case law, and other EU legal instruments to back its interpretation of the Convention.[90]

Since its inception, for its part, the IACtHR has cited the ECtHR profusely. Ferrer McGregor felt comfortably affirming that 'the reference to the experience of an already established regional tribunal proved to be a strategy that legitimized the work of the Inter-American Court, both from a substantive perspective (in the strength of its conclusions) and a practical one (in the resolution of specific questions)'.[91] While the IACtHR often quotes the ECtHR, however, the ECtHR cites IACtHR case law much more selectively,[92] in most cases to better ground a shift in its doctrine.[93] Over time, with the development of its own doctrine, the IACtHR's references to the ECtHR seem less prominent in its jurisprudence.[94] While the reference to the more consolidated Strasbourg case law might have bolstered the authority of the IACtHR in an initial period, it seems a perception that the IACtHR might overly depend on European precedents became a risk that could actually undermine the American court's authority. Despite the growing reliance on its own regional legitimacy, the IACtHR still seeks affirmation in international law.

[89] Gráinne De Búrca, 'After the EU Charter of Fundamental Rights: The Court of Justice as a Human Rights Adjudicator?' (2013) 20 Maastricht Journal of European and Comparative Law 168; Romain Tinière, 'The Use of ECtHR Case Law by the CJEU: Instrumentalisation or Quest for Autonomy and Legitimacy?' (2023) 8 European Papers—A Journal on Law and Integration 323.

[90] Sionaidh Douglas-Scott, 'A Tale of Two Courts: Luxembourg, Strasbourg and the Growing European Human Rights *Acquis*' (2006) 43 Common Market Law Review 629; Tobias Lock, 'The ECJ and the ECtHR: The Future Relationship Between the Two European Courts' (2009) 8 The Law & Practice of International Courts and Tribunals 375.

[91] Eduardo Ferrer Mac Gregor Poisot, 'What Do We Mean When We Talk About Judicial Dialogue?: Reflections of a Judge of the Inter-American Court of Human Rights' (2017) 30 Harvard Human Rights Journal 89, 100.

[92] ibid 105: 'The European Court has used the jurisprudence of the Inter-American Court on those "paths" where the latter has already walked. For example, in a particularly serious matter for the respect of human rights—the enforced disappearances of individuals—one can suggest that the jurisprudence of the Inter-American Court "inspired" the European Court in the construction of its own jurisprudence.'

[93] Nicolás Montoya Céspedes and Laurence Burgorgue-Larsen, 'El diálogo judicial entre la Corte Interamericana de Derechos Humanos y la Corte Europea de Derechos Humanos' in George Rodrigo Bandeira Galindo and others (eds), *Protección multinivel de derechos humanos* (Universitat Pompeu Fabra 2013).

[94] ibid 196–97.

Another important contribution by Huneeus points out the mutual reinforcement of the legitimacy of the IACtHR and the International Criminal Court in the context of the peace process in Colombia: 'the overlap of the courts' work has benefitted the sociological legitimacy of each in a dynamic of constructive interference.'[95] In other words, and again, the clear patterns of interdependency and reliance vary over time and context.

To bring the case law of the ATJ, it has, like the IACtHR in its early days, heavily relied on the case law of the CJEU. For instance, the incorporation of the doctrines of primacy and direct effect by the ATJ has closely followed the reasoning of the CJEU. Saldías goes as far as to claim that the reference to CJEU case law has reached the point of 'epistemic dependence',[96] which is particularly problematic when foreign decisions are cited authoritatively. For that reason, Saldías argues for the ATJ's need to engage more directly with domestic courts instead.[97]

4.2. Epistemic and deliberative values through judicial dialogue

As shown above, domestic and other international and regional courts shape the decisions of regional courts in multiple ways. Broadly speaking, through mechanisms of direct or indirect collaboration, domestic and other international and regional courts can influence the interpretative strategies of other regional courts, all the while alerting them to potential pitfalls. At the same time, these forms of collaboration mutually empower courts vis-à-vis other political branches, in particular state governments. In general, regional courts might be influenced by the decisions of other international or regional courts, but have more leeway to make use of (or ignore) those decisions, while domestic courts enjoy a greater capacity to countervail the decisions of the regional courts to which they are parties. These forms of interaction, encompassing both collaboration and constraint, may well be conceived as forms of interdependence justified on grounds of the epistemic and deliberative values associated with judicial dialogue.

[95] Alexandra Huneeus, 'Legitimacy and Jurisdictional Overlap: The ICC and the Inter-American Court in Colombia' in Nienke Grossman and others (eds), *Legitimacy and International Courts* (Cambridge University Press 2018) 116.
[96] Saldías (n 88) 65.
[97] ibid 63–65.

As I have argued elsewhere,[98] from a normative perspective, judicial dialogue is understood as a source of legitimacy that involves communication and exchange of arguments between courts in order to reach common understandings of mutually acceptable outcomes. The legitimating potential of dialogue mainly resides in two features. First, judicial dialogue, as an ongoing exchange of arguments, represents an optimal means to reach better-reasoned outcomes for a certain community as a whole. Second, judicial dialogue promotes participation in the interpretive activity so that the outcome emerges from a collective communicative enterprise.

From an epistemic perspective, dialogue improves interpretative outcomes, particularly when it takes place between regional courts and the domestic courts in the corresponding regional organization. Certain features, endogenous to the practice of dialogue, improve the quality of the decisions and lead to better-reasoned outcomes for that community or region. First of all, dialogue brings to the fore information about the views and concerns of the participants. Communication between national and regional courts thus promotes knowledge and sustains a better understanding of competing interests and values at different levels of governance. Thus, by dialoguing with domestic courts, regional courts better understand those courts' claims and underlying motivations. In this vein, as the interlocutors have the possibility to check the arguments expounded by others, dialogue brings out mistakes or misunderstandings about factual or normative claims, thus permitting them to revise those interpretations with added insights. Second, dialogue necessarily gives attention to differing views and voices and enriches the debate by including diverse participants and arguments unanticipated by others.[99] Including the unanticipated often leads to new possibilities and solutions. In the settings under examination, the voices coming from domestic and regional courts reflect vastly different experiences and viewpoints, which are grounded in different institutional roles and positions in the overall system. Third, engaging in dialogue forces courts to justify, again and again if need be, their interpretation of the law and respond to the arguments advanced by other courts. The need to give reasons and the scrutiny to which all participants' assertions are subject promotes a particular mode of justification that reveals the shallowness of

[98] Aida Torres Pérez, *Conflicts of Rights in the European Union* (Oxford University Press 2009), 109–16.

[99] Paul W Kahn, 'Interpretation and Authority in State Constitutionalism' (1993) 106 Harvard Law Review 1147, 1155.

self-interested claims and advances impartiality.[100] Although courts might have their own policy interests, they are compelled, more than any other branch of government, to present their views in terms of legal principles and arguments to persuade others that their interpretation is the best outcome for the community as a whole.[101] Persuasiveness is particularly relevant for regional courts, which do not possess coercive means to enforce their decisions.

At the same time, judicial dialogue also embodies values related to deliberation and participation. Dialogue contributes to the normative legitimacy of the outcome because it gives participants the opportunity to offer input on the interpretive decision and to join the interpretation as a shared result. In addition, the intersubjective construction of meaning through dialogue allows participants to see the outcome as the result of a collective enterprise.[102] In this vein, the importance of genuine dialogue between domestic and regional courts, as opposed to monological reflections handed down by a regional court, can be appraised. If meaningful participation is assured, those affected by international norms will be more inclined to support the results as fair. Participation through dialogue in interpreting fundamental rights and other international norms thus not only contributes to the legitimacy of the interpretive outcome but also compounds the perception of the court's legitimacy among those bound by its decisions. This perception, as argued before, is relevant for the effectiveness of norms, which benefits from both the participatory nature of the process of interpretation and the synthetic nature of outcomes enhances compliance.[103] These observations are the reason we argue that cooperation in the construction of regional norms through dialogue would contribute to the legitimacy of the decisions of regional courts. The interpretive outcome, after all, would not represent the product reached by isolated regional courts and imposed summarily through a top-down process. Rather, the interpretive outcome would be the product of a much larger judicial and democratic community, built through a bottom-up process that gives voice to domestic courts.[104]

[100] Jon Elster, 'Strategic Uses of Argument' in Kenneth Joseph Arrow and others (eds), *Barriers to Conflict Resolution* (W W Norton & Company 1995) 250; James D Fearon, 'Deliberation as Discussion', in Jon Elster (ed), *Deliberative Democracy* (Cambridge University Press 1998).

[101] Rodger A Payne and Nayef H Samhat, *Democratizing Global Politics: Discourse Norms, International Regimes, and Political Community* (State University of New York Press 2004) 20–21.

[102] Jürgen Habermas, *Moral Consciousness and Communicative Action* (Polity Press 1990) 67.

[103] Thomas de la Mare, 'Article 177 in Social and Political Context' in Paul Craig and Gráinne De Búrca (eds), *The Evolution of EU law* (Oxford University Press 1999).

[104] Miguel Maduro, 'As Formas Del Poder Constitucional de La Unión Europea' (2003) 119 Revista de Estudios Políticos 11, 31.

The actual degree to which such judicial dialogue goes on in practice is an open question, one which exceeds our scope. The goal here was to argue that constraints from other courts might be justified as forms of interdependence under the epistemic and deliberative values associated with judicial dialogue. It is also important to remember the importance of dissent. Dialogical interaction includes defiance or patterns of contestation. Dialogue is driven by the underlying threat of open conflict, which furthers the exchange of arguments to reach better-reasoned outcomes for the community as a whole. Dialogue must be conceived as a process that evolves imperfectly over time. Judicial dialogue will necessarily develop in a fragmented manner since the exchanges of arguments among national and regional courts occur case by case. The crucial element as a precondition for a workable dialogue is mutual recognition and respect. As argued above, that respect involves recognition of the other as part of a common enterprise and engaging the other's arguments in good faith and offering reasons for the course of action imposed or recommended. In that regard, it is important to distinguish the role of dialogue in the interpretive process and the role it might have once a judgment has already been issued.

Domestic courts may well be critical of a regional court judgment, or even defiant, but reticence can be understood as a form of constraint in light of checks and balances, as long as it is argued in reasons that address those of the regional court. For instance, in an analysis of the interaction between the highest courts in Argentina, Brazil, Colombia, and Mexico and the IACtHR, Maués and other co-authors found that all of those apex courts directly engaged the IACtHR's decisions, giving direct effect to the IACHR doctrine and acknowledging its case law as critical to consistent interpretation and conventionality control, but nonetheless advancing 'safeguard arguments' to retain their authority to disagree with the IACtHR when their own constitutional structures required it:

> These safeguard arguments enable domestic courts to control the reception of international precedents. Safeguard arguments appear in the jurisprudence of national courts through the use of expressions or statements that indicate relational engagement, instead of complete convergence, with San José's jurisprudence.[105]

[105] Antonio Moreira Maués and others, 'Judicial Dialogue Between National Courts and the Inter-American Court of Human Rights: A Comparative Study of Argentina, Brazil, Colombia and Mexico' (2021) 21 Human Rights Law Review 108.

On balance, domestic and international courts affect the decision-making process of regional courts in many ways. However, that influence is not necessarily undue in terms of the regional courts' independence. Often, the interactions can be justified under the epistemic and deliberative values of dialogue. In alliance with domestic courts, moreover, such dialogue might shield the courts from improper executive interference. At the same time, in certain scenarios, epistemic dependence might also, contrary to the intention, undermine the authority and even the independence of the regional courts in the eyes of its audience. In terms of compliance, meanwhile, some forms of resistance might be more difficult to justify under the principle checks and balances, as will be examined in Chapter 6.

5

Judicial Selection and Appointment

1. Introduction

Chapter 4 explored the main institutions that provide sources of constraint to the action of regional courts and the values that they embody, and may well justify those constraints. Now, in the remaining chapters, we turn to specific mechanisms that might discipline the power of regional courts by formalizing channels for institutional interaction and, by consequence, constrain regional courts under the principle of checks and balances. Many scholars have identified several types of constraining mechanisms. Notably, Helfer and Slaughter[1] mapped out many of the various mechanisms for state control, using as organizing principles the distinctions between formal and political mechanisms, and whether the mechanisms are *ex ante* or *ex post*. For his part, Ginsburg[2] also identified several forms of political constraint, drawing distinctions between *ex ante* mechanisms such as appointment procedures, judicial terms and jurisdiction and *ex post* constraints in the form of exit or voice, which also include overrule and non-compliance.[3] Other scholars include among the mechanisms legal discretion and control over material and human resources,[4] or inter-state and inter-branch competition.[5]

Given the concern over the democratic deficit implied by international courts whose judges are largely unknown to their constituencies, the analysis

[1] Laurence Helfer and AM Slaughter, 'Why States Create International Tribunals: A Response to Professors Posner and Yoo' (2005) 93 California Law Review 899.

[2] Tom Ginsburg, 'Political Constraints on International Courts' in Cesare PR Romano, Karen J Alter, and Yuval Shany (eds), *The Oxford Handbook of International Adjudication* (1st edn, Oxford University Press 2014).

[3] Clifford J Carrubba, Matthew Gabel, and Charles Hankla, 'Judicial Behavior Under Political Constraints: Evidence from the European Court of Justice' (2008) 102 The American Political Science Review 435; Alec Stone Sweet and Thomas Brunell, 'The European Court of Justice, State Noncompliance, and the Politics of Override' (2012) 106 The American Political Science Review 204.

[4] Robert O. Keohane, Andrew Moravcsik, and Anne-Marie Slaughter, 'Legalized Dispute Resolution: Interstate and Transnational Legalization and World Politics' (2000) 54(3) International Organization 457.

[5] Eyal Benvenisti and George W Downs, 'Prospects for the Increased Independence of International Tribunals' (2011) 12 German Law Journal 1057.

Balancing International Judicial Independence. Aida Torres Pérez, Oxford University Press.
 DOI: 10.1093/oso/9780198852544.003.0005

will focus on constraining mechanisms justifiable on democratic grounds, specifically judicial selection (Chapter 5) and political override (Chapter 6).[6] Both judicial selection and political override potentially influence and constrain the action of regional courts. Then, we examine the extent to which the two mechanisms are justifiable as forms of interdependence or, to put it another way, the point at which they become undue forms of influence that undermine judicial independence. An understanding of the risks of abuse from the perspective of safeguarding judicial independence can be sought in the design and implementation of these mechanisms.

This chapter focuses on the selection processes for judges in the regional courts under analysis. Our inquiry adopts a normative perspective in a critical assessment of judicial selection as a constraining mechanism on regional courts in light of the checks and balances principle. The model of judicial selection employed affects both the institutional independence of the court and the appearance of independence in the eyes of those under its jurisdiction and public opinion more broadly. From the perspective of sociological legitimacy, the selection process is key to the perception of independence by individuals. If the perception is that political considerations are more important than competence and merit in the selection process, the overall perception of the court's legitimacy in public opinion might suffer. Furthermore, in courts that possess jurisdiction over individuals, such as the regional courts under examination in this analysis, appointment by governments creates the risk that the court will be perceived as representing the interests of the state parties.

Judicial appointment power is usually attributed to either the member states or an intergovernmental body of the respective international organization. In either case, state governments play a significant role in the process. By consequence, judicial appointment is generally regarded as a principal mechanism through which state governments influence international courts and rein in their independence,[7] for it can be assumed that the individuals or parties in control of national governments will tend to appoint politically aligned judges.[8] In practice, judicial nominations are advanced for a wide range of varied motives. As Voeten succinctly put it, 'governments are neither simply picking the best qualified candidates nor are they singularly obsessed with

[6] Ginsburg (n 2).
[7] Helfer and Slaughter (n 1); Ginsburg (n 2).
[8] Aida Torres Pérez, 'Can Judicial Selection Secure Judicial Independence? Constraining State Governments in Selecting International Judges' in Michal Bobek (ed), *Selecting Europe's Judges* (Oxford University Press 2015).

limiting sovereignty costs'.[9] Motives for judicial selection might include a desire to signal a credible commitment to a certain cause, concerns over the implications of court rulings, and rewards for political loyalty, but may well also be influenced by local norms regarding the appropriate profile for an international judge and an aspiration to advance specific norms related to the liberal international order.[10]

We should also keep in mind that, once appointed, the capacity of governments to influence judges,[11] as well as the capacity of those judges to influence court decisions, depends on a wide set of factors which includes term length, the possibility of reappointment, the size and composition of the court, the particular decision-making process within collegial bodies, and whether dissenting opinions are allowed. The many different possible combinations of these institutional arrangements modulate the real impact of judicial appointments and government influence.

Attributing power to select regional judges to states parties may be an appropriate mechanism to counterbalance regional courts' powers justified on democratic grounds. For the value of democratic legitimacy to be realized, however, the institutions that are granted that power and the procedures that they follow must be carefully assessed. Not only the design of the mechanism for judicial appointment but also how the power of appointment is exercised in practice must be considered.

In what follows, our reflection focuses on the selected regional courts for a critical analysis of current institutional arrangements. We look at the design of the mechanisms for judicial selection and, more specifically, the institutions that participate in it and the values or interests they represent. We wish to determine whether, to the extent that power is concentrated in the hands of state governments, other institutions may counterbalance executive power. We also examine how the mechanisms for judicial selection are implemented in practice with an eye toward identifying potential improvements that enhance democratic accountability and favour the selection of competent and independent judges.

[9] Erik Voeten, 'The Politics of International Judicial Appointments' (2009) 9 Chicago Journal of International Law 387, 389.
[10] ibid 391–92.
[11] ibid 403.

2. Selecting Regional Judges: The Legal Framework and Practice

The selection of judges for regional courts takes place in two stages: first, nomination of the candidates at the national level; and second, election or appointment at the regional level. State governments generally play a relevant role at both levels. In the regional courts under analysis, the selection of judicial candidates at the national level always corresponds to the respective state government, although the states might have in place instruments and procedures that enhance transparency and promote the selection of candidates on the basis of merit and competence. For instance, some states include public calls for candidates, or form selection committees of a governmental or mixed composition, usually from representatives of parliament and sometimes including external experts, which interview candidates. In any case, governments tend to enjoy broad leeway. The main power for appointment or election on the international stage also tends to lie with state governments. In the Court of Justice of the European Union (CJEU) and the Andean Tribunal of Justice (ATJ), appointment requires unanimous approval by the state governments. For its part, election to the Inter-American Court of Human Rights (IACtHR) corresponds to the General Assembly, the intergovernmental institution of the Organization of American States (OAS). The European Court of Human Rights (ECtHR) stands out, since the election corresponds to the Parliamentary Assembly of the Council of Europe.

One can distinguish between full representation and selective representation courts. On courts with full representation sit one judge per member state, which is the case of the ECtHR, CJEU, and the ATJ. Selective representation courts are those on which fewer judges sit than there are member states, and for that reason, not all states may appoint a judge on the court, as is the case on the IACtHR. Correspondingly, the dynamics of appointment greatly differ in practice. In selective representation courts, such as the IACtHR, campaigning and vote trading are central practices for candidate success.[12] The IACtHR is composed of seven judges elected by an absolute majority of the states parties to the Convention in the General Assembly by secret ballot.[13] Each of the state parties may propose two candidates from its country, plus a third from another state.[14] In practice, however, state governments tend to propose only

[12] Ruth Mackenzie, Kate Malleson, Penny Martin, and Philippe Sands, *Selecting International Judges: Principle, Process, and Politics* (Oxford University Press 2010) 100–28, with regard to the International Court of Justice and the International Criminal Court.

[13] American Convention on Human Rights (ACHR) 1969 art 53(2).

[14] ibid art 53(1).

one candidate, most often of the respective nationality.[15] Faúndez Ledesma has strongly denounced the consequent practice of vote trading among state governments that dilutes considerations of merit or competence. The practice leads governments to back the candidate of another state in exchange for its support for their respective candidate to international bodies.[16] The election of judges does not differ much from the election of members to other international bodies.[17] Its ubiquity attests to the highly politicized nature of the selection processes. Many scholars and several organizations have demanded greater transparency and participation both at the national and international levels.[18]

In contrast, in full representation courts, state governments do not need to campaign for their respective candidate's appointment. At the same time, however, this leaves no incentives for states to appraise candidates from other member states or to seek support for their own.[19] The CJEU thus comprises twenty-seven judges appointed by common accord of the member states.[20] The ATJ, in turn, is composed of four judges[21] appointed by the representatives of the member states by unanimity.[22] Requiring unanimity means that any single state can veto other governments' candidates, although the incentive is not to object to other candidates, since doing so might cause one of those states to reject their candidate. As the selection process is, by consequence, less constrained by the need to gain the support of others, governments enjoy wider discretion in the choice of their nominees.

[15] Héctor Faúndez Ledesma, 'La independencia e imparcialidad de los miembros de la comisión y de la corte: paradojas y desafíos' in Juan E Méndez and Francisco Javier Cox (eds), *El futuro del sistema interamericano de protección de los derechos humanos* (Primera reimpresion, IIDH 1999).

[16] ibid 187; Centro por la Justicia y el Derecho Internacional (CEJIL), *Aportes Para El Proceso de Selección de Miembros de La Comisión y La Corte Interamericanas de Derechos Humanos* (Centro por la Justicia y el Derecho Internacional 2005) 9 <https://cejil.org/wp-content/uploads/pdfs/Documento_1_sp_0.pdf>.

[17] 'The practice of "vote exchange" has historically dominated these processes. States exchange promises of political support for votes in other elections, and this practice often ignores the capabilities and suitability of the candidates. The previous Panels have made detailed criticisms of these practice' (Evaluation Panel, 'Final Report of the Independent Panel for the Election of Inter-American Commissioners and Judges' (2015) 21 <https://www.justiceinitiative.org/uploads/34b476e4-dd7b-431e-acd4-e25fbff100cc/iachr-panel-report-eng-20150603.pdf>.

[18] Faúndez Ledesma (n 15); Judith Schönsteiner, 'Alternative Appointment Procedures for the Commissioners and Judges in the Inter-American System of Human Rights' (2007) 46 Revista IIDH 195; Oswaldo Ruiz-Chiriboga, 'The Independence of the Inter-American Judge' (2012) 11 The Law and Practice of International Courts and Tribunals 111.

[19] Voeten (n 9) 401–02.

[20] Consolidated Version of the Treaty on the Functioning of the European Union 2012 art 253.

[21] Tratado de Creación del Tribunal de Justicia de la Comunidad Andina 1999 art 6. According to Article 6, the number of judges is five. Initially, Chile was also a state party, but withdrawn. At present, there are four judges corresponding to the four state parties.

[22] ibid 7.

In the case of the ECtHR, the Parliamentary Assembly elects the forty-six judges, one per member state. It is by a majority of votes cast from a list of three candidates nominated by each state party.[23] Therefore, the states do not compete for seats on the Court but may engage in lobbying for their preferred candidate among the three nominations. Within the Parliamentary Assembly, as mentioned in the last chapter, the Committee on the Election of Judges interviews and assesses the candidates. This Committee may exert some constraint on the choices of the state governments, for it looks for any procedural or substantive grounds which might lead to the objection of anyone in the list before even interviewing the candidates.[24] Procedural grounds for rejection include national selection procedures that do not satisfy the minimum requirements of fairness and transparency, the absence of publicity of the call for candidates, or not holding interviews during the national selection procedure. The committee may also recommend rejecting a list on substantive grounds when the curricula vitae of at least one of the candidates clearly does not fulfil the requirements of Article 21(1) of the European Convention on Human Rights (ECHR). Indeed, the Committee has rejected candidates for those reasons on several occasions since 2016.[25]

In sum, state governments dominate at the national and international stages of the selection process (see Table 5.1). To the extent that selection is allocated to political actors, political considerations cannot be excluded from the process. This shortfall is not problematic in itself. Exercising appointment power to influence the overall direction of the court may in many cases be legitimate, and, for instance, counter undesired judicial activism, or legitimately check ideological shifts by the court that governments perceive as too progressive or conservative. At the same time, once appointed, judges should be shielded from undue pressure, interference or instructions from the institution or authorities that appointed them. The judges must not, for the sake of the court's legitimacy, behave as representative of the interests of their respective government.

Granting selection power to governments can easily be justified from the perspective of democratic accountability, but the design and implementation of selection mechanisms must ensure that value is realized in practice. At the international stage, the procedures are highly politicized. Vote trading, for

[23] European Convention on Human Rights 1950 art 22.

[24] Secretary General of the Parliamentary Assembly of the Council of Europe, 'Memorandum on the Procedure for the Election of Judges to the European Court of Human Rights' <https://rm.coe.int/procedure-for-the-election-of-judges-to-the-european-court-of-human-ri/1680aa8ddf>.

[25] ibid para 20.

Table 5.1 Judicial appointment and mandate

	Institution responsible for selection	Institution that nominates candidates	Number of judges	Length of term	Reelection
ECtHR	The Parliamentary Assembly elects one of the three nominations by a majority of votes (Art 22 ECHR)	The list of three candidates is nominated by the corresponding High Contracting Party (Art 22 ECHR)	Forty-six, one for each of the High Contracting Parties (Art 20 ECHR)	Nine years (Art 23(1) ECHR)	No reelection permitted (Art 23(1) ECHR)
IACtHR	General assembly by absolute majority (Art 53(1) ACHR)	Each state party may propose up to three candidates (Art 53(2) ACHR)	Seven (Art 52 ACHR)	Six years with partial replacement every three years (Art 54 ACHR)	Judges may be reelected only once (Art 54 ACHR)
CJEU	State governments by common accord (Art 253 TFEU)	Each state government proposes one candidate	The Court of Justice consists of one judge from each member state (Art 19(2) TEU)	Six years Partial renewal every three years (Art 253 TFEU)	Judges can be reelected indefinitely (Art 253 para 4 TFEU)
ATJ	Representatives of state governments must elect the judges by unanimity (Art 7 ATJ Treaty)	Lists of three candidates are submitted by each member state (Art 7 ATJ Treaty)	Four, one per each member state (Art 6 ATJ Treaty)	Six years Partial renewal every three years (Art 8 ATJ Treaty)	Judges may be reelected only once (Art 8 ATJ Treaty)

appointments to selective representation courts, has become the unwritten norm, while governments are given broad discretion to choose their judge in full representation courts where unanimity is required for election. Open deliberation and transparency are lacking in either case. That is the main reason why the grant of appointment power to state governments does not necessarily deliver the optimal degree of democratic legitimacy. Only in the case of the ECtHR is the appointment power granted to the corresponding regional parliamentary body, which itself might sometimes suffer shortcomings from a democratic perspective, as argued in the previous chapter. The Parliamentary

Assembly at least furthers (internal) deliberation and provides some check on state governments.

In all of the cases under study, the concentration of appointment power in the hands of state governments entails potential for abuse and diverts focus from the judicial candidates' competence and merit. In seeking to address those issues, a general observation is that multiplying number of actors that participate in the process of selection creates incentives for mutual control.[26] In that regard, the establishment of advisory expert panels might contribute to constraining the power of state governments, which is addressed in section 3. Greater transparency may well enhance public scrutiny and confidence, as discussed in section 4. In the end, the mechanisms of judicial selection must be assessed together with other structural elements, such as tenure, re-appointment, and the availability of dissenting opinions, which are examined in section 5. As these diverse structural arrangements do not work in isolation, we need to consider their interaction to assess their impact upon judicial independence.[27]

3. Advisory Expert Panels

Advisory expert panels have been set up in several international and regional courts to assess the suitability of judicial candidates.[28] The panels carry out a screening process that potentially constrains executive power in the judicial selection process and advances judicial independence. With regard to the selected regional courts, advisory expert panels participate in the judicial selection process for the ECtHR, the IACtHR, and the CJEU, although each is of a very different nature.

For the CJEU, the expert panel was introduced by the Lisbon Treaty (Article 255 of the Treaty on the Functioning of the European Union (TFEU)), which entered into force in 2009. According to Article 253 TFEU, judges and advocates general 'shall be appointed by common accord of the governments of the Member States [...] after consultation of the panel provided for in Article 255'. Hence, consultation of the Panel is an obligation directly rooted in the Treaty itself. The introduction of this Panel represented a ground-breaking step forward, in that it removed judicial selection from the exclusive power of state

[26] James Melton and Tom Ginsburg, 'Does De Jure Judicial Independence Really Matter?: A Reevaluation of Explanations for Judicial Independence' (2014) 2 Journal of Law and Courts 187.

[27] ibid 194.

[28] Torres Pérez (n 8) 193.

governments.[29] Article 255 establishes that the seven-member Panel be formed by former judges from, first, the Court of Justice and General Court, national supreme courts and, lastly, lawyers of recognized competence. Six of the members of the Panel are proposed by the CJEU President and one by the European Parliament, and they are appointed by the Council to four-year mandates which can be renewed once.[30] The function of the Panel, as laid down in Article 255 of the TFEU, is 'to give an opinion on candidates' suitability' to perform their duties 'before the governments of the Member States make the appointments'. To perform the assessment, the Panel may ask for additional information from the corresponding state government. The candidate will appear before the Panel, unless the appointment is under review for renewal, in a closed camera.[31] The Panel will issue a reasoned opinion. Opinions shall be forwarded to the member states' governments,[32] but they are not published or accessible to the public.

In the case of the ECtHR, the advisory expert panel is designed following the model of the CJEU. It was established in 2010 by a Resolution of the Committee of Ministers *on the establishment of an Advisory Panel of Experts on candidates for the Election as Judge to the European Court of Human Rights.*[33] The Panel's mandate is to advise the state parties whether candidates meet the criteria stipulated in Article 21(1) of the ECHR for moral character, competence, and merit. The Panel is composed of seven members, 'chosen among members of the highest national courts, former judges of international courts, including the European Court of Human Rights and other lawyers of recognised competence'.[34] The Resolution on the establishment of the Advisory Panel specifies that the composition of the Panel shall be geographically and gender balanced. The members of the Panel are appointed by the Committee of Ministers' following consultation with the President of the ECtHR. Also, proposals for appointment may be submitted by the High Contracting Parties,[35] in contrast to the Article 255 Panel. Before submitting a list of three candidates to the Parliamentary Assembly, each government transmits to the Panel

[29] Marijn Van Der Sluis, Tomáš Dumbrovský, and Bilyana Petkova, 'Judicial Appointments: The Article 255 TFEU Advisory Panel and Selection Procedures in the Member States' (2014) 51 Common Market Law Review 455.

[30] Council Decision of 25 February 2010 relating to the operating rules of the panel provided for in Article 255 of the TFEU 2010 art 3.

[31] ibid 7.

[32] ibid 8.

[33] Resolution CM/Res(2010)26 on the establishment of an Advisory Panel of Experts on Candidates for Election as Judge to the European Court of Human Rights 2010.

[34] ibid 2.

[35] ibid 3.

the names and curricula vitae of the respective candidates. If the Panel deems the candidates acceptable, it informs the state without further comment. If the Panel finds one or more candidates unsuitable, however, it may request further information from the state. If, after that information is received, the Panel still deems any of the candidates unsuitable, it is to inform the state of the reasons for its finding, which remain confidential.[36] In addition, once a list has been submitted to the Parliamentary Assembly by the corresponding state government, the Panel shall make available to the Parliamentary Assembly its views on the candidates' satisfaction of the criteria stipulated in Article 21(1) of the ECHR.[37] In this process, the Panel itself does not conduct any interviews, but the candidates will be interviewed by the Selection Committee of the Parliamentary Assembly.

Regarding the IACtHR, the Independent Panel to Evaluate Candidates to the Inter-American Human Rights System Bodies was convened for the first time in 2015, after its creation was advocated by prominent non-governmental organizations (NGOs), namely, the Open Society Justice Initiative, the Center for Justice and International Law, and the Due Process of Law Foundation.[38] Over time, it has gained the support of many more NGOs, universities, and legal clinics throughout the region.[39] Since 2018, the American University Washington College of Law houses the Panel's Secretariat,[40] which has enhanced the Panel's independence vis-à-vis the states and the powerful civil society organizations.[41] The main purpose of this Panel is improving the transparency of the process of judicial selection. In particular, as stated in its 2015 Report, 'The purpose of the Independent Panel is to improve the visibility, transparency, consistency, and legitimacy of elections to the Commission and Court.'[42] As expressly stated in the Report, it is inspired by the implementation of similar actions taken by other international institutions, such as the ICC and

[36] ibid 5.

[37] ibid.

[38] Evaluation Panel, 'Final Report of the Independent Panel of Experts for the Evaluation of Candidates for Election to the Inter-American Court of and Commission on Human Rights' (2021) 5 <https://www.american.edu/wcl/impact/initiatives-programs/center/publications/documents/upload/final-report-of-the-2021-independent-panel-of-experts.pdf>.

[39] Evaluation Panel, 'Final Report of the Independent Panel for the Election of Inter-American Commissioners and Judges' (n 17) 2.

[40] All the information about the Panel and the Final Reports can be found at: https://www.american.edu/wcl/impact/initiatives-programs/independent-panel-to-evaluate-candidates-to-the-iahrs-bodies/.

[41] Evaluation Panel, 'Final Report of the Independent Panel of Experts for the Evaluation of Candidates for Election to the Inter-American Court of and Commission on Human Rights' (n 38).

[42] Evaluation Panel, 'Final Report of the Independent Panel for the Election of Inter-American Commissioners and Judges' (n 17) 2.

the ECtHR.[43] The 2021 Report also emphasizes the Panel's goal to review the processes of nomination and election, evaluate the qualifications of the candidates, and make recommendations on how to improve future nominations and elections.[44]

The Panel was established as an independent entity that was to comprise five members with unquestionable experience and knowledge of human rights law and the Inter-American Human Rights System.[45] At present, it has six members.[46] While they were initially nominated by the NGOs that advocated the Panel's creation considering criteria of expertise in the field of human rights, geographical and gender balance, at present they are selected by the American University. The Panel conducts its evaluations using the curricula vitae and information provided by the candidates that includes responses to a questionnaire elaborated by the Panel.[47] The Panel also interviews willing candidates, although some candidates decline. Additionally, the Panel looks at verifiable information submitted by civil society groups.[48] The Panel's Reports, including the evaluation of the candidates, are publicly available on the website of the American University Washington College of Law.[49] The Reports provide detailed assessments on the candidates' expertise in human rights, their knowledge of the Inter-American System, and their independence, impartiality, and any conflicts of interests.

From a comparative perspective, the European and Inter-American Panels differ significantly. While the CJEU Panel is established by Treaty and the ECtHR by Resolution of the Committee of Ministers, the IACtHR Panel is not an institutionalized body established by a legal instrument, but instead was created by a group of NGOs and civil society organizations and is maintained at a private university. Another important difference involves the level of transparency of their activities, since the IACtHR's Panel Reports include detailed assessments of the candidates, while the CJEU and ECtHR Panel opinions are not publicly available.

[43] ibid.

[44] Evaluation Panel, 'Final Report of the Independent Panel of Experts for the Evaluation of Candidates for Election to the Inter-American Court of and Commission on Human Rights' (n 38) 5.

[45] Evaluation Panel, 'Final Report of the Independent Panel for the Election of Inter-American Commissioners and Judges' (n 17) 2.

[46] Evaluation Panel, 'Final Report of the Independent Panel to Evaluate Candidatures for the Bodies of the Inter-American Human Rights System' (2024) 4 <https://www.american.edu/wcl/impact/initiatives-programs/independent-panel-to-evaluate-candidates-to-the-iahrs-bodies/past-reports/upload/2024-iahrs-panel-final-report.pdf>.

[47] ibid. The questionnaire is included in annex 3.

[48] ibid 4–5.

[49] https://www.american.edu/wcl/impact/initiatives-programs/independent-panel-to-evaluate-candidates-to-the-iahrs-bodies/ (Accessed 24 November 2025).

Given the non-binding force of all those Panels' opinions, one might question their effectiveness in practice. In the case of the CJEU, this concern seems unnecessary, for every candidate who received a negative opinion was replaced by the corresponding government.[50] In total, the Panel has issued opinions on 243 candidates since it started functioning in 2010, 215 of which have been favourable and 28 unfavourable.[51] In other words, slightly more than one in five candidates (21.5%) for a first term of office received an unfavourable opinion, and always led the corresponding government to propose someone else.[52]

This is not the case of the ECtHR, where negative Panel opinions have not always led state parties to change their candidates. The Fifth Activity Report, corresponding to the period from 7 May 2019 to 1 July 2022, indicates that the Panel issued an unfavourable opinion in 47% of the presented lists, meaning that at least one of the candidates was not considered qualified to serve on the court.[53] The Report identifies some resistance of state governments against negative assessments by the Panel. The Report specifies that 'In eight cases the Panel expressed a negative opinion on 12 candidates. Four of these candidates were replaced by the Government. In one case the candidate withdrew but the replacement candidate was likewise considered by the Panel to be non-qualified.'[54] Therefore, eight candidates who received a negative opinion were not replaced. Indeed, the Report specifies that, during this period, three state parties submitted to the Parliamentary Assembly a list which had previously been totally or partially rejected by the Panel. In those cases, in two instances, the governments failed to replace the candidates who had received a negative opinion from the Panel.[55] In the third case, the government replaced two of the initial candidates, but not another whom the Panel had deemed unqualified. In two of these cases, the Parliamentary Assembly rejected the lists, while in one case it was accepted.

At the IACtHR, the Reports do not offer statistical information on the number of candidates who received negative opinions and whether they were in the end appointed, but each Report includes very detailed assessments of

[50] Panel provided for by Article 255 of the TFEU, 'Seventh Activity Report' (2022) 9 <https://curia.europa.eu/jcms/upload/docs/application/pdf/2022-07/2022.2597-qcar22002enn_002.pdf>.
[51] ibid 10. No unfavourable opinions have been delivered on candidates for renewal of a term of office.
[52] ibid.
[53] Advisory Panel of Experts on Candidates for Election as Judge to the European Court of Human Rights, 'Fifth Activity Report for the Attention of the Committee of Ministers' (2022) 17–18. Out of seventeen candidate lists, nine received a favourable opinion and eight received an unfavourable one. With regard to individual judges, twelve out of forty-five received a negative opinion.
[54] ibid 17.
[55] ibid 18.

the candidates. For instance, in the last 2024 Report, the Panel concluded that all candidates met the evaluation criteria established by the Inter-American instruments for appointment to a judgeship at the IACtHR. At the same time, the Report raised concerns over the independence of two candidates. Questions were raised about the Colombian nominee Carlos Rodríguez Mejía on account of his current position as Ambassador of Colombia to Costa Rica,[56] while the Paraguayan nominee Diego Moreno Rodríguez was questioned over his family connections to the executive branch.[57] In the end, Rodríguez Mejía was not elected, but Moreno Rodríguez was.

Clearly then, independence is a criterion that the Panels explicitly take into consideration. The IACtHR Panel holds that independence and impartiality, on the one hand, and high moral authority and recognized expertise in human rights, on the other, are the main criteria for assessment,[58] but recognizes that the former is more difficult to assess.[59] As mentioned above, the IACtHR Panel Reports offer very detailed information about prior positions or connections between the government and the candidate, or even members of the candidate's family.

In the case of the CJEU, the Panel also emphasized the difficulties in assessing independence:

> The requirement of impartiality and independence being beyond doubt is explicitly referred to in the criteria for assessment of candidates set out in Articles 253 and 254 of the Treaty. […] The fulfilment of this requirement, which is essential, is undoubtedly difficult to assess solely on the basis of candidates' files as submitted by Member States' governments and hearings conducted by the panel where appropriate. The panel does, however, endeavour to establish whether there are factors of any kind which are likely to lead it to express reservations as to the ability of candidates to perform the duties of Judge with independence, impartiality, integrity and probity. The panel may therefore need to question a candidate or the government which submitted the proposal on one or more aspects of an application which might give rise

56 Evaluation Panel, 'Final Report of the Independent Panel to Evaluate Candidatures for the Bodies of the Inter-American Human Rights System' (n 46) 15.

57 ibid 20.

58 Evaluation Panel, 'Final Report of the Independent Panel of Experts for the Evaluation of Candidates for Election to the Inter-American Court of and Commission on Human Rights' (n 38) 19–20.

59 Advisory Panel of Experts, 'Abridged Version of the Report from The Independent Panel of Experts for The Evaluation of Candidates for The Inter-American Commission on Human Rights' (2019) <https://www.american.edu/wcl/impact/initiatives-programs/center/publications/documents/upload/final-report-of-the-2021-independent-panel-of-experts.pdf>.

> to doubts as to whether the candidate concerned would be able to perform the duties of a Judge completely independently and impartially, or doubts as to the candidate's integrity or probity.[60]

Also, the Panels might take into consideration the domestic process of selection as a proxy for judicial independence. The CJEU Panel highlights the importance of an open, transparent, rigorous, and independent national selection procedure. At the same time, the Panel specifies that the lack of a procedure enabling the merits of the candidate selected at the national level to be assessed in an independent and objective manner may not in itself constitute a disadvantage,[61] but it may work in the candidate's favour as a rigorous national procedure could help allay the Panel's doubts and questions.[62]

The IACtHR Panel claims that the domestic selection procedures are crucial to improve the suitability, independence, and impartiality of the candidates, but that the lack of such procedures does not exclude any candidate categorically.[63] The Panel noted the largely discretionary and exclusive control over domestic nomination procedures by the executive power.[64] For that reason, the IACtHR Panel Reports include recommendations regarding domestic selection procedures. For the ECtHR, the Parliamentary Assembly has gone even further by requiring that, when submitting the names of candidates to the Assembly, state governments describe the selection process they followed, to the point of concluding that, 'in the absence of a fair, transparent and consistent national selection procedure, the Assembly may reject such lists'.[65]

In the end, despite the differences among the Panels, they all contribute to constraining the broad discretion of state governments in the process of selecting regional judges and thereby further the cause of judicial independence. Moreover, they might contribute to improving selection procedures at the domestic level by emphasizing the need to set up open and transparent procedures and recommending specific measures for that purpose.

[60] Panel provided for by Article 255 of the TFEU (n 50) 19.

[61] ibid 11.

[62] ibid.

[63] Evaluation Panel 'Final Report of the Independent Panel of Experts for the Evaluation of Candidates for Election to the Inter-American Court of and Commission on Human Rights' (n 38) 20.

[64] ibid 6.

[65] Resolution 1646 (2009) on Nomination of candidates and election of judges to the European Court of Human Rights 2009 para 2.

4. Transparency

The selection of international judges is usually conducted through political negotiations in dark corners far from reporters and public interest groups, both at the domestic and regional stages. In the vivid wording of Dehousse, 'it is in the muffled atmosphere of ministerial cabinets and diplomatic meetings, sheltered from the public gaze, that the members of the Court of Justice are appointed'.[66] Over time, some elements of transparency have been introduced, though they remain limited. The transparency of the processes for selecting regional judges may well contribute to the independence and perception of independence in the eyes of the public opinion, and it might favour selection based upon competence and merit. A transparent process of judicial selection may well bolster judicial independence by publicly revealing the connections between judicial candidates and the governments that proposed them, as well as facilitating scrutiny by other actors. In addition, transparency might actually counteract to some degree the dominance of governments or the political institutions of the corresponding international organizations.[67] Indeed, greater transparency could consequently improve both the independence of the judges selected and the legitimacy of regional courts in the eyes of the public.

Instruments for transparency might be introduced at different levels and moments. At the domestic stage of the process, mechanisms to enhance the transparency of the selection process might include public announcements or calls in newspapers, the specialized press, or on the internet, by consulting civil society organizations, or holding public hearings before parliamentary or advisory bodies.[68] At the regional stage, the procedures, overall, remain quite obscure. Yet transparency might be improved at several points in the process of judicial selection. First, with regard to the judicial candidates in the Council of Europe, the curricula vitae of the three candidates proposed by each state are published on the Council of Europe's website. Thus, fairly detailed information about all candidates' backgrounds is available to the public. In the case of the IACtHR, in order to promote transparency and the participation of civil society, the candidates' curriculum vitae are published on the OAS website. The General Secretary issues a press release notifying the publication of the

[66] Renaud Dehousse, *The European Court of Justice: The Politics of Judicial Integration* (Macmillan 1998) 14.

[67] Paul Mahoney, 'The International Judiciary—Independence and Accountability' (2008) 7 Law and Practice of International Courts and Tribunals 346.

[68] Alberto Alemanno, 'How Transparent Is Transparent Enough?: Balancing Access to Information Against Privacy in European Judicial Selections' in M. Bobek (ed), *Selecting Europe's Judges* (Oxford University Press 2015).

CVs in order to make sure that civil society was adequately informed. Such a requirement on its own, however, does not guarantee adequate scrutiny of all candidates, in particular those from countries in which society is less mobilized.[69] In the case of the CJEU and the ATJ, in contrast, no information about the judicial candidates' profiles is published before the appointment and therefore there is no prior scrutiny by civil society that is even possible.

Second, hearings with the candidates are held before the Selection Committee in the Parliamentary Assembly of the Council of Europe (PACE) and also by the CJEU and the IACtHR Expert Panels. The interviews of candidates to the ECtHR and the CJEU, however, are held in closed sessions. Arguably, private hearings allow for more open and flexible discussion. In the EU, there was a proposal to hold public hearings before the European Parliament, but it was rejected by the CJEU using the argument that the public hearings would undermine judicial independence and run the risk of prejudging issues that might subsequently be brought before the court.[70] Given the character of the CJEU Panel that is more technically than politically designed to assess the suitability of the member states' candidates, there may well be good reason to hold the interviews in private. In contrast, given the political nature of the PACE Sub-Committee, public hearings would almost certainly strengthen the democratic legitimacy of the process. Questions that might reveal judges' ideological positions towards certain issues, after all, do not necessarily undermine their independence.[71] In the case of the IACtHR, where the main goal is increasing the transparency of the process, public hearings seem pertinent and appropriate.

An important difference between the Inter-American and European courts should also be noted with regard to the publicity of Panel opinions. The Opinions of the CJEU and ECtHR Panels are confidential. The respective Activity Reports provide information about the process and outcome, but in a general way. The Reports do not identify the candidates or reveal their assessment. They refer to the general reasons for the rejection of candidates. In contrast, the IACtHR Panel Reports include the individual assessment of the candidates and are publicly accessible on the website of the American University Washington College of Law. The evaluations are very detailed and individualized. The Reports include the reasoning behind the assessment of the candidates' high moral character; recognized competence in human rights;

[69] Schönsteiner (n 18).

[70] Anthony Arnull, *The European Union and Its Court of Justice* (2nd ed, Oxford University Press 2006).

[71] Torres Pérez (n 8) 196.

independence, impartiality, and absence of conflicts of interest; contribution to the balanced and representative composition of the organization; and the national nomination process.[72] For instance, the 2024 Report revealed the Panel's concern over the competence of Alberto Borea Odría: the candidate's unfamiliarity with the IACtHR's most recent jurisprudential acquis regarding sexual and reproductive rights and the right to protest. Also, with regard to Carlos Rodríguez Mejía, the Panel expressed concern over his independence from the Colombian President and potential conflict of interests arising from his position as Colombia's Ambassador to Costa Rica. The candidate's promise to resign upon election as a judge was deemed insufficient, since candidate eligibility was a prerequisite for consideration. Adding to the concern of the Panel, the Report mentions that he formerly served as the President of the Republic's lawyer. Given the absence of a public and participatory nomination mechanism in Colombia, the Report highlighted the 'discretionary nature of candidate selection by the Executive'.

The confidentiality of the CJEU and the ECtHR Panel opinions has been defended on several grounds. First, it has been argued that making public the entirety of the Panel opinions might damage the reputation of the candidates, producing a chilling effect that discourages qualified candidates hesitant to expose themselves to the level of scrutiny of an Expert Panel. Lord Mance, who was a member of the CJEU, claimed that 'it would deter and be unfair to candidates if [the opinions] were to be public'.[73] As for the Strasbourg Panel, the Steering Committee for Human Rights has stated that publication might discourage potential candidates who risk serious reputational costs if given a negative assessment.[74] Apparently, however, it is only when the candidates' merits are clearly inadequate for judicial office that the advisory panels issue negative opinions. According to its Second Activity Report, the CJEU Panel rejected candidates who demonstrated 'complete absence of any professional experience relevant to EU law' or whose legal abilities were found 'inadequate'. To the extent that the Panel only rejects candidates who fail to meet the minimum requirements for judges on the respective court, the deterrent effect should only affect low-profile candidates.[75]

[72] Evaluation Panel, 'Final Report of the Independent Panel to Evaluate Candidatures for the Bodies of the Inter-American Human Rights System' (n 46) 15.

[73] Lord Mance, 'The Composition of the European Court of Justice' 9 (2011) <https://supremecourt.uk/uploads/speech_111019_b490b98938.pdf>.

[74] Steering Committee for Human Rights (CDDH), Draft CDDH report on the review of the functioning of the Advisory Panel of experts on candidates for election as judge to the European Court of Human Rights, CDDH(2013)R79 Addendum II, 29 November 2013 ('CDDH report'), para 54.

[75] Torres Pérez (n 8) 197.

Another argument calls for keeping the Reports confidential to protect the privacy and personal data of the candidates. In its Seventh Activity Report, the CJEU Panel argued that requests for access to the Panel's opinions must be handled according to the framework laid down by Regulation (EC) No 1049/2001, regarding public access to European Parliament, Council and Commission documents, which provides for some exceptions to the obligation to disclose documents when their dissemination may affect the protection of private life and integrity.[76] The Panel claimed that, in light of the judgment of the CJEU *Commission v Bavarian Lager*,[77] 'the disclosure of its opinions—which pertain to an assessment of candidates' suitability to perform the duties of Judge and Advocate-General of the Court of Justice and the General Court, and therefore contain personal data—would be likely to undermine the privacy of the candidates'.[78]

At the same time, disclosure of the opinions could arguably hinder the effectiveness and quality of the procedure. The CJEU Panel itself has asserted that: 'the full disclosure of its opinions would undermine the aims and quality of the consultation and appointment procedures provided for in Articles 253 to 255 TFEU, notably because it would jeopardise the secrecy of the panel's deliberations and of the intergovernmental conference at which the Member States appoint the Judges and Advocates-General (Article 4(2) and (3) of Regulation (EC) No 1049/2001)'.[79] Along very similar lines, the Steering Committee in the Council of Europe expressed its concerns regarding the publication of the Advisory Panel's evaluations, which included the negative consequences of doing so would have for its effectiveness vis-à-vis state parties. Confidentiality, the argument goes, allows for more room for manoeuvre. Furthermore, publishing the reports could have a 'chilling effect' on the Advisory Panel's own willingness to issue unfavourable opinions.

In our opinion, the publication of the candidates' assessment would not necessarily infringe on the candidates' right to privacy or the functions of those Panels. With regard to the protection of privacy grounded in EU law,[80] the Panel's opinions on the suitability of the candidates indisputably contain

[76] Article 4(1)(b) of Regulation (EC) No 1049/2001.

[77] C-28/08 Commission v Bavarian Lager https://curia.europa.eu/juris/document/document.jsf?text=&docid=84752&pageIndex=0&doclang=EN&mode=lst&dir=&occ=first&part=1&cid=7342180 (Accessed 24 November 2025).

[78] Panel provided for by Article 255 of the TFEU (n 50) 16. The panel's approach has been supported by the European Ombudsman's decision in case 1955/2017/THH on the Council's refusal to grant public access to opinions evaluating the merits of candidates for appointment to the Court of Justice and the General Court.

[79] ibid.

[80] See the analysis by Alemanno in Bobek, 213–14.

personal data within the meaning of Article 2(1) Regulation 45/2001.[81] This potential risk, however, does not automatically mean that the publication should be rejected. Under Regulation 45/2001, personal data may be considered if its 'processing is necessary for the performance of a task carried out in the public interest on the basis of the Treaties'.[82] In other words, the public interest could outweigh the candidates' right to privacy and justify the publication of the Panel's assessment. Access to the information behind the Panel's assessment of whether the candidates appointed were suitable is certainly in the public interest.

The argument has also been made that the purpose of the Panel is to advise the state governments on the suitability of the candidates, and that making the evaluation available to third parties would therefore imply processing the data for purposes other than those for which it was collected.[83] However, the role of the Panel may be conceived more broadly as ensuring that the candidates fulfil the conditions set out by the Treaties. From this perspective, publication would reinforce the role of the expert panel: ensuring the candidates' suitability to sit on the court in question. As it is, negative evaluations do not necessarily prevent candidates from taking up their appointments, and this currently might occur outside public knowledge. Publishing the opinions could reinforce the role of expert panels because, if the opinions were made public, state governments would feel more pressure to withdraw candidates who receive negative assessments. Publishing the panel opinions and evaluations, or at least their conclusions, with regard to specific candidates would put not only *ex post* but also *ex ante* pressure on state governments to choose suitable candidates. Publication of the opinions could enhance the deterrent effect of the panel by discouraging state governments from selecting candidates on the sole basis of political loyalty if that motive were liable to become public knowledge. The same reasoning applies to the ECtHR Panel. In addition, given the ultimate responsibility of the PACE for the election of the judges, more transparency in the process could be demanded from this parliamentary body as well. One possible measure could be making public the report issued by the Sub-Committee after the interviews are held, as this report contains its recommendations and reasoning, instead of transmitting the report exclusively to the members of the PACE. This report would ideally also include the conclusions reached by the Expert Panel.[84] As for the IACtHR, on balance, making public the Panel

[81] Regulation 45/2001 https://eur-lex.europa.eu/eli/reg/2001/45/oj/eng (Accessed 24 November 2025).
[82] Art 5(a) Regulation 45/2001.
[83] Art 6(1).
[84] Torres Pérez (n 8) 198.

Reports does not seem an unjustified restriction on personal data or as undermining the advisory function of the Panel, since the overall goal behind its establishment was precisely improving the transparency of the selection process.

5. Tenure, Reappointment, and Dissenting Opinions

Judicial selection is an important constraining mechanism from the perspective of structural judicial independence, but it does not operate in isolation. Besides the selection process, other institutional features are relevant in safeguarding judicial independence. Whether or not judges' mandates are limited and the possibility of reappointment are especially pertinent. In these areas, different institutional arrangements might bolster judicial independence and counterbalance the dominance of state executives in the appointment process.

The terms of office of international judges are generally limited (ranging from four to nine years) and renewable.[85] All the judges in the selected regional courts under analysis have limited tenure. The length of each judge's term is six years at the IACtHR, the CJEU, and the ATJ; and nine years at the ECtHR. The mandate is renewable at all the courts studied here except the ECtHR. The CJEU stands out from the others in being the only court where reappointment is unlimited. At the ATJ and the IACtHR, judicial mandates can only be renewed once.[86] Focusing on institutional design, short terms and the possibility of reappointment seem potential risks for judicial independence[87] in that judges may seek to curry the favour of the state government (or other actors) that supported their candidature in order to obtain reappointment or future job prospects after the term ends.

On the other hand, limited tenure and reappointment of regional judges might find justification in a democratic perspective. Limited tenure facilitates the renewal of the composition of regional courts according to the evolution of the political communities under their jurisdiction. At the domestic level, while ordinary judges tend to enjoy life tenure, the mandates of constitutional court judges are usually limited. The main reason is precisely to avoid a gap from

[85] Daniel Terris, Cesare Romano, and Leigh Swigart, *The International Judge: An Introduction to the Men and Women Who Decide the World's Cases* (Oxford University Press 2007) 155; Dinah Shelton, 'Legal Norms to Promote the Independence and Accountability of International Tribunals' (2003) 2 The Law and Practice of International Courts and Tribunals 27, 37–38.

[86] See Table 5.1.

[87] Terris, Romano, and Swigart (n 85) 155; Ruth Mackenzie and Philippe Sands, 'International Courts and Tribunals and the Independence of the International Judge' (2003) 44 Harvard International Law Journal 271, 279; Voeten (n 9) 400; Mahoney (n 67).

arising between the court and the basic beliefs of the people and their political representatives.[88] As regional courts are even further removed from the respective constituencies, the possibility of periodically renewing the judges according to the will of the state parties serves democratic interests. As already argued, however, it is very important, if the democratic value is to be realized, for the procedures for judicial selection and appointment to lie outside the sole prerogative of state governments through negotiations carried out behind closed doors.

In turn, going back to the value of judicial independence and the risk that judges might be tempted to please the state government that proposed them in order to be reappointed, we should also examine closely the potential justification of reappointment.[89] Dunoff and Pollack have looked at reappointment as a means to ensure some accountability that had to be balanced with the value of judicial independence.[90] In our opinion, however, reappointment as a form of accountability constraint could unduly interfere with judicial independence by making it easier for state executives to sideline judges who do not promote their interests and reward those who do. Seen this way, reappointment could be employed to punish or reward judges on the basis of their decisions. Showing how complex the issue is, Hermansen and Naurin's[91] findings challenge the belief that renewable terms weaken judicial independence and argue that governments prioritize factors in deciding whether to request reappointment beyond the specific content of their decisions and the preferences of the government in power for specific policies.[92]

Their argument, nevertheless, does not negate the concerns that the possibility of reappointment raises from the perspective of judicial independence. These concerns can be seen behind Protocol No 14 that amended the ECHR in order to extend the length of judicial mandates from six to nine years and ban reappointment. The explanatory report emphasizes that this amendment is aimed at strengthening the independence and impartiality of the ECtHR.[93]

[88] Victor Ferreres Comella, *Constitutional Courts and Democratic Values: A European Perspective* (Yale University Press 2009) 100–01.

[89] Faúndez Ledesma (n 15) 191 recommended abandoning the practice of reelection.

[90] Jeffrey L Dunoff and Mark A Pollack, 'The Judicial Trilemma' (2017) 111 The American Journal of International Law 225.

[91] Silje SL Hermansen and Daniel Naurin 'Shaping the Bench: The Effect of Ideology and Performance on Judicial Reappointments' (2024) *APSA Preprints*. doi: 10.33774/apsa-2024-kvbc9.

[92] ibid.

[93] Explanatory Report to Protocol No 14 to the Convention for the Protection of Human rights and Fundamental Freedoms, amending the control system of the Convention, para 50: 'The judges' terms of office have been changed and increased to nine years. Judges may not, however, be reelected. These changes are intended to reinforce their independence and impartiality, as desired notably by the Parliamentary Assembly in its Recommendation 1649 (2004).'

Ultimately, we find that institutional design involving lengthy mandates without renewal is advisable.

Adding to the need for careful design and nuance is the potential risk to judicial independence, even when regional judges cannot be reappointed for a second term.[94] After all, if the judges must leave the regional court, they will likely seek positions of equal or prestige when they do. In terms of their career prospects, judges might seek appointment to other international or national courts or public institutions. Voeten argues that there is some evidence that career insecurity makes judges more likely to favour their national government when it is a party to a dispute.[95]

A possible counterweight against the risks involved in limited mandates, whether reappointment is available or not, but especially when it is, would be the exclusion of dissenting opinions, because dissenting opinions enable governments to monitor the position of individual judges on specific disputes. The possibility of issuing dissenting opinions might expose judges from the state involved in the dispute to undue pressure.[96] Of the selected regional courts under analysis, the human rights courts, the ECtHR[97] and IACtHR, allow dissenting opinions, while the regional integration courts, the CJEU[98] and the ATJ,[99] do not.

From the standpoint of judicial independence, dissenting opinions might expose international judges and jeopardize their independence, in particular vis-à-vis their state of nationality. If dissenting opinions are not allowed, the position of individual judges will remain unknown. When dissenting opinions are allowed, judges might reasonably fear 'retaliation' for signing on to opinions against the interests of the respective state; or, conversely, might decide to make strategic use of dissenting opinions to curry favour. Given the lack of tenured judges in regional courts, the ban on dissenting opinions might help shield the independence of the court from an institutional perspective.

There are other reasons to prohibit dissenting opinions as well. A main argument against issuing dissenting opinions at the CJEU and the ATJ is preserving the authority of the court.[100] This argument is formulated from the perspective

[94] Ferreres Comella (n 88) 101.

[95] Eric Voeten, 'The Impartiality of International Judges: Evidence from the European Court of Human Rights' (2008) 102 American Political Science Review 417, 417.

[96] In the case of the IACtHR, judges may not participate in cases against the state of nationality.

[97] ECHR art 45(2).

[98] Article 36 of the Consolidated version of Protocol (No. 3) on the Statute of the Court of Justice of the European Union.

[99] ATJ Treaty art 17.

[100] See the discussion in Armin von Bogdandy and Ingo Venzke, *In Whose Name? A Public Law Theory of International Adjudication* (Oxford University Press 2016) 177.

of the civil law tradition, in which courts are expected to speak the law in one voice. The rulings are presented as incontrovertible interpretations of the text. The lack of dissent fosters the perception of the law as an undisputed mandate, and thus divisions are not to be disclosed.

On the other hand, arguments in favour of allowing dissenting opinions are usually made from the perspective of judicial reasoning and transparency.[101] In terms of the judicial reasoning, and from an internal perspective, the prospect of confronting a dissenting opinion may encourage the majority of the judges to make extra effort for the clarity and sharpness of its opinions.[102] Indeed, it has been argued that the lack of dissenting opinions and the need to reach a compromise among judges that might have different positions regarding the outcome (or might agree with the outcome, but not the reasoning) explains the occasionally cryptic reasoning of the CJEU. From an external perspective, the opportunity for the judges in the minority to present their counterarguments enables litigants and the public to better understand the terms of the debate. Also, dissenting opinions often foreshadow a shift in the case law.

In addition, dissenting opinions may well serve the interest of transparency,[103] which furthers both epistemic and democratic values. From an epistemic perspective, dissenting opinions improve our knowledge of the decision-making process, the arguments that were confronted within the court and the reasons for the final ruling. In democratic terms, publishing dissenting opinions allows greater public scrutiny of the judicial activity. While increased transparency and public scrutiny might exacerbate the risks of public pressure for specific outcomes, by allowing scrutiny by a broad range of actors, it enhances the openness and responsiveness of the institution to the citizens.[104] In this way, greater transparency might bolster the democratic legitimacy of courts.[105]

In the end, from the perspective of institutional design, limited tenure, reappointment, and dissenting opinions all risk, in certain circumstances, undermining judicial independence. Dunoff and Pollack characterized the ensuing trade-offs between independence, accountability, and transparency as a 'judicial trilemma'.[106] Judicial independence is compromised if reappointment is

[101] Ruth B Ginsburg, 'The Role of Dissenting Opinions' (2010) 95 Minnesota Law Review 1–8.
[102] ibid.
[103] Dunoff and Pollack (n 90).
[104] Bruno de Witte, 'Democratic Adjudication in Europe: How Can the European Court of Justice Be Responsive to the Citizens?' in Michael Dougan, Niam Nic Shuibhne, and Eleanor Spaventa (eds), *Empowerment and Disempowerment of the European Citizen* (Hart Publishing 2012).
[105] Bogdandy and Venzke (n 100).
[106] Dunoff and Pollack (n 90) 226. The contribution of Dunoff and Pollack raised awareness of the trade-offs that international courts confront regarding institutional design. The understanding of the variables offered, however, was limited, in that accountability was reduced to the structural checks

possible (accountability) and individual positions are public (transparency). In terms of design, several institutional combinations are possible. In all the selected regional courts, judicial mandates are limited. In the CJEU and the ATJ, judges can be reappointed, but dissenting opinions are not issued. In the ECtHR, issuing dissenting opinions is allowed, but judges cannot be reappointed. In the IACtHR, judges can be reappointed, and dissenting opinions are allowed, which might be the worst combination from the perspective of independence. The judges on the IACtHR, however, may not participate in cases against the respective state of nationality, which at least partially shields them from undue pressure by their 'home state', although their reasoning in cases against other states still certainly remains relevant for the evolution of the case law.

In sum, although no single best model can be celebrated, instituting lengthy mandates without the possibility of reappointment and allowing the issuance of dissenting opinions strikes a good balance in terms of the trade-offs. Limited, but longer, mandates further democratic legitimacy by facilitating the renewal over time of the court's composition. Allowing reappointment in order to make judges politically accountable for the content of judicial decisions should be rejected because it risks unduly undermining judicial independence. Dissenting opinions, while exposing the position of individual judges, can be justified in terms of promoting transparency and thereby epistemic and democratic values. This line of argumentation was, in fact, the path followed by the ECtHR in Protocol No 14 that proscribed the reappointment of judges and lengthened the mandates of ECtHR judges, in a court in which dissenting opinions are allowed. Whichever institutional design is chosen, attentiveness to the risks of that design for independence and the countervailing values enables an informed, critical assessment of current arrangements and should guide proposals for reform.

found in reappointment; and transparency to the mechanisms that permit the identification of individual judicial positions such as dissenting opinions.

6
Political Override and Non-Compliance

1. Introduction

The dependence of regional courts on the member states for effective compliance with their judgments might be regarded as a form of constraint from an institutional perspective. Ginsburg conceptualized *ex post* political constraints within the framework outlined by Hirschman of 'exit, voice and loyalty'.[1] Exit refers to the most extreme response open to member states: withdrawal from the jurisdiction of the regional court and the corresponding treaty. Yet withdrawal carries high political costs, which states might avoid by articulating their concerns through a variety of mechanisms that involve, in one way or another, ignoring, obstructing, or misapplying specific court judgments, or potentially even by effectively overruling a court decision by amending a treaty or legislation. Also, such mechanisms might be formal or informal, ranging from the formal amendment of relevant treaty stipulation to informal behaviours such as disregarding court decisions, publicly voicing discontent or mobilizing public opinion against the international court. The mere prospect of non-compliance or political override through treaty or legislative amendment might have an impact on the regional courts' adjudicative function.

Threats of political override and non-compliance have been examined by political scientists empirically. Indeed, several studies have examined legislative override and non-compliance regarding the Court of Justice of the European Union (CJEU), often reaching divergent conclusions. Carrubba, Gabel, and Hankla claimed to have found evidence of systematic sensitivity on the part of the CJEU to threats of both legislative override and non-compliance, and that those threats had a substantive effect on judicial rulings.[2] In contrast, Stone Sweet and Brunell[3] argued that threats of override were not

[1] Tom Ginsburg, 'Political Constraints on International Courts' in Cesare PR Romano, Karen J Alter, and Yuval Shany (eds), *The Oxford Handbook of International Adjudication* (1st edn, Oxford University Press 2014) 490.

[2] Clifford J Carrubba, Matthew Gabel, and Charles Hankla, 'Judicial Behavior Under Political Constraints: Evidence from the European Court of Justice' (2008) 102 The American Political Science Review, 435, 449.

[3] Alec Stone Sweet and Thomas Brunell, 'The European Court of Justice, State Noncompliance, and the Politics of Override' (2012) 106 The American Political Science Review 204, 205.

Balancing International Judicial Independence. Aida Torres Pérez, Oxford University Press.
 DOI: 10.1093/oso/9780198852544.003.0006

considered credible and did not constrain the court in any systematic way.[4] They also claimed that state non-compliance, rather than hindering the development of the EU's legal system, stimulated it.[5] For his part, Larsson suggested that the disagreements in the literature over when and how override occurs, its effects, and normative implications are partly because override has been defined in very different ways.[6]

Focusing on the normative dimension, several questions seem worthy of attention. First, do constraints derived from political override, however realistic the threat is, undermine judicial independence or provide an adequate check on the power of regional courts and contribute to containing unwanted forms of judicial activism? May political override or non-compliance as forms of constraint be justified on grounds of democratic or epistemic values? To elucidate these questions, our analysis distinguishes between political override (section 2) and non-compliance (section 3). Political override involves the use of mechanisms provided by the legal order itself to amend the relevant rules. In contrast, non-compliance amounts to infringing (or the threat thereof) a treaty obligation to abide by the regional court's judgments.

2. Forms of Political Override of Regional Courts' Judgments

There are mechanisms in place that allow political authorities to respond to a court judgment by amending the relevant rules being interpreted and applied. At the domestic level, we can distinguish between legislative and constitutional amendments in response to court decisions.[7] At the international level, political authorities may either react to a regional court judgment by amending the text of the corresponding treaty or the relevant law in force. Accordingly, in our analysis, we distinguish between treaty and legislative overrides. While treaty override involves the amendment of the respective international treaty in response to a regional court judgment, legislative override is mainly relevant for those regional legal orders in which the respective regional institutions enact legislation, as is the case for the systems of economic and political

[4] ibid 212.
[5] ibid.
[6] Olof Larsson, 'Political and Constitutional Overrides: The Case of the Court of Justice of European Union' (2021) 28 Journal of European Public Policy 1932, 1933.
[7] Victor Ferreres Comella, *Constitutional Courts and Democratic Values: A European Perspective* (Yale University Press 2009) 96–97.

integration under analysis: the EU and the Andean Community. In general terms, following Larsson, 'override occurs when politicians change the text of laws or treaties (or produces new ones) in order to undo or limit an unwanted implication of a court's [...] decision'.[8] Regarding the content of the treaty or legislative amendment, another distinction can be made between substantive and structural overrides. The former refers to amendments on substantive policy, usually regarding a particular norm and how it is to be interpreted, while the latter refers to amendments that modify the institutional framework, especially those that affect the court itself, for example, by changing the court's composition or the scope of its jurisdiction.[9]

How often overrides occur and how effective an influence the threat of override is on judicial behaviour are empirical issues that remain contested.[10] Given the potential impact upon judicial independence, we are more concerned with the normative dimension and so turn our attention to the extent to which political overrides, as checks on the action of regional courts, are justified, and under what conditions.

Political scientists tend to view threats of political override and non-compliance as compromising judicial independence inasmuch as those threats might affect the judicial decision-making processes by factoring in consideration of member states' preferences. This risk leads Larsson to claim that '[Overrides] are potentially a threat to the independence of courts, and by extension to the rule of law, as the threat of override can lead to political considerations crowding out the role of the law in the process of adjudication'.[11] In this way, state preferences might influence the court's reasoning, by giving weight to factors beyond the interpretation of the law.

These risks notwithstanding, here we argue that some forms of political override may be justified as mechanisms that fortify institutional interdependence from a checks and balances perspective. The potential impact of political override (or the threat thereof) upon the process of adjudication does not, after all, necessarily undermine judicial independence. As argued earlier, judicial independence requires that judges be free from *undue* influences or constraints. Political constraints that take the form of treaty or legislative amendments are not necessarily undue, as they can be understood as democratic responses to

[8] Larsson (n 6) 1933.

[9] In that regard, Larsson distinguishes between political and constitutional overrides: 'I will define political override as 'any legislative or treaty act which affects the policy impact of a court decision in some material way'; while constitutional override is defined as 'any legislative or treaty act which contests and revises the mandate of a court'. (ibid 1936).

[10] Carrubba, Gabel, and Hankla (n 2); Stone Sweet and Brunell (n 4).

[11] Larsson (n 6) 1933.

court decisions using the procedural mechanisms offered by the legal system. Such responses differ significantly from, for instance, pressures from state governments seeking economic advantage or to impose an ideological position. In sum, the availability of a treaty or legislative amendment, even if it potentially influences the process of adjudication, does not necessarily undermine judicial independence from a normative perspective.

At the domestic level, the mechanism for constitutional amendment has been regarded as a democratic check capable of bolstering the democratic legitimacy of the judicial review of legislation.[12] It enables the institutions directly representing the people to, following the procedures constitutionally established, respond to a constitutional court interpretation by amending the constitution. The constitutional amendment procedure is usually arduous, requiring supermajority approval from several institutions, and often a referendum by popular vote as well. The outcome may thus be regarded as an expression of the will of the political community as a whole. In this way, constitutional amendment offers a democratic check on the action of constitutional courts (or any courts with the power of reviewing legislation) that alleviates the counter-majoritarian difficulty of judicial review.[13] Accordingly, a constitutional amendment might be conceived as a mechanism of inter-institutional dialogue within a system of checks and balances.

Legislative amendment may also offer means for the political branches to respond to court decisions, but in such cases, the line between legitimate response to a court decision and disobedience is less clear. If a constitutional court annuls a law because it violates the constitution, for example, and the parliament immediately responds by effectively re-enacting the law in an only superficially different form, the legislative response amounts to an act of disobedience. Notwithstanding, after sufficient time has elapsed, parliament could legitimately pass a new law 'to generate a second round of debate that will give the court the opportunity to reconsider its earlier holdings'.[14] If the legislative response is more nuanced and seeks to clarify or specify certain aspects that remain open or to fill a lacuna, particularly when the law was not struck down by the constitutional court, but was rather interpreted in a certain way with which the legislator disagrees, the legislative bypass might be legitimate. The ensuing analysis will examine more closely the distinctions

[12] Ferreres Comella (n 7) 96, 104–07.
[13] ibid 104–05.
[14] ibid 96.

between treaty override and legislative override of regional courts' rulings as forms of interdependence.

2.1. Treaty amendment

Treaty amendment enables the parties of treaties to respond to a regional court's interpretation they regard as incorrect or unfavourable (though usually both). The availability of the treaty amendment procedure can be regarded as a democratically legitimate check on regional courts. Still, the democratic legitimacy of treaty amendment at the international level is not equivalent to that of constitutional amendment at the domestic level. Constitutional amendment usually involves far greater deliberation and consensus-building, in addition to direct participation of the people. Treaty amendment procedures also tend to require a high degree of consensus, often unanimity of the states' parties, but they usually require much less, if any, open, public deliberation.

The requirement of unanimity, if anything, preserves state sovereignty and gives all state parties a veto power. The negotiations to amend an international treaty, however, almost always take place among the representatives of the state governments behind closed doors. At the same time, the ratification process at the national level might require supermajorities in parliament, or even an approval referendum, as do the EU Treaties in some member states. Indeed, the level of openness and citizen involvement in treaty amendment procedures varies across states. While treaty amendment as a constraining mechanism on regional courts might be justified as a democratic check, much room remains for improving the procedures for treaty amendment both at the regional and domestic levels in terms of democratic legitimacy.

If we look at the treaty amendment procedures from a different perspective, however, it might appear that the requirement of unanimity or a very high threshold for treaty amendment might render treaty amendment a hardly effective constraining mechanism in practice, given the diversity of member state preferences and every single member state's veto power. Because of these factors, correcting the interpretation of a regional court using treaty amendment may actually be much more difficult than constitutional amendment at the domestic level. And yet, the high activation threshold of this constraining mechanism can be justified in the interests of ensuring broad consensus and the court's authority. Were it easier to amend treaties, regional courts might show greater deference to state authorities in order to preserve their authority and avoid overrule.

In sum, the normative justification of treaty amendment in response to regional courts' judgments as a democratic check holds, although the democratic credentials of the process could stand strengthening to better ground it. At the same time, the participation of multiple institutions and a high threshold promote both the democratic values as well as the authority of the court.

In practice, treaty amendment in response to a regional court judgment, as already intimated, rarely occurs, but some instances are worth noting. In the European Union, in *Grogan*,[15] the CJEU was asked to decide whether medical termination of pregnancy, performed according to the law of the state in which it takes place, constituted a service within the terms of Article 60 of the former European Economic Community Treaty.[16] The case concerned the legality of a measure in Ireland prohibiting student associations from distributing information about clinics in another member state where voluntary termination of pregnancy was lawfully carried out. In Ireland, abortion was banned under Article 40(3)(3) of the Constitution, and Irish courts interpreted the provision as extending to assisting pregnant women obtain abortions abroad. Even providing detailed information about the clinics was deemed a violation under Article 40(3)(3) of the Constitution.

The CJEU affirmed the position that abortion was to be regarded as a service but concluded that the prohibition of the distribution of information by student associations was not contrary to EU law because the clinics performing the abortions were not involved in the distribution of the information. Following this judgment, and during the Maastricht Treaty negotiations, Ireland managed to obtain support for a Protocol declaring that nothing in the EU Treaties affected the Irish constitutional ban on abortion.[17] Here, the Protocol did not override the CJEU's judgment, but clarified that it did not put in question Ireland's constitutional ban on abortion. The Protocol's assurance that the abortion ban would not be overridden proved crucial, politically speaking, in securing Ireland's support for the Maastricht Treaty. Some twenty-five years later, in 2018, Ireland held a referendum that led to the repeal of its constitutional ban on abortion.

One clear case of override through treaty amendment occurred in response to *Kalanke*.[18] In *Kalanke*, the CJEU confronted an affirmative action measure

[15] *The Society for the Protection of Unborn Children Ireland Ltd v Stephen Grogan and Others* [1991] European Court of Justice C-159/90.

[16] EC Treaty.

[17] Protocol No. 17 annexed to the Treaty on the European Union in Maastricht.

[18] *Eckhard Kalanke v Freie Hansestadt Bremen* [1995] European Court of Justice C-450/93.

that automatically gave priority to women in sectors where they were under-represented when the candidates for promotion were equally qualified. The CJEU ruled that the affirmative action measure in question was not compatible with the principle of equal treatment for men and women as enshrined in Article 2(1) and (4) of Council Directive 76/207/EEC.[19] Article 2(1) establishes the principle of equal treatment, understood as no discrimination on grounds of sex either directly or indirectly, while Article 2(4) qualified that: 'This Directive shall be without prejudice to measures to promote equal opportunity for men and women, in particular by removing existing inequalities which affect women's opportunities.' Thus, Paragraph 4 opened the door for affirmative action measures that promoted equal opportunity. Notwithstanding, the CJEU went on to argue in *Kalanke* that Article 2(4) of the Directive must be interpreted strictly and that national rules 'which guarantee women absolute and unconditional priority for appointment or promotion go beyond promoting equal opportunities and overstep the limits of the exception in Article 2(4) of the Directive'.[20] This CJEU judgment directly impacted social policies in several member states where robust programmes that included affirmative action measures to promote equal opportunities were in place. In response, a new paragraph (4) was added to Article 141 of the Treaty of the European Community in the treaty reform of Amsterdam (now Article 157 of the Treaty on the Functioning of the European Union (TFEU)) to explicitly allow for national affirmative action measures. Article 141(4) stated that: 'With a view to ensuring full equality in practice between men and women in working life, the principle of equal treatment shall not prevent any Member State from maintaining or adopting measures providing for specific advantages in order to make it easier for the underrepresented sex to pursue a vocational activity or to prevent or compensate for disadvantages in professional careers.'

In this case, the treaty amendment fulfilled its potential as a legitimate response to the CJEU's interpretation of a sensitive issue that directly impacted national public policy. It showed that the possible influence of state preferences made available by the treaty amendment procedure may be regarded as a legitimate constraint over judicial power. This episode showed that the treaty amendment circuit could channel a form of democratic response to the CJEU's interpretation.

[19] Council Directive 76/207/EEC of 9 February 1976 on the implementation of the principle of equal treatment for men and women as regards access to employment, vocational training and promotion, and working conditions 1976.

[20] *Eckhard Kalanke v Freie Hansestadt Bremen* (n 18) para 22.

2.2. Legislative override

Legislative override, understood as the amendment of the legislative provision that has been interpreted or annulled, is another possible response to a regional court judgment. This constraining mechanism is particularly relevant in regional systems of integration in which the respective institutions enact legislative acts, meaning the EU and the Andean Community, for the purpose of this analysis. Political scientists have devoted much attention to legislative override in the EU, as mentioned before, when I noted that the claims as to the impact of legislative override or the threat of override upon court judgments are contested.[21] Larsson has recently given evidence of actual political override, in the form of legislative amendments to adjust policy outcomes that do not necessarily question the court's mandate.[22] Larsson does not, however, make any claim as to the impact of potential override upon the court's decision-making process. Looking at legislative amendment more closely, we might understand it as a direct challenge to the court's authority, though it often adopts a more nuanced form. If a regional court decision declares null and void some legislative act, immediately re-enacting that piece of legislation (or a very similar one) would amount to an act of non-compliance (see section 3 below). However, new legislation might aim to clarify or specify the judicial doctrine, fill a gap or distinguish circumstances that set certain cases apart. Also, after time, re-enacting the overturned law might better be regarded as an invitation to revise the previous court interpretation and initiate a second round of debate in light of new information and experience, as mentioned before regarding debates at the domestic level.

If the regional court directly interprets a Treaty clause, however, legislative override is more difficult to justify. In the EU, this issue is particularly controversial, since the Treaties tend to cover policy goals, thus bringing them into constitutional applicability. Such 'over-constitutionlization' of basic policies makes it more difficult for political institutions to counter CJEU case law by changing the law[23] and then process political disagreement through ordinary channels.[24] On occasion, the CJEU has adapted its interpretation of

[21] Carrubba, Gabel, and Hankla (n 2); Stone Sweet and Brunell (n 4).

[22] Larsson (n 6).

[23] Michael Blauberger and Susanne K Schmidt, 'Free Movement, the Welfare State, and the European Union's Over-constitutionalization: Administrating Contradictions' (2017) 95 Public Administration (London) 437, 439.

[24] Elise Muir, 'EU Citizenship, Access to "Social Benefits" and Third-Country National Family Members: Reflecting on the Relationship Between Primary and Secondary Rights in Times of Brexit' (2018) 3 European Papers 1353, 1353.

the Treaties in response to the enactment of new legislation. For instance, in the field of EU citizenship and the access to welfare benefits for mobile non-economically active citizens, the CJEU and the EU legislature have carried on an ongoing exchange. At first, the CJEU interpreted that the EU citizenship was enough for an EU citizen lawfully residing in another member state to obtain a benefit covered by specific EU legislation on the basis of the prohibition of nationality discrimination (ex Art 18(1) of the TFEU).[25] The EU legislation then attempted to constrain the implications of the CJEU doctrine on the right to non-discrimination on grounds of nationality regarding access to welfare benefits by means of Directive 2004/38.[26] The enactment of this Directive, particularly its exception to equal treatment in Article 24(2), carved out the possibility to deny aid to those who did not hold permanent residence and were not working. As Blauberger and Schmidt surmised: 'Member states took the legislative process as an occasion to signal to the Court that they did not want to grant social assistance to economically inactive EU migrants.'[27] At first, the CJEU maintained its reasoning on the basis of treaty provisions with regard to equal treatment on grounds of nationality,[28] though, as Muir notes, '[i]n doing so it largely disregarded the concern expressed by political institutions to make non-economically active migrants' residence—and therefore equal treatment rights under EU law—conditional upon having a "sufficient" level of resources.'[29] Nonetheless, in a later series of cases on the rights of mobile non-economically active EU citizens,[30] again borrowing Muir's summation, 'the CJEU "deconstitutionalised" its understanding of key aspects of the prohibition of nationality discrimination.'[31] The CJEU focused on secondary legislation and, in particular, the goals and text of Directive 2004/38[32] in order to interpret restrictively the scope and content of the right to non-discrimination on grounds of nationality with regard to mobile non-economically active EU citizens.

[25] *María Martínez Sala v Freistaat Bayern* [1998] European Court of Justice C-85/96 [635].

[26] Directive 2004/38/EC of the European Parliament and of the Council of 29 April 2004 on the right of citizens of the Union and their family members to move and reside freely within the territory of the Member States amending Regulation (EEC) No 1612/68 and repealing Directives 64/221/EEC, 68/360/EEC, 72/194/EEC, 73/148/EEC, 75/34/EEC, 75/35/EEC, 90/364/EEC, 90/365/EEC and 93/96/EEC 2004.

[27] Blauberger and Schmidt (n 23) 443.

[28] *Michel Trojani v Centre public d'aide sociale de Bruxelles (CPAS)* [2004] European Court of Justice C-456/02 [39].

[29] Muir (n 24) 1362–63.

[30] *Pensionsversicherungsanstalt v Peter Brey* [2013] European Court of Justice C-140/12.

[31] Muir (n 24) 1360.

[32] ibid 1363–64.

Directive 2004/38 can be viewed as a form of legislative override with an impact upon the subsequent CJEU case law. Instead of sticking to its prior interpretation of the relevant Treaty provisions, the CJEU was sensitive to the approach of the political institutions expressed in secondary legislation.[33] Certainly, the shift of the CJEU has been criticized for lessening the protection of mobile EU citizens.[34] However, this sort of political override, and its potential effects upon subsequent cases, does not necessarily undermine the independence of the CJEU. The approval of new legislation cannot be regarded as undue influence upon the court unless it directly disobeys a prior judgment, such as would be the case of new legislation immediately re-enacting a legislative provision the CJEU declared nulled and void. Legislative override embodies democratic value, even if the legislative procedures differ from the domestic ones and the European Parliament does not play a primary role. Various institutions do participate in it, institutions that represent different constituencies and interests. In certain contexts, legislative override can therefore be regarded as part of an inter-institutional dialogue under a system of checks and balances. Moreover, the complexity of the legislative process, in terms of the number and diversity of the actors involved and the thresholds required for collective decisions, makes it difficult for member states to impose their preferences systematically.[35] It is important to be aware of all the actors and processes that might have an impact upon regional courts, but legislative override does not necessarily undermine independence from a normative perspective.

2.3. Substantive and structural override

With regard to the content of overrides, a relevant distinction should be made between substantive and structural overrides. Treaty or legislative amendment might offer one recourse to overturn or revise the substantive policies and interpretations stemming from specific regional court judgments, as discussed above. In contrast, structural override refers to treaty or legislative amendments addressed to institutional reform of the court itself.[36] Those structural overrides would normally represent instances of backlash, as opposed to

[33] Larsson (n 6) 1945.

[34] Niamh Nic Shuibhne, 'Limits Rising, Duties Ascending: The Changing Legal Shape of Union Citizenship' (2015) 52 Common Market Law Review 889, 889.

[35] R Daniel Kelemen, 'The Political Foundations of Judicial Independence in the European Union' (2012) 19 Journal of European Public Policy 43, 46.

[36] Larsson (n 6) 1936.

pushback, according to the terminology of Madsen, Cebulak, and Wiebusch. These scholars offered an analytical framework to elucidate the forms and patterns of resistance to international courts that distinguishes between pushback and backlash: 'There is a difference between mere pushback from individual Member States or other actors, seeking to influence the future direction of an IC's case-law and actual backlash in terms of critique triggering significant institutional reform or even the dismantling of tribunals.'[37] Treaty and legislative amendments on substantive issues would be included within the notion of pushback, whereas institutional reforms of regional courts could be seen as a form of backlash. Yet, the notions of pushback and backlash include diverse forms of resistance to international courts coming from a variety of actors that go beyond treaty and legislative amendment.

With regard to judicial independence, structural amendments are particularly concerning when they are aimed at controlling the court or undermining its power and authority, which may involve reducing the scope of the court's jurisdiction, packing the court with judges aligned with the member states' interests, punishing the court by depriving it of resources, or any amendments that attack the institutional foundations or the mandate of the court. At the domestic level, recent examples of constitutional and legislative amendments to capture the courts and undermine their independence have been witnessed in the context of the rule of law backsliding in several EU member states, such as the Polish law that reduced the retirement age of judges in order to allow the government in power to appoint new judges more sympathetic to its interests.

Regional courts might be, in contrast to domestic courts, particularly resilient in this regard. As mentioned earlier, treaty amendment is particularly onerous. Unanimity is usually required, which effectively gives every member state veto power. The high threshold for collective decisions, the many veto points, and the wide variety of conflicting state preferences make enacting legislative or treaty amendments to reverse court decisions or attack its institutional foundations extremely difficult.[38]

In the case of the European Court of Human Rights (ECtHR), the Brighton Declaration and subsequent Protocol 15 might be regarded as a form of structural treaty override. The Brighton Declaration was the outcome of a High-level Conference in Brighton held at the behest of the UK government in April 2012. The UK government had criticized certain decisions of the ECtHR that stirred

[37] Mikael Rask Madsen, Pola Cebulak, and Micha Wiebusch, 'Backlash Against International Courts: Explaining the Forms and Patterns of Resistance to International Courts' (2018) 14 International Journal of Law in Context 197, 198.

[38] Kelemen (n 35) 45–46.

political indignation, especially the *Hirst* judgment that overruled Britain's general rule depriving prisoners of voting rights.[39] The UK government successfully mobilized a political reaction that led to the Brighton Declaration, endorsed by all forty-seven-member states. The Brighton Declaration emphasized the principle of subsidiarity and the margin of appreciation doctrine, which already had a foothold in ECtHR doctrine, encouraging 'the Court to give great prominence to and apply consistently these principles in its judgments'.[40] The Declaration also called for explicitly including the principle of subsidiarity and the margin of appreciation doctrine in the Preamble of the European Convention on Human Rights (ECHR).[41] Subsequently, Protocol 15[42] amended the ECHR to introduce just such a reference to the principle of subsidiarity and the doctrine of the margin of appreciation in the Preamble to the Convention. In the end, therefore, Protocol 15 amounted to a structural treaty override. Even though the episode did not strip the ECtHR of any jurisdiction, it certainly aimed at reducing the level of scrutiny and putting limits on the power of the ECtHR.[43]

Normatively, going back to the main thread of my analysis, does this treaty amendment undermine the independence of the ECtHR? Though a plausible critical assessment of Protocol 15 can be made from the perspective of the mandate of the ECtHR and a robust protection of human rights, such a treaty amendment does not necessarily undermine the ECtHR's independence to adjudicate free from undue influence or pressure. Since both the Brighton Declaration and the ensuing treaty amendment expressed the unanimous will of all the states' parties, the argument behind it enjoys solid democratic grounding. Another factor to take into consideration is that, in contrast to just voicing states' discontent, the institutionalized process for treaty amendment launched by the Declaration was premised upon mutual recognition and respect.[44] The contested point was the institutional role of the ECtHR and the

[39] Mikael Rask Madsen, *The European Court of Human Rights*, vol 1 (Oxford University Press 2018) 267.

[40] Brighton Declaration 2012 para 12.

[41] ibid.

[42] Protocol No. 15 amending the Convention on the Protection of Human Rights and Fundamental Freedoms 2021: 'Affirming that the High Contracting Parties, in accordance with the principle of subsidiarity, have the primary responsibility to secure the rights and freedoms defined in this Convention and the Protocols thereto, and that in doing so they enjoy a margin of appreciation, subject to the supervisory jurisdiction of the European Court of Human Rights established by this Convention'.

[43] Madsen (n 39) 245: 'Brighton Declaration "began an institutionalized process that aimed to limit the ECtHR's power. The process before and after the Brighton Declaration raises the fundamental question of whether the overall authority of the Court has changed".'

[44] ibid 271: 'Compared to the discourse of discontent, the Brighton Declaration, adopted by consensus, provides a different but more robust empirical indicator of the general recognition of the ECtHR by key constituencies—the member states' governments (...).'

degree of deference towards the states in the exercise of the courts' power of review.

3. Non-Compliance

. To the extent that international courts do not possess coercive powers to enforce their decisions, and therefore require the collaboration of state authorities, the threat of non-compliance is liable to constrain the decision-making process. Resisting regional court judgments could be used in isolated cases or strategically to challenge the legitimacy of the court.[45] Non-compliance or partial compliance might be conceived as a form of political *ex post* mechanism that constrains the independence of international courts.[46] We should thus reflect upon the extent to which non-compliance (or the threat thereof) undermines judicial independence from a normative perspective or whether, under certain circumstances, it can be justified in light of the checks and balances doctrine.

Going back to our foundational definition, judicial independence requires freedom from undue influences or constraints that distort the decision-making process, but that does not mean freedom from any form of constraint whatsoever. Most commonly, political scientists have approached political override and non-compliance without distinction as mechanisms that might, empirically speaking, constrain judicial independence.[47] As argued above, political override, in the form of a treaty or legislative amendment that follows the established procedural requirements, does not necessarily undermine independence, however consequential it might be on a regional court's behaviour. Political override might thus be regarded as a form of inter-institutional dependence capable of providing a democratic check on the action of regional courts. Compared to a treaty or legislative amendment, threats of non-compliance are normatively more problematic, since non-compliance with court decisions amounts to failure to fulfil state's obligations under the respective international treaty. In such a legal framing, non-compliance would thus comprise an undue constraint on regional courts.

[45] Ginsburg (n 1) 490.
[46] Laurence Helfer and AM Slaughter, 'Why States Create International Tribunals: A Response to Professors Posner and Yoo' (2005) 93 California Law Review 899, 54: 'State responses range from outright recalcitrance and defiance at one extreme to partial or delayed compliance at the other.'
[47] Carrubba, Gabel, and Hankla (n 2); Stone Sweet and Brunell (n 4).

Still, we should ask ourselves if non-compliance with regional court judgments can be justified under certain circumstances. Several authors have developed arguments to justify non-compliance on democratic grounds,[48] although those who conclude that non-compliance with international courts' judgments may be justified restrict legitimate non-compliance to exceptional circumstances. While some studies focus on threats of non-compliance by state governments, compliance with regional court judgments often involves the action of various national authorities, going beyond the executive to include the legislature, domestic courts, or other national authorities, such as public prosecutors or independent agencies. This underscores the need to disaggregate our conception of the states, since the various authorities occupy very different institutional positions.

The specific circumstances advanced by scholars who have defended non-compliance on democratic grounds are restricted to the action of state parliaments. Accordingly, Follesdal has claimed that 'states might not be suitable actors in a system of checks to ensure that ICs interpret in appropriate ways. Yet checks and balances should be developed in our multi-level legal order to alleviate these risks wrought by ICs' interpretation and law making'.[49] In his view, state governments are not well-positioned to oppose the decisions of international courts, but state parliaments might provide a valid democratic check. The direct election of members of parliament and the extensive public deliberation and justification in which they engage affords them greater democratic legitimacy.[50] Follesdal argued that domestic parliaments may, in the right circumstances, therefore deliberately and justifiably disobey an international court judgment in an effort to correct the interpretation or application of international law by the international court.[51] In order to determine those legitimating circumstances for such non-compliance by national parliaments, Follesdal followed Rawls' theory of civil disobedience and adapted the relevant criteria to the international sphere.[52] In particular, he emphasized

[48] Colm O'Cinneide, 'Saying "No" to Strasbourg: When Are National Parliaments Justified in Refusing to Give Effect to Judgments of International Human Rights Courts?' in Matthew Saul, Andreas Follesdal, and Geir Ulfstein (eds), *The International Human Rights Judiciary and National Parliaments* (Cambridge University Press 2017).

[49] Andreas Follesdal, 'Law Making by Law Breaking? A Theory of Parliamentary Civil Disobedience Against International Human Rights Courts' in Matthew Saul, Andreas Follesdal, and Geir Ulfstein (eds), *The International Human Rights Judiciary and National Parliaments* (Cambridge University Press 2017) 331.

[50] ibid 335.

[51] ibid 331, 334.

[52] ibid 340–44.

the need for public justification for non-compliance.[53] The emphasis on public justification frames non-compliance as a judicial control mechanism that is only valid if the reasons for non-compliance are publicly elaborated and go beyond the state's self-interests and current ideological position. According to Follesdal's analysis, the failure of the UK parliament to comply with *Hirst* is not justifiable on the basis of those criteria.[54] O'Cinneide has also argued that non-compliance by national parliaments and other state organs with international human rights court decisions may be justified 'in the interest of maintaining fidelity to the principle of popular sovereignty. However, this "red line" should only be crossed in exceptional circumstances—and national authorities should have to bear a heavy burden of justification in this regard'.[55] O'Cinneide argues that states cannot justify disobedience every time a court decision goes against them under the principle of popular sovereignty. The manner in which he develops the circumstances under which non-compliance would be justified reduces non-compliance to a 'nuclear option'.[56] In sum, despite the greater degree of deference due to national parliaments because of their democratic pedigree, the specific conditions that potentially would justify their non-compliance with regional court decisions remain extremely qualified.

In the context of the IACtHR, the recent enactment of an Amnesty Law in Peru offers an example of legislative override that amounts to sheer non-compliance that cannot be justified. On 1 July 2024,[57] the IACtHR issued a decision requiring Peru not to enact or give effect to a legislative proposition for the prescription of the crimes against humanity committed in Peru in the cases that had already been examined in *Barrios Altos v Perú*[58] and *La Cantuta v Perú*.[59] Nonetheless, in direct opposition to the IACtHR decision, Law No. 6951/2023 was anyhow enacted. Moreover, about a year later, the Peruvian Parliament initiated the process to pass an Amnesty Law addressed to the members of armed forces, national police, and self-defence committees that participated in the fight against terrorism between 1980 and 2000. On 9 July 2025, the law was enacted by the Peruvian Congress without a broad deliberation by

[53] ibid 342, 346.
[54] ibid 348.
[55] O'Cinneide (n 48) 327–28.
[56] ibid 322–27.
[57] Resolution of the IACtHR (1 July 2024) (interim measures and monitoring compliance)https://corteidh.or.cr/docs/medidas/barrioscantuta_06.pdf>.
[58] *Barrios Altos v Perú* [2001] Inter-American Court of Human Rights.
[59] *La Cantuta v Perú* [2007] Inter-American Court of Human Rights.

sixteen deputies in the permanent commission.[60] On 24 July 2025, a new resolution of the President of the IACtHR required that the state of Peru suspend the legislative process to enact the Amnesty Law or otherwise that the authorities did not enforce that law until a decision on the merits by the IACtHR was taken.[61] In response to the IACtHR resolution, two days later, the Ministry of Justice issued a Declaration rejecting it and invoking its popular sovereignty.[62] Finally, on 13 August, the Peruvian President promulgated the law, which has been in force since then. In the end, this is a case of non-compliance that would not fulfil the conditions to be regarded as a legitimate response to the regional court. On the contrary, it amounts to a direct challenge to the court's authority on grounds of state sovereignty.

Sometimes the source of non-compliance might actually be national courts.[63] As argued already, dialogue between courts often has significant epistemic and deliberative value. Despite the space for disagreement and partial contestation that such judicial dialogue opens, however, judicial dialogue cannot be invoked as a value in itself to justify purposeful non-compliance. Domestic courts might comply, or partially comply, without forfeiting their ability to voice disagreement with the regional court decision and influence the court's reasoning in future cases. Dialogue requires conditions of mutual recognition, respect and attentive argumentation. A case in point is *Fontevecchia*, in which the Argentine Supreme Court challenged the position of the IACtHR. The case concerned the publication of information about Carlos Menem, then the President of Argentina, and a son he had not recognized. The journalists behind the story were convicted in Argentina of violating Menem's right to privacy to pay a fine. The case was then brought before the IACtHR, which found that the domestic judgment breached the right to freedom of thought and expression enshrined in Article 13 of the American Convention on Human Rights (IACHR). The IACtHR ordered Argentina to render without effect the civil sanction, giving one year from notification of the judgment to comply.[64]

[60] CEJIL, Corte Interamericana ordena frenar Ley de Amnistía por riesgo de impunidad en graves violaciones a derechos humanos en Perú (30 July 2025)https://cejil.org/comunicado-de-prensa/corte-interamericana-ordena-frenar-ley-de-amnistia-por-riesgo-de-impunidad-en-graves-violaciones-a-derechos-humanos-en-peru> (Accessed 24 November 2025).

[61] Resolution of the President of the IACtHR (24 July 2025) (adoption of urgent measures) <https://corteidh.or.cr/docs/medidas/barrioscantuta_se_07.pdf>.

[62] <https://www.gob.pe/institucion/minjus/noticias/1215483-comunicado> (Accessed 24 November 2025).

[63] Alexandra Huneeus, 'Courts Resisting Courts: Lessons from the Inter-American Court's Struggle to Enforce Human Rights' (2011) 44 Cornell International Law Journal 493.

[64] *Fontevecchia y D'Amico vs. Argentina* [2011] Inter-American Court of Human Rights.

Argentina's Ministry of Foreign Affairs accordingly asked the Supreme Court to remove all legal effects stemming from its prior judgment.

In response, the Supreme Court argued that the IACtHR did not represent a fourth judicial instance capable of reviewing or annulling state judgments, and that, given its subsidiary role, the state parties must be given some margin of appreciation. Using a nuanced argument, the Argentine Supreme Court denied that it was failing to recognize the obligatory nature of the IACtHR judgments under Article 68(1) of the IACHR. Instead, it was insisting that the obligation to comply was conditioned on the IACtHR's competences and remedial capacities. The response of the IACtHR to the Argentine Supreme Court took the form of a monitoring compliance order.[65] In it, the IACtHR reiterated the obligation of state parties to comply with its judgments, and that compliance could not be subject to any restrictions by state authorities. Still, at the same time, the IACtHR also acknowledged that Argentina's Supreme Court had autonomous authority to determine the means by which it could fulfil its obligation and suggested several alternatives. In the end, the Supreme Court issued a resolution[66] stating that its previous judgment had been declared incompatible with the IACtHR, following the template for compliance offered by the IACtHR.[67]

From the perspective of judicial independence, then, non-compliance can be generally regarded as an undue pressure on the court's decision-making autonomy. Even if non-compliance with regional court decisions by parliaments could be justified on democratic grounds, the justification only holds under exceptional circumstances. For its part, a degree of contestation by national courts may also be accommodated in the interest of fomenting judicial dialogue, as long as the criteria of mutual recognition and respect are met and the arguments advanced appeal to public reason.

[65] Resolution of the IACtHR, 18 October 2017 (monitoring compliance with judgment *Fontevecchia and D'Amico v Argentina*).

[66] *Resolución Nro 4015/17* [2017] Corte Suprema de Justicia de la Nación Argentina ESC/4218/2017.

[67] Antonio Moreira Maués and others, 'Judicial Dialogue Between National Courts and the Inter-American Court of Human Rights: A Comparative Study of Argentina, Brazil, Colombia and Mexico' (2021) 21 Human Rights Law Review 108, 121, 124–25.

Afterword

As I was finishing the manuscript of this book, nine member states issued an open letter to the European Court of Human Rights (ECtHR) on 22 May 2025.[1] Denmark and Italy initiated the declaration that Austria, Belgium, Czech Republic, Estonia, Latvia, Lithuania, and Poland signed onto. In it, they denounced the overreach of the ECtHR in matters pertaining to immigration and asylum, which they believe is undermining democracy at the domestic level. They demanded greater discretion for their national asylum and immigration policies without the interference of the ECtHR to better protect their democracies. Two days later, the Secretary General of the Council of Europe issued a statement invoking the ECtHR's independence and denouncing political pressure on the court: 'Upholding the independence and impartiality of the Court is our bedrock. Debate is healthy, but politicizing the Court is not. In a society governed by the rule of law, no judiciary should face political pressure.'[2]

Similarly, in 2019, Argentina, Brazil, Chile, Colombia, and Paraguay, all states parties under the jurisdiction of the IACtHR, issued a joint declaration on the Inter-American System of Human Rights.[3] The statement emphasized the importance of the principle of subsidiarity, respect for state autonomy and their democratic processes, and demanded the recognition of a margin of appreciation for state policies implementing their treaty obligations. The declaration also argued that the effects of IACtHR judgments ought to be limited

[1] Prime Minister of Denmark and others, 'Letter to the ECtHR on the Initiative of Denmark and Italy' (22 May 2025) <https://www.governo.it/sites/governo.it/files/Lettera_aperta_22052025.pdf> accessed 19 March 2026.

[2] Council of Europe, 'Alain Berset on the Joint Letter Challenging the European Court of Human Rights' (*Council of Europe Newsroom*, 24 May 2025) <https://www.coe.int/en/web/portal/-/alain-berset-on-the-joint-letter-challenging-the-european-court-of-human-rights> (Accessed 24 November 2025).

[3] Ministerio de Relaciones Exteriores de Paraguay, 'Gobiernos de Argentina, Brasil, Chile, Colombia y Paraguay Se Manifiestan Sobre El Sistema Interamericano de Derechos Humanos' (*Ministerio de Relaciones Exteriores de Paraguay*, 23 April 2019) <https://www.mre.gov.py/index.php/noticias-de-embajadas-y-consulados/gobiernos-de-argentina-brasil-chile-colombia-y-paraguay-se-manifiestan-sobre-el-sistema-interamericano-de-derechos-humanos>(Accessed 24 November 2025).

to the parties to the case, and that the forms of reparation imposed needed to respect the principle of proportionality.

We might consider whether these statements undermine judicial independence or might be justified on grounds of checks and balances. The governments issuing them clearly seek to influence the regional court in question, though the extent to which their action might attain their objective is highly uncertain. The declarations might also seek to mobilize public opinion as a source of pressure on the court. Notwithstanding, in our opinion, those public statements may not be conceived as institutionalized constraints justified under the checks and balances principle, but rather as informal means for a minority of state governments to express disagreement with the judgments or general practices and stance of a regional court. Indeed, the analysis hinges on the limits to the freedom of expression of public authorities regarding court judgments. Just as at the domestic level, mutual recognition and respect among institutions require authorities to exercise a degree of restraint from public criticism of court decisions.

In the end, regional courts carry out their functions while simultaneously developing them under multiple forms of formal and informal constraint. Some constraints might undermine judicial independence, while others might be justifiable in the interest of legal or political accountability. My understanding is that the interplay between independence and accountability does not always involve a trade-off where one value must be sacrificed in favour of the other. To put it another way, the balance between judicial independence and accountability does not have to be a zero-sum game when the checks and balances principle is adapted to the much more complex international level. Constraints that are normatively justified do not undermine judicial independence, since independence does not require freedom from any influence or constraint whatsoever, but only freedom from constraints that unduly distort the decision-making process. This book demonstrates how the checks and balances principle, despite the added layers of complexity, offers a useful framework of analysis for the normative justification of power constraints.

The delicate balance between independence and power constraints is crucial for the overall legitimacy of regional courts. Independence lies at the core of any court's authority, including that of international regional courts. Although the domestic and international judiciaries differ in many respects, the differences between them are often overstated,[4] particularly when the spotlight is

[4] Tom Ginsburg, 'Political Constraints on International Courts' in Cesare PR Romano, Karen J Alter, and Yuval Shany (eds), *The Oxford Handbook of International Adjudication* (Oxford University Press 2014) 486.

on multilateral regional courts with compulsory jurisdiction and individual access. Nonetheless, as intimated above, the conceptualization of international judicial independence, and particularly its implementation, faces various challenges that are quite distinct from those faced at the domestic level, particularly in terms of the dominance or at least primary role of state governments in the design and composition of the courts and the sheer diversity across courts in terms of institutional setting, mandate, and functions. At the heart of my study is a normative quest to identify and disentangle many of the power constraints in a context of intimately intertwined politics and law.

Reflexively, constraints might be justified on grounds of the value of accountability. However, mechanisms to ensure legal accountability in the international sphere are currently limited. The shortfalls often occur because, by design, available legal accountability mechanisms imply a trade-off between internal and external judicial independence. As argued, given the context in which regional courts operate, prioritizing external judicial independence by denying political actors a direct role in the disciplinary regime seems appropriate.

Also, amid the increasing power and influence of regional courts and growing concerns about their democratic legitimacy, we need to take another look at political constraints rather than rejecting them outright. A more nuanced recasting of the checks and balances principle for the international sphere conceptualizes appropriate political constraints in terms of institutional interdependence. In this monograph, I have dissected the complexities of this principle at the regional level, arguing for a more granular, disaggregated view of the state and its constituent institutions than has been previously employed in this field. The approach facilitates a nuanced analysis of the competing institutional sources of constraint on regional courts and the values that they embody, and might justify the allocation of constraint mechanisms. The study specifically focused on two mechanisms: judicial selection and political override. In the end, the extent to which those mechanisms not only constrain judicial power but also reinforce democratic accountability by rooting it in institutional interdependence determines the overall legitimacy of the court. A persistent challenge has been keeping sight of all relevant interacting institutions, given the predominance of state governments in international relations. Considering the relevance of diverse institutions and their multiple conjugations requires extending the scope of analysis from the legal rules to how those rules are operationalized in formal procedures and informal practices.[5]

[5] Bruno De Witte, 'Legal Methods for the Study of EU Institutional Practice' (2022) 18 European Constitutional Law Review 637.

In the end, the analytical framework developed here offers a means to critically evaluate existing institutional arrangements and guide institutional design and practice. It can then be applied to the analysis of specific international and regional courts, and it serves as a robust frame of reference to bolster future comparative studies, including those focused on regional courts from other parts of the world. Also, future works could expand and deepen the study of other mechanisms of constraint, such as regional courts' financing, or the role of other institutions relevant to the functioning of regional and international courts, such as specific treaty bodies and commissions, domestic constitutional courts, or even non-institutional actors.

In addition, more empirical studies on the impact of political constraints on judicial behaviour would be welcome. Quantitative and qualitative research could contribute to empirically testing how the risk of political constraints affects the strategic decision-making of regional court judges, especially in politically salient cases. Empirical data on the actual use of those constraints and their impact could then be examined under the normative framework provided here.

Ultimately, the end goal from the perspective of institutional design should be to 'optimize, rather than maximize independence',[6] and the optimal degree of independence for each regional court can only be assessed based on its institutional context.

[6] Owen M Fiss, 'The Right Degree of Independence', in Irwin P Stotzky (ed) *Transition to Democracy in Latin America: The Role of the Judiciary* (Routledge 1993) 56.

Bibliography

Aguilar Feijoó LF, 'El Parlamento Andino, un órgano del Sistema Andino de Integración moldeado por el Tribunal de Justicia de la Comunidad Andina' in Hugo R Gómez Apac and others (eds), *Tribunal de Justicia de la Comunidad Andina: 1979–2024: 45 años de creación y 40 años al servicio del derecho y la integración* (Tribunal de Justicia de la Comunidad Andina 2024)

Alemanno A, 'How Transparent Is Transparent Enough?: Balancing Access to Information Against Privacy in European Judicial Selections' in M Bobek (ed), *Selecting Europe's Judges* (Oxford University Press 2015)

Alter KJ, 'Explaining National Court Acceptance of European Court Jurisprudence: A Critical Evaluation of Theories of Legal Integration' in Anne-Marie Slaughter, Alec Stone Sweet, and Joseph Weiler (eds), *The European Courts and National Courts* (Hart Pub 1998)

Alter KJ, *Establishing the Supremacy of European Law: The Making of an International Rule of Law in Europe* (Oxford University Press 2003)

—— 'Agents or Trustees? International Courts in Their Political Context' (2008) 14 European Journal of International Relations 33

Alter KJ, 'The Multiplication of International Courts and Tribunals After the End of the Cold War' in Cesare PR Romano, Karen J Alter, and Yuval Shany (eds), *The Oxford Handbook of International Adjudication* (Oxford University Press 2014)

—— *The New Terrain of International Law: Courts, Politics, Rights* (Princeton University Press 2014)

Alter KJ and Helfer LR, 'Nature or Nurture? Judicial Lawmaking in the European Court of Justice and the Andean Tribunal of Justice' (2010) 64 International Organization 563

Alter KJ, Helfer LR, and Madsen MR, 'How Context Shapes the Authority of International Courts' (2016) 79 Law and Contemporary Problems 1

Alter KJ, Helfer LR, and McAllister JR, 'A New International Human Rights Court for West Africa: The ECOWAS Community Court of Justice' (2013) 107 The American Journal of International Law 737

Andrade Moreno M, 'El liberalismo según Gargarella: tradición, hegemonía y crítica' (2021) 49 Revista Derecho del estado 59

Anne-Marie Slaughter, 'Sovereignty and Power in a Networked World Order' (2004) 40 Stanford Journal of International Law 283

Arnull A, *The European Union and Its Court of Justice* (2nd edn, Oxford University Press 2006)

Avbelj M and Komárek J, *Constitutional Pluralism in the European Union and Beyond* (Hart 2012)

Baetens F and Baetens F, 'Unseen Actors in International Courts and Tribunals: Challenging the Legitimacy of International Adjudication', *Legitimacy of Unseen Actors in International Adjudication* (Cambridge University Press 2019)

Barendt E, 'Separation of Powers and Constitutional Government' (1995) Winter Public Law 599

Başak Ç, Anne K, and Nicola B, 'The Legitimacy of the European Court of Human Rights: The View from the Ground' (Department of Political Science, University College London 2011)

Bates E, 'Democratic Override (or Rejection) and the Authority of the Strasbourg Court: The UK Parliament and Prisoner Voting' in Matthew Saul, Andreas Follesdal, and Geir Ulfstein (eds), *The International Human Rights Judiciary and National Parliaments* (Cambridge University Press 2017)

Benvenisti E and Downs GW, 'Prospects for the Increased Independence of International Tribunals' (2011) 12 German Law Journal 1057

Besselink LFM, *A Composite European Constitution: Een Samengestelde Europese Constitutie* (Europa Law Publishing 2008)

Besson S and others, 'Legal Philosophical Issues of International Adjudication: Getting Over the Amour Impossible Between International Law and Adjudication' in Cesare PR Romano, Karen J Alter, and Yuval Shany (eds), *The Oxford Handbook of International Adjudication* (Oxford University Press 2014)

Bingham, Lord, 'The Rule of Law' (2007) 66 The Cambridge Law Journal 67

Blauberger M and Schmidt SK, 'Free Movement, the Welfare State, and the European Union's Over-Constitutionalization: Administrating Contradictions' (2017) 95 Public Administration 437

Blokker N, 'The Governance of International Courts and Tribunals: Organizing and Guaranteeing Independence and Accountability' in Andreas Follesdal and Geir Ulfstein (eds), *The Judicialization of International Law* (Oxford University Press 2018)

Bodansky D, 'The Legitimacy of International Governance: A Coming Challenge for International Environmental Law?' (1999) 93 American Journal of International Law 596

—— 'Legitimacy in International Law and International Relations' in Jeffrey L Dunoff and Mark A Pollack (eds), *Interdisciplinary Perspectives on International Law and International Relations* (Cambridge University Press 2012)

Bogdandy A von and Krenn C, 'On the Democratic Legitimacy of Europe's Judges' in Michal Bobek (ed), *Selecting Europe's Judges* (Oxford University Press 2015)

Bogdandy A von and Venzke I, *In Whose Name? A Public Law Theory of International Adjudication* (Oxford University Press 2016)

Bohlander M, 'Separation of Powers and the International Judiciary—A Vision of Institutional Judicial Independence in International Law' in Shimon Shetreet and Christopher Forsyth (eds), *The Culture of Judicial Independence* (Brill | Nijhoff 2012)

Buchanan A and Keohane RO, 'The Legitimacy of Global Governance Institutions' (2006) 20 Ethics & International Affairs 405

Bühlmann M and Kunz R, 'Confidence in the Judiciary: Comparing the Independence and Legitimacy of Judicial Systems' (2011) 34 West European Politics 317

Burbank S, 'The Architecture of Judicial Independence' (1999) 72 Southern California Law Review 315

—— 'Judicial Independence, Judicial Accountability and Interbranch Relations' (2008) 137(4) Georgetown Law Journal 16

Burbank S and Friedman B, *Judicial Independence at the Crossroads: An Interdisciplinary Approach* (SAGE Publications 2002)

—— 'Reconsidering Judicial Independence' in Stephen Burbank and Barry Friedman, *Judicial Independence at the Crossroads: An Interdisciplinary Approach* (SAGE Publications 2002)

Burley A-M and Mattli W, 'Europe Before the Court: A Political Theory of Legal Integration' (1993) 47 International Organization 41

Bustos Gisbert R, *La Constitución Red: Un Estudio Sobre Supraestatalidad y Constitución* (Instituto Vasco de Administración Pública 2005)

—— 'La Influencia de Los Textos No Vinculantes Del Consejo de Europa Sobre Independencia Judicial En El TEDH y En La UE' [2021] Teoría y realidad constitucional 161

—— *Independencia judicial e integración Europea* (1ª edición, Tirant lo Blanch 2022)

—— 'Política, Independencia y Autogobierno Judicial: Cuatro Miradas' (2022) 198 Revista de estudios políticos 93

Çalı B and Cunningham S, 'Judicial Self Government and the Sui Generis Case of the European Court of Human Rights' (2018) 19 German Law Journal 1977

Cappelletti M, '"Who Watches the Watchmen?" A Comparative Study on Judicial Responsibility' (1983) 31 The American Journal of Comparative Law 1

Carolan E, *The New Separation of Powers: A Theory for the Modern State* (Oxford University Press 2009)

Carrubba CJ, Gabel M, and Hankla C, 'Judicial Behavior Under Political Constraints: Evidence from the European Court of Justice' (2008) 102 The American Political Science Review 435

Cartabia M, 'The Italian Constitutional Court and the Relationship Between the Italian Legal System and the European Union' in Slaughter AM, Stone Sweet A, and Weiler J (eds), *The European Court and National Courts—Doctrine and Jurisprudence: Legal Change in Its Social Context* (Hart Pub 1998)

Centro por la Justicia y el Derecho Internacional (CEJIL), *Aportes Para El Proceso de Selección de Miembros de La Comisión y La Corte Interamericanas de Derechos Humanos* (Centro por la Justicia y el Derecho Internacional 2005) <https://cejil.org/wp-content/uploads/pdfs/Documento_1_sp_0.pdf>

Chesterman S, 'An International Rule of Law?' (2008) 56 The American Journal of Comparative Law 331

Cohen HG and others, 'Legitimacy and International Courts—A Framework' in Nienke Grossman and others (eds), *Legitimacy and International Courts* (1st edn, Cambridge University Press 2018)

Crawford J and McIntyre J, 'The Independence and Impartiality of the "International Judiciary"' in Christopher Forsyth and Shimon Shetreet (eds), *The Culture of Judicial Independence* (Brill 2011)

De Búrca G, 'After the EU Charter of Fundamental Rights: The Court of Justice as a Human Rights Adjudicator?' (2013) 20 Maastricht Journal of European and Comparative Law 168

de la Mare T, 'Article 177 in Social and Political Context' in Paul Craig and Gráinne De Búrca (eds), *The Evolution of EU Law* (Oxford University Press 1999)

De Witte B, 'Legal Methods for the Study of EU Institutional Practice' (2022) 18 European Constitutional Law Review 637
Dehousse R, *The European Court of Justice: The Politics of Judicial Integration* (Macmillan 1998)
Delbruck J, 'Exercising Public Authority Beyond the State: Transnational Democracy and/or Alternative Legitimation Strategies?' (2003) 10 Indiana Journal of Global Legal Studies 29
—— 'Transnational Federalism: Problems and Prospects of Allocating Public Authority Beyond the State' (2004) 11 Indiana Journal of Global Legal Studies 30
Douglas-Scott S, 'A Tale of Two Courts: Luxembourg, Strasbourg and the Growing European Human Rights *Acquis*' (2006) 43 Common Market Law Review 629
Dunoff JL and Pollack MA, 'The Judicial Trilemma' (2017) 111 The American Journal of International Law 225
Dzehtsiarou K and Coffey DK, 'Legitimacy and Independence of International Tribunals: An Analysis of the European Court of Human Rights' (2014) 37 Hastings International & Comparative Law Review 271
Ebobrah ST, 'International Human Rights Courts' in Cesare PR Romano, Karen J Alter, and Yuval Shany (eds), *The Oxford Handbook of International Adjudication* (Oxford University Press 2014)
Elster J, 'Strategic Uses of Argument' in Kenneth Joseph Arrow and others (eds), *Barriers to Conflict Resolution* (W W Norton & Company 1995)
Ervin SJ, 'Separation of Powers: Judicial Independence' (1970) 35 Law and Contemporary Problems 108
European Commission for Democracy Through Law (Venice Commission), 'Report on the Rule of Law' (2011) <https://rm.coe.int/1680700a61>
Faúndez Ledesma H, 'La independencia e imparcialidad de los miembros de la comisión y de la corte: paradojas y desafíos' in Juan E Méndez and Francisco Javier Cox (eds), *El futuro del sistema interamericano de protección de los derechos humanos* (IIDH 1999)
Fearon JD, 'Deliberation as Discussion' in Jon Elster (ed), *Deliberative Democracy* (Cambridge University Press 1998)
Feld LP and Voigt S, 'Economic Growth and Judicial Independence: Cross-Country Evidence Using a New Set of Indicators' (2003) 19 European Journal of Political Economy 497
Ferejohn J, 'Independent Judges, Dependent Judiciary: Explaining Judicial Independence' (1999) 72 University of Southern California 353
Ferejohn JA, 'Accountability in Global Context' (2007) 5 International Law and Justice Working Papers
Ferejohn JA and Kramer LD, 'Independent Judges, Dependent Judiciary: Institutionalizing Judicial Restraint' (2002) 77 New York University Law Review 962
Ferrer Mac Gregor Poisot E, 'What Do We Mean When We Talk About Judicial Dialogue?: Reflections of a Judge of the Inter-American Court of Human Rights' (2017) 30 Harvard Human Rights Journal 89
Ferreres Comella V, *Constitutional Courts and Democratic Values: A European Perspective* (Yale University Press 2009)
—— *The Constitution of Arbitration* (Cambridge University Press 2022)
Fiss OM, 'The Right Degree of Independence' in Irwin P Stotzky (ed), *Transition to Democracy in Latin America: The Role of the Judiciary* (Westview Press 1993)
Follesdal A, 'The Legitimacy of International Human Rights Review: The Case of the European Court of Human Rights' (2009) 40 Journal of Social Philosophy 595
—— 'The Legitimacy Deficits of the Human Rights Judiciary: Elements and Implications of a Normative Theory' (2013) 14 Theoretical Inquiries in Law 339
—— 'Independent yet Accountable: Stress Test Lessons for the European Court of Human Rights' (2017) 24 Maastricht Journal of European and Comparative Law 484
—— 'Law Making by Law Breaking? A Theory of Parliamentary Civil Disobedience Against International Human Rights Courts' in Matthew Saul, Andreas Follesdal, and Geir Ulfstein (eds), *The International Human Rights Judiciary and National Parliaments* (Cambridge University Press 2017)
Follesdal A and Ulfstein G (eds), *The Judicialization of International Law*, vol 1 (Oxford University Press 2018)
García Ramírez S, 'Raíz, Actualidad y Perspectivas de La Jurisdicción Interamericana de Derechos Humanos' (2009) 1 Cuestiones constitucionales 149
Gardbaum S, 'Comparative Political Process Theory' (2020) 18 International Journal of Constitutional Law 1429
Geyh C, 'Rescuing Judicial Accountability from the Realm of Political Rhetoric' (2006) 56(4) Case Western Reserve Law Review 911

Ginsburg T, 'Political Constraints on International Courts' in Cesare PR Romano, Karen J Alter, and Yuval Shany (eds), *The Oxford Handbook of International Adjudication* (Oxford University Press 2014)
Goldstein J and others, 'Introduction: Legalization and World Politics' (2000) 54 International Organization 385
Grant R and Keohane R, 'Accountability and Abuses of Power in World Politics' (2005) 99 The American Political Science Review 29
Habermas J, *Moral Consciousness and Communicative Action* (Polity Press 1990)
Halberstam D, 'Constitutional Heterarchy: The Centrality of Conflict in the European Union and the United States' in Jeffrey L Dunoff and Joel P Trachtman (eds), *Ruling the World?* (Cambridge University Press 2009)
Hamilton A and others, *The Federalist Papers* (New American Library 1961)
Helfer L and Alter KJ, 'The Andean Tribunal of Justice and Its Interlocutors: Understanding Preliminary Reference Patterns in the Andean Community' (2009) 41 NYU Journal of International Law and Politics 871
—— 'Legitimacy and Lawmaking: A Tale of Three International Courts' (2013) 14 Theoretical Inquiries in Law 479
—— and Slaughter A-M, 'Why States Create International Tribunals: A Response to Professors Posner and Yoo' (2005) 93 California Law Review 899
—— and Slaughter A-M, 'Toward a Theory of Effective Supranational Adjudication' (1997) 107 The Yale Law Journal 273
Hermansen SSL and Naurin D, 'Shaping the Bench: The Effect of Ideology and Performance on Judicial Reappointments' (2024) APSA Preprints. doi: 10.33774/apsa-2024-kvbc9.
Huneeus A, 'Courts Resisting Courts: Lessons from the Inter-American Court's Struggle to Enforce Human Rights' (2011) 44 Cornell International Law Journal 493
—— 'Legitimacy and Jurisdictional Overlap: The ICC and the Inter-American Court in Colombia' in Nienke Grossman and others (eds), *Legitimacy and International Courts* (Cambridge University Press 2018)
Hurd I, 'The International Rule of Law: Law and the Limit of Politics' (2014) 28 Ethics & International Affairs 39
Iglesias Sánchez S, *La independencia judicial ante el Tribunal de Justicia de la UE* (Aranzadi Thomson Reuters 2023)
Jackson VC, 'Judicial Independence: Structure, Context, Attitude' in Anja Seibert-Fohr (ed), *Judicial Independence in Transition*, vol 233 (Springer Berlin Heidelberg 2012)
—— 'Comparative Constitutional Law: Methodologies' in Rosenfeld M and Sajó A (eds), *The Oxford Handbook of Comparative Constitutional Law* (Oxford University Press 2012)
Kahn PW, 'Interpretation and Authority in State Constitutionalism' (1993) 106 Harvard Law Review 1147
Kanstantsin D and Coffey DK, 'Legitimacy and Independence of International Tribunals: An Analysis of the European Court of Human Rights' (2014) 37 UC Law SF International Law Review 271
Kavanagh A, 'The Constitutional Separation of Powers' in David Dyzenhaus and Malcolm Thorburn (eds), *Philosophical Foundations of Constitutional Law* (Oxford University Press 2016)
—— *The Collaborative Constitution* (Cambridge University Press 2024)
Kelemen RD, 'The Political Foundations of Judicial Independence in the European Union' (2012) 19 Journal of European Public Policy 43
Kelemen RD, 'Selection, Appointment, and Legitimacy' in Michal Bobek (ed), *Selecting Europe's Judges* (Oxford University Press 2015)
Keller H and Stone Sweet A (eds), *A Europe of Rights: The Impact of the ECHR on National Legal Systems* (Oxford University Press 2008)
Kenney SJ, 'Breaking the Silence: Gender Mainstreaming and the Composition of the European Court of Justice' (2002) 10 Feminist Legal Studies 257
Keohane RO, 'Sovereignty, Interdependence, and International Institutions' in Michael Joseph Smith and Linda B Miller (eds), *Ideas And Ideals: Essays on Politics in Honor of Stanley Hoffmann* (Routledge 1991)
—— Moravcsik A, and Slaughter AM, 'Legalized Dispute Resolution: Interstate and Transnational Legalization and World Politics' (2000) 54(3) International Organization 457
Kingah S and Molano-Cruz G, 'Addressing Human Rights in the Court of Justice of the Andean Community and the Tribunal of the Southern African Development Community' (2014) 81 Colombia Internacional 99
Kingsbury B, Krisch N, and Stewart RB, 'The Emergence of Global Administrative Law' (2005) 68 Law and Contemporary Problems 15

Klabbers J, 'Constitutionalism Lite' (2004) 1 International Organizations Law Review 31
Kochenov DV and Butler G, 'Independence of the Court of Justice of the European Union: Unchecked Member States Power After the Sharpston Affair' (2021) 27 European Law Journal 262
Kokott J, 'Report on Germany' in Anne-Marie Slaughter, Alec Stone Sweet, and Joseph Weiler (eds), *The European Court and National Courts—Doctrine and Jurisprudence: Legal Change in Its Social Context* (Hart Pub 1998)
Kornhauser LA, 'Is Judicial Independence a Useful Concept?' in Stephen Burbank and Barry Friedman, *Judicial Independence at the Crossroads: An Interdisciplinary Approach* (SAGE Publications 2002)
Kosař D, 'Judicial Accountability in the (Post)Transitional Context: A Story of the Czech Republic and Slovakia' [2010] SSRN Electronic Journal <http://www.ssrn.com/abstract=1689260> accessed 27 January 2025
—— 'Selecting Strasbourg Judges' in Michal Bobek (ed), *Selecting Europe's Judges* (Oxford University Press 2015)
—— *Perils of Judicial Self-Government in Transitional Societies: Holding the Least Accountable Branch to Account* (Cambridge University Press 2016)
Krenn C, 'The European Court of Justice's Financial Accountability' (2017) 13 European Constitutional Law Review 453
Krisch N, 'The Open Architecture of European Human Rights Law' (2008) 71 The Modern Law Review 183
Krisch Nico, *Beyond Constitutionalism: The Pluralist Structure of Postnational Law* (Oxford University Press 2012)
Krsticevic V, 'El Papel de Las ONG En El Sistema Interamericano de Protección de Los Derechos Humanos', *El Sistema interamericano de protección de los derechos humanos en el umbral del siglo XXI* (Corte Interamericana de Derechos Humanos 2003)
Larsson O, 'Political and Constitutional Overrides: The Case of the Court of Justice of European Union' (2021) 28 Journal of European Public Policy 1932
—— Squatrito T, Stiansen Ø, and St John T, 'Selection and Appointment in International Adjudication: Insights from Political Science' (2022) 14(2) Journal of International Dispute Settlement 134
Lemmens K, '(S)Electing Judges for Strasbourg: A (Dis)Appointing Process?' in Michal Bobek (ed), *Selecting Europe's Judges* (Oxford University Press 2015)
Limbach J and others, 'Judicial Independence: Law and Practice of Appointments to the European Court of Human Rights' (2003) <https://www.corteidh.or.cr/tablas/32795.pdf>
Lock T, 'The ECJ and the ECtHR: The Future Relationship Between the Two European Courts' (2009) 8 The Law & Practice of International Courts and Tribunals 375
Lord Mance, 'The Composition of the European Court of Justice' (2011) <https://supremecourt.uk/uploads/speech_111019_b490b98938.pdf> accessed 19 March 2026
MacCormick N, *Questioning Sovereignty: Law, State, and Nation in the European Commonwealth* (Oxford University Press 1999)
Mackenzie R and Sands P, 'International Courts and Tribunals and the Independence of the International Judge' (2003) 44 Harvard International Law Journal 271
Mackenzie R, Malleson K, Martin P, and Sands P, *Selecting International Judges* (Oxford University Press 2010)
Madsen MR, 'Sociological Approaches to International Courts', in Cesare PR Romano, Karen J Alter, and Yuval Shany (eds) *The Oxford Handbook of International Adjudication* (Oxford University Press 2014)
—— 'The Challenging Authority of the European Court of Human Rights: From Cold War Legal Diplomacy to the Brighton Declaration and Backlash' (2016) 79 Law and Contemporary Problems 141
—— *The European Court of Human Rights*, vol 1 (Oxford University Press 2018)
Madsen MR, Cebulak P, and Wiebusch M, 'Backlash Against International Courts: Explaining the Forms and Patterns of Resistance to International Courts' (2018) 14 International Journal of Law in Context 197
Maduro M, 'As Formas Del Poder Constitucional de La Unión Europea' (2003) 119 Revista de Estudios Políticos 11
Mahoney J, Goertz G, and Vogt WP, 'A Tale of Two Cultures: Contrasting Quantitative and Qualitative Research', *Selecting Research Methods*, vol 4 (SAGE Publications 2008)
Mahoney P, 'The International Judiciary—Independence and Accountability' (2008) 7 The Law and Practice of International Courts and Tribunals 313
Mak E, 'Researching Judicial Ethical Codes, or: How to Eat a Mille-Feuille?' (2018) 9 International Journal for Court Administration 55

—— 'A Code of Judicial Ethics as a Signpost and a Beacon: On Virtuous Judgecraft and Dutch Climate Litigation' (2023) 26 Legal Ethics 97
Makris S, 'EU Competition Law as Responsive Law' (2021) 23 The Cambridge Yearbook of European Legal Studies 228
Maués AM and others, 'Judicial Dialogue Between National Courts and the Inter-American Court of Human Rights: A Comparative Study of Argentina, Brazil, Colombia and Mexico' (2021) 21 Human Rights Law Review 108
McCorquodale R, 'Defining the International Rule of Law: Defying Gravity?' (2016) 65 The International and Comparative Law Quarterly 277
McDermott Y, *Fairness in International Criminal Trials* (Oxford University Press 2016)
Melton J and Ginsburg T, 'Does De Jure Judicial Independence Really Matter?: A Reevaluation of Explanations for Judicial Independence' (2014) 2 Journal of Law and Courts 187
Meron T, 'Judicial Independence and Impartiality in International Criminal Tribunals' (2005) 99 American Journal of International Law 359
Möllers C, *The Three Branches: A Comparative Model of Separation of Powers* (1st edn, Oxford University Press 2013)
Montesquieu CL de S de, *The Spirit of the Laws* (Anne M Cohler, Basia Carolyn Miller, and Harold Samuel Stone eds, Cambrigde University Press 1989)
Montoya Céspedes N and Burgorgue-Larsen L, 'El diálogo judicial entre la Corte Interamericana de Derechos Humanos y la Corte Europea de Derechos Humanos' in George Rodrigo Bandeira Galindo and others (eds), *Protección multinivel de derechos humanos* (Universitat Pompeu Fabra 2013)
Moravcsik A, 'The Origins of Human Rights Regimes: Democratic Delegation in Postwar Europe' (2000) 54 International Organization 217
Muir E, 'EU Citizenship, Access to "Social Benefits" and Third-Country National Family Members: Reflecting on the Relationship Between Primary and Secondary Rights in Times of Brexit' (2018) 3 European Papers 1353
Naurin D and Voeten E, 'Transcending the Domestic-International Divide in the Study of Judicial Behavior' [2023] SSRN Electronic Journal <https://www.ssrn.com/abstract=4507034> accessed 26 January 2025
Nollkaemper A, 'Conversations Among Courts: Domestic and International Adjudicators' in Cesare PR Romano, Karen J Alter, and Yuval Shany (eds), *The Oxford Handbook of International Adjudication* (Oxford University Press 2014)
O'Cinneide C, 'Saying "No" to Strasbourg: When Are National Parliaments Justified in Refusing to Give Effect to Judgments of International Human Rights Courts?' in Matthew Saul, Andreas Follesdal, and Geir Ulfstein (eds), *The International Human Rights Judiciary and National Parliaments* (Cambridge University Press 2017)
Oteiza E, 'El deber de respetar la independencia judicial. Esfuerzos y ambigüedades de los Estados en el plano internacional' in Jordi Nieva Fenoll and Eduardo Oteiza (eds), *La independencia judicial: un constante asedio* (Marcial Pons 2019)
Pasquino P, 'Prolegomena to a Theory of Judicial Power' (2003) 2 The Law and Practice of International Courts and Tribunals 11
Payne RA and Samhat NH, *Democratizing Global Politics: Discourse Norms, International Regimes, and Political Community* (State University of New York Press 2004)
Pernice I, 'Multilevel Constitutionalism and the Treaty of Amsterdam: European Constitution-Making Revisited?' (1999) 36 Common Market Law Review 703
Peters A, 'Compensatory Constitutionalism: The Function and Potential of Fundamental International Norms and Structures' (2006) 19 Leiden Journal of International Law 579
—— 'The Merits of Global Constitutionalism' (2009) 16 Indiana Journal of Global Legal Studies 397
—— 'Global Constitutionalism' in Michael T Gibbons and Diana H Coole (eds), *The Encyclopedia of Political Thought*, vol 8 (Wiley-Blackwell 2014)
—— 'International Organizations: Effectiveness and Accountability' [2016] SSRN Electronic Journal <http://www.ssrn.com/abstract=2770606> accessed 27 January 2025
Piana D, *Judicial Accountabilities in New Europe: From Rule of Law to Quality of Justice* (Routledge 2016)
Pollack MA, 'Political Science and International Adjudication' in Cesare Romano, Karen J Alter, and Yuval Shany (eds), *The Oxford Handbook of International Adjudication* (Oxford University Press 2014)
Posner EA and Vermeule Adrian, *The Executive Unbound: After the Madisonian Republic* (1st edn, Oxford University Press 2010)
Posner EA and Yoo JC, 'Judicial Independence in International Tribunals' (2005) 93 California Law Review 1

Ragin CC and Ragin CC, *The Comparative Method: Moving Beyond Qualitative and Quantitative Strategies* (First paperback edition, University of California Press 1989)

Romano C, Alter KJ, and Shany Y, 'Illustrations: A Reader's Guide' in Cesare Romano, Karen J Alter, and Yuval Shany (eds), *The Oxford Handbook of International Adjudication* (Oxford University Press 2014)

Romano CPR, 'The Proliferation of International Judicial Bodies: The Pieces of the Puzzle' (1999) 31 New York University Journal of Internatinal Law & Politics 709

—— 'The Shift from the Consensual to the Compulsory Paradigm in International Adjudication: Elements for a Theory of Consent' (2007) 39 New York University Journal of International Law & Politics 791

Romano CPR, Alter KJ, and Shany Y, 'Mapping International Adjudicative Bodies, the Issues, and Players' in Karen J Alter, Yuval Shany, and Cesare PR Romano (eds), *The Oxford Handbook of International Adjudication* (Oxford University Press 2014)

Ruiz-Chiriboga O, 'The Independence of the Inter-American Judge' (2012) 11 The Law and Practice of International Courts and Tribunals 111

Saldías O, '¿Refugiándose En Redes Epistémicas? El Tribunal de La Comunidad Andina y La Independencia Judicial' in Santiago Deluca and others (eds), *Tribunales en organizaciones de integración: Mercosur, Comunidad Andina y Unión Europea* (Thomson Reuters/Aranzadi 2012)

Saul M, 'Conclusion: How Does, Could and Should the International Human Rights Judiciary Interact with National Parliaments?' in Matthew Saul, Andreas Follesdal, and Geir Ulfstein (eds), *The International Human Rights Judiciary and National Parliaments* (Cambridge University Press 2017)

Saul M, Follesdal A, and Ulfstein G (eds), *The International Human Rights Judiciary and National Parliaments: Europe and Beyond* (Cambridge University Press 2017)

Saunders C, 'Separation of Powers and the Judicial Branch' (2006) 11 Judicial Review 337

Sauvé J-M, 'Selecting the European Union's Judges' in Michal Bobek (ed), *Selecting Europe's Judges* (Oxford University Press 2015)

Schönsteiner J, 'Alternative Appointment Procedures for the Commissioners and Judges in the Inter-American System of Human Rights' (2007) 46 Revista IIDH 195

Seibert-Fohr A, 'Judicial Independence—The Normativity of an Evolving Transnational Principle' in Anja Seibert-Fohr (ed), *Judicial Independence in Transition*, vol 233 (Springer Berlin Heidelberg 2012) <https://link.springer.com/10.1007/978-3-642-28299-7_29> accessed 26 January 2025

—— (ed), *Judicial Independence in Transition*, vol 233 (Springer Berlin Heidelberg 2012)

—— 'International Judicial Ethics' in Cesare PR Romano, Karen J Alter, and Yuval Shany (eds), *The Oxford Handbook of International Adjudication* (Oxford University Press 2014)

Shany Y, 'No Longer a Weak Department of Power? Reflections on the Emergence of a New International Judiciary' (2009) 20 European Journal of International Law 73

—— *Assessing the Effectiveness of International Courts* (Oxford University Press 2014)

Shapiro MM, *Courts: A Comparative and Political Analysis* (University of Chicago Press 1981)

Shelton D, 'Legal Norms for Independence and Accountability of International Tribunals' (2003) 2 The Law and Practice of International Courts and Tribunals 27

Shetreet S, 'The Normative Cycle of Shaping Judicial Independence in Domestic and International Law: The Mutual Impact of National and International Jurisprudence and Contemporary Practical and Conceptual Challenges' (2009) 10 Chicago Journal of International Law 275

—— 'The Significance of the Independence of the Judiciary Creating a Culture of Judicial Independence: The Practical Challenge and the Conceptual and Constitutional Infrastructure' in Shimon Shetreet and Christopher Forsyth (eds), *The Culture of Judicial Independence* (Brill | Nijhoff 2012)

—— and Forsyth C (eds), 'The Culture of Judicial Independence: Conceptual Foundations and Practical Challenges' (2013) 76 The Modern Law Review 181

Shuibhne NN, 'Limits Rising, Duties Ascending: The Changing Legal Shape of Union Citizenship' (2015) 52 Common Market Law Review 889

Sifris R, 'Weighing Judicial Independence Against Judicial Accountability: Do the Scales of the International Criminal Court Balance?' (2013) 8 Chicago-Kent Journal of International and Comparative Law 88

Slaughter A-M, 'The Real New World Order' (1997) 76(5) Foreign Affairs 183

—— 'The Accountability of Government Networks' (2001) 8 Indiana Journal of Global Legal Studies 347

—— *A New World Order* (Princeton University Press 2004)

Squatrito T, 'Conceptualizing, Measuring and Mapping the Formal Judicial Independence of International Courts' [2018] SSRN Electronic Journal <https://www.ssrn.com/abstract=3131557> accessed 26 January 2025

Stone Sweet A and Brunell T, 'The European Court of Justice, State Noncompliance, and the Politics of Override' (2012) 106 The American Political Science Review 204
Strauss PL, 'The Place of Agencies in Government: Separation of Powers and the Fourth Branch' (1984) 84 Columbia Law Review 573
Takata H, 'Separation of Powers in a Globalized Democratic Society: Theorizing the Human Rights Treaty Organs' Interactions with Various State Organs' (2024) 13 Global Constitutionalism 458
Terris Daniel, Romano C, and Swigart Leigh, *The International Judge: An Introduction to the Men and Women Who Decide the World's Cases* (Oxford University Press 2007)
Thomas of Cwmgiedd J, 'The Judiciary Within the State—the Relationship Between the Branches of the State' (2017) <https://www.judiciary.uk/wp-content/uploads/2022/07/lcj-michael-ryle-memorial-lecture-20170616.pdf> accessed 19 March 2026
Tinière R, 'The Use of ECtHR Case Law by the CJEU: Instrumentalisation or Quest for Autonomy and Legitimacy?' (2023) 8 European Papers—A Journal on Law and Integration 323
Torres Pérez A, 'The Internationalization of Lawmaking Processes: Constraining or Empowering the Executive' (2006) 14 Tulsa Journal of Comparative & International Law 1
—— *Conflicts of Rights of Conflict in the European Union: A Theory of Supranational Adjudication* (Oxford University Press 2009)
—— 'Can Judicial Selection Secure Judicial Independence? Constraining State Governments in Selecting International Judges' in Michal Bobek (ed), *Selecting Europe's Judges* (Oxford University Press 2015)
—— 'From Judicial Independence to Interdependence in the International Sphere' (2017) 24 Maastricht Journal of European and Comparative Law 462
—— 'In Nobody's Name: A Checks and Balances Approach to International Judicial Independence' in Hélène Ruiz Fabri and others (eds), *International Judicial Legitimacy* (Nomos Verlagsgesellschaft mbH & Co KG 2020)
Tyler TR, 'Psychological Perspectives on Legitimacy and Legitimation' (2006) 57 Annual Review of Psychology 375
Ulfstein G, 'International Courts and Judges: Independence, Interaction, and Legitimacy' (2014) 46 New York University Journal of International Law & Politics 849
Van Der Sluis M, Dumbrovský T, and Petkova B, 'Judicial Appointments: The Article 255 TFEU Advisory Panel and Selection Procedures in the Member States' (2014) 51 Common Market Law Review 455
Ventura Robles M, 'La Legitimidad de Los Jueces de La Corte Interamericana de Derechos Humanos' (2016) 145(46) Revista de derecho público 11
Vile MJC, *Constitutionalism and the Separation of Powers* (Liberty Fund 1998)
Voeten E, 'The Impartiality of International Judges: Evidence from the European Court of Human Rights' (2008) 102 The American Political Science Review 417
—— 'The Politics of International Judicial Appointments' (2009) 9 Chicago Journal of International Law 387
—— 'Borrowing and Nonborrowing Among International Courts' (2010) 39 The Journal of Legal Studies 547
—— 'International Judicial Independence' in Jeffrey L Dunoff and Mark A Pollack (eds), *Interdisciplinary Perspectives on International Law and International Relations: The State of the Art* (Cambridge University Press 2012)
—— 'Public Opinion and the Legitimacy of International Courts' (2013) 14 Theoretical Inquiries in Law 411
Voigt S, Gutmann J, Feld LP, 'Economic Growth and Judicial Independence, a Dozen Years on: Cross-Country Evidence Using an Updated Set of Indicators' CESifo Working Paper 5010 (2014) <https://www.ifo.de/DocDL/cesifo1_wp5010.pdf> accessed 19 March 2026
von Bogdandy A, 'Globalization and Europe: How to Square Democracy, Globalization, and International Law' (2004) 15 European Journal of International Law 885
—— 'Pluralism, Direct Effect, and the Ultimate Say: On the Relationship Between International and Domestic Constitutional Law' (2008) 6 International Journal of Constitutional Law 397
Waldron J, 'Separation of Powers in Thought and Practice?' (2013) 54 Boston College Law Review 433
Walker N, 'The Idea of Constitutional Pluralism' (2002) 65 Modern Law Review 317
Weber M, *Economy and Society* (University of California Press 1968)
Weiler JHH, 'A Quiet Revolution: The European Court of Justice and Its Interlocutors' (1994) 26 Comparative Political Studies 510
Zimmermann D, *The Independence of International Courts: The Adherence of the International Judiciary to a Fundamental Value of the Administration of Justice* (Nomos 2014)

Index

For the benefit of digital users, indexed terms that span two pages (e.g., 52–53) may, on occasion, appear on only one of those pages.

Tables are indicated by an italic *t* following the page number.

a contrario interpretation 36
abortion 132
abuse of power 58–59, 62–63, 71–72
access 15
accountability ix, 11, 22–24, 27–51
  behavioural 30–31
  concept of 27, 28–29
  context 27–30
  decisional 30–31
  definition of 29
  definitional ambiguity 34
  democratic 52, 64–65, 105, 147
  ex post 23
  forms of 29–30
  independence and 27–28
  legal 29–40, 147
  managerial 33
  political 29–30
  public 50
  regional judges 30–40
  societal 29–30
additional activity, duty to disclose 31–32
adjudication model 8, 18–19, 55
advisory expert panels 64–65, 110–16
  function of 110–11
  reasoned opinions 110–11
  Resolution of the Committee of Ministers (2010) 111–12
affirmative action policies 132–33
African Court on Human and Peoples' Rights (ACtHPR) 7–8
aims of international judicial independence 18–22
Alter, Karen J. ix–x, 8, 14–15, 95–96
American University Washington College of Law 112–13, 118–19
Amnesty Law 141–42
Andean Community 16, 95–96, 128–29, 134
Andean Parliament 84–85
Andean Presidential Council of the Andean Community 78
Andean Tribunal of Justice (ATJ) xi, 7, 16, 17*t*, 22, 31
  accountability holders 38*t*
  Andean Community 95–96
  budget 79
  CJEU case law, dependence on 98
  codes of conduct 46–47
  composition 107
  disciplinary regime 38*t*
  disqualification regime 35–36
  dissenting opinions 124–25
  full representation 106–7
  institutional design 79
  institutional functions 78, 84–85
  intellectual property agencies 95–96
  judicial appointment and mandate 79–80, 106, 109*t*, 117–18
  judicial selection 106–7, 109*t*
  preliminary reference 94
  purely political model 36–37
  reappointment of judges 122, 125–26
  recusal, requests for 36
  removal of judges 34–35
  sanctions 38*t*
  serious misconduct 34–35
  standards 38*t*
apex courts 101
Appellate Body of the World Trade Organization (WTO AB) 7, 14, 16
appointment, judicial *see* judicial selection and appointment
arbitral bodies 13
arbitration model 8
Argentina 39–40, 68, 101, 145–46
  Fontevecchia decision 142–43
Assembly of States Parties 42–44
asylum policy 145
Austria 41–42, 145
authoritarianism 41–42

backlash 136–37
bad behaviour 34–35
Bangalore Principles of Judicial Conduct 11–12
Belgium 145
Besson, Samantha 22
bias 22–23
bilateral cooperation 6
bilateral treaties 62
Bingham, Lord 20
Blauberger, Michael 134–35
Blokker, Niels 77–78, 83
Bohlander, Michael 33, 41, 45
Bolivia 40
Borea Odría, Alberto 118–19
Boudou, Amado 39
Brazil 101, 145–46
Brexit 16
Brighton Declaration (and Protocol 15) 137–39
Brunell, Thomas 127–28
budgets 78–79, 84–85
Bureau 49–50
Burgh House Principles on the Independence of the International Judiciary 4, 12–13

Çalı, Başak 40
Cappelletti, Mauro 29–30
Caribbean Community 45–46
Caribbean Court of Justice (CCJ) 7, 45–46
Carolan, Eoin 54
Caroline, Princess of Monaco 94
Carruba, Clifford J. 127–28
Cartagena Agreement (1969) 16
Cebulak, Pola 136–37
Center for Justice and International Law 112–13
Charter of Fundamental Rights of the European Union 21–22, 96–97
checks and balances approach xi–xii, 23–24, 30, 52–72, 146, 147
  see also separation of powers principle
  context 52–53
  dynamic perspective 66–67
  functional separation 53–59
  global constitutionalism 59–63
  indeterminacy 70–72
  institutional constraints 53–59, 75, 76, 77, 80, 91–92
  institutional mutual recognition and respect as preconditions 67–69
  interdependence 63–72
  judicial selection and appointment 103
  political override 139
  power constraints, allocation of 70–72
  spheres and actors, multiplicity of 65–66
Chile 145–46
citizenship 134–36
civil disobedience theory 140–41
civil law countries 11
civil society organizations 75, 86–87, 113, 117–18
civil-continental bureaucratic model 10–11
codes of conduct and ethics 33, 46–51
coercive powers 5
Cold War 16, 82
Colombia 97–98, 101, 114–15, 118–19, 145–46
comity 67–68
common law professional model 10–11
common standards 10–18, 50–51
communism 41–42
comparative approach 17–18
competence 33, 49, 106–7, 118–19
competition
  inter-branch 103
  interstate 103
compliance 9–10, 85–86, 143
  see also non-compliance
compulsory jurisdiction 5, 13, 146–47
  state consent 5, 7–8
confidentiality 88, 114
consensual jurisdiction 7
consent of the parties 8
consent *see* state consent
constitutional amendment procedure 130
constitutional courts x, 130–31
constitutional perspective x
constitutional pluralism 60–61
constitutionalism
  composite 60–61
  global *see* global constitutionalism
  multilevel 60–61
  network 60–61
constrained independence 22–24
  theory of ix–x
constraints, freedom from 146–47
  see also institutional constraint
contextual approach 11
cooperative regimes 14–15
corporate solidarity 41, 46, 51
corporativism 42
corruption 39
Costa Rica 114–15, 118–19
Council of Europe 11–12, 15
  Committee of Ministers 9–10, 78–79
  Secretary General 145
Council of Ministers of the European Union (EU) 78
counter-majoritarian difficulty 22
Court of Justice of the European Union (CJEU) xi, 7, 8, 10, 11–12, 16, 17*t*, 21–22, 31

255 panel 45–46
abortion decisions 132
accountability holders 38*t*
advisory expert panels 110–12, 113–14, 115–16, 117–20
affirmative action measures 132–33
benefits and pensions, deprival of judges' 35, 36–37
budget 84–85, 89–90
case law, epistemic dependence on 98
Code of Conduct for Members and Former Members (CJEU Code) 46–47, 48, 49–50
composition 107
confidentiality 118–19
conflict of interests, disqualification in case of 35n.48
disciplinary regime 38*t*
disclosure 120
dissenting opinions 124–25
equal treatment of men and women 132–33
EU citizenship 134–37
full representation 106–7
fundamental rights, protection of 95, 96–97
General Court 30–31
institutional design, compared with ATJ 79, 95–96
judicial appointment and mandate 79–80, 106, 109*t*
judicial selection 89
nationality of judges 36
non-discrimination principle 134–35
parliamentary/political critique of 90
political/legislative override 127–28, 134–36, 137–38
preliminary reference 68–69, 94–95
President 111–12
reappointment of judges 122, 125–26
removal of judges 34–35
sanctions 38*t*
standards 38*t*
transparency 117–19
treaty amendment 133, 138–39
treaty interpretation 134–35
Crawford, James 3
criminal responsibility 14–15
cross-citation 96–97
Cunningham, Stewart 40
Czech Republic 145

de facto rules 66
de iure legal rules 66
deconstitutionalization 134–35
deference 66–67
see also mutual deference
definition of judicial independence 4, 55
Dehousse, Renaud 117
deliberation 86–91
deliberative values 98–102
democracy 15, 70–71
see also liberal democracy
theories of 82
democratic deficit 103–4
democratic legitimacy 80–83, 86–91, 105, 125, 126, 131
democratic override 90–91
democratic rejection 90–91
democratic rule ix
Denmark 145
depoliticization 82–83
dialogue 98–102, 142–43
disciplinary regimes 37
breakdown of 38*t*
in practice 38–40
disclosure 120
discretion 55–56
dispute settlement x, 14–15
disqualification 34, 37, 39, 46
dissenting opinions 40, 110, 122–26
diversity 50–51
see also institutional diversity
domestic and international judiciary 91–102
collaboration and resistance, patterns of 92–98
epistemic and deliberative values through judicial dialogue 98–102
domestic courts 3–4
due diligence process 45–46
Due Process of Law Foundation 112–13
Dunoff, Jeffrey L. 123, 125–26

economic and political integration 14–15, 17*t*, 31, 68
effectiveness ix–x, 10, 27, 28–29, 85–86, 92
enforcement 9–10, 92–93
epistemic values 98–102
Estonia 145
ethics 46–51
Ethics Council 49–50
EU *see* European Union (EU)
European Coal and Steel Community (ECSC) 16
European Commission (EC) 120
European Community of Atomic Energy (ECAE) 16
European Convention on Human Rights (ECHR) 15, 21–22, 94, 108, 112–13, 123–24, 137–38
European Council of the European Union 78, 120

European Court of Human Rights (ECtHR) xi, 7, 8, 10, 11–12, 15, 17*t*, 22, 31
accountability holders 38*t*
advisory expert panels 110, 111–13, 114, 118–19
Belgium selection panel 86n.40
Brighton Declaration 137–39
budget 78–79
confidentiality 118–19
democratic overreach 90–91
disciplinary regime 38*t*
dissenting opinions 40, 124, 125–26
ECHR and 94, 96–97
freedom of information, right to 94
full representation 106–7
fundamental rights 96–97
IACtHR, citation by 97–98
immigration and asylum 145
impartiality of 123–24, 145
independence of 123–24, 138–39, 145
institutional role 138–39
internal review processes 30–31
judicial appointment and mandate 79–80, 108–10, 109*t*, 126
judicial selection 78–79, 89, 106, 110
Limbach Report 87
margin of appreciation doctrine 66–67, 69, 137–38
mutual support 68–69
nomination of candidates 86n.39
open letter (2025) 145
PACE Committee on the Election of Judges 84–85, 87, 88, 106, 108, 109*t*, 116, 121–22
President 111–12
prisoners' voting rights 90–91, 137–38
privacy, right to 94
purely judicial model 36–37
reappointment of judges 122, 126
removal of judges 34–35
res judicata 93
Resolution of the Committee of Ministers 113
Resolution on Judicial Ethics 46–47, 48–50
Rules of Procedure 36
sanctions 38*t*
scope of power 137–39
standards 38*t*
structural override 137–38
UK role and function 90–91
European Economic Community Treaty 16, 132
European Parliament (EP) 84–85, 89–90, 120
European Union (EU)
annual budget 84–85
citizenship 134–36
composition 16
EU law implementation 95
general EU law principles 94–95
political override 128–29, 134–35
ex ante constraints 6, 66, 103, 121–22
ex post constraints 6, 66, 85–86, 103, 121–22, 139
executive power 62–63, 64–65, 83, 85–86
see also checks and balances approach; separation of powers principle
'exit, voice and loyalty' 127
external judicial independence 41–46

fair trial, right to a 21–22
fairness 88–89
Federalist Papers 56–57
Feld, Lars P. 17–18
Ferejohn, John A. 29–30, 56–59, 66–67
Follesdal, Andreas 90–91, 140–41
freedom from preferences of other actors 4
freedom of thought and expression, right to 142–43
functional perspective 55
fundamental rights 11, 21–22, 94–95, 96–97, 100
see also human rights

Gabel, Matthew 127–28
gender balance 88–89, 113, 132–33
General Council of the International Judiciary 41
Germany 41–42, 95
von Hannover saga 94
Geyh, Charles 34
Ginsburg, Tom 66, 103, 127
global constitutionalism 59–63
globalization 60, 62–63, 82
governmental institutions 76–83
democratic legitimacy 80–83
intergovernmental bodies 77–80
judicial governance 77–80
state sovereignty 80–83
Grant, Ruth W. 23, 27, 29

Hankla, Charles 127–28
Helfer, Laurence R. ix–x, 6, 66, 95–96, 103
Hermansen, Silje S. L. 123
High Contracting Parties 113
Hirschmann, Albert O. 127
holistic approach 11
homophobia 40
horizontal integration 59–60
human resources 103
human rights xi, 15, 31
courts 14, 17*t*, 21–22
organizations 11–12
protection of 14–15, 21–22
Huneeus, Alexandra 93

immigration 145
impartiality principle 3, 19–20
in camera meetings 88
incompatibilities 34–35
independence, principle of 3
Independent Expert Review 44
Independent Oversight Mechanism (IOM) 42–44, 45–46
indeterminacy 70–72
influence on judges 105
institutional constraint
  domestic and international judiciary 91–102
  governmental institutions 76–83
  parliamentary institutions 84–91
  sources of 75–102
institutional design 125–26
institutional diversity 10–18
institutional perspective 55
instrumental approach 70–71
insularity 23–24
integrity of the judiciary 55
intellectual property agencies 95–96
Inter-American Commission on Human Rights 75–76, 142–43
Inter-American Convention on Human Rights (IACHR) 7–8, 16, 21–22
Inter-American Court of Human Rights (IACtHR) xi, 7–8, 9–10, 15–16, 17*t*, 22, 31, 75–76
  accountability holders 38*t*
  advisory expert panels and reports 110, 112–13, 114–15, 116, 118–19, 121–22
  Amnesty Law, Peru 141–42
  budget 78–79
  CJEU case law, reliance on 98
  Code of Ethics for the Judges (IACtHR Code) 46–50
  compliance role 78–79, 143
  composition 106–7
  disciplinary regime 38*t*, 39
  disqualification 35n.48, 39
  dissenting opinions 124
  domestic courts, relationship with 93, 101–2
  ECtHR, citation of 97–98
  Fontevecchia (Argentinian case) 68, 142–43
  full representation 106–7
  General Assembly 78–79
  incompatibilities 34–35
  Inter-American System of Human Rights 145–46
  judicial appointment and mandate 79–80, 109, 122
  judicial selection 106–7
  limits on judges' positions and activities 32–33
  multiplicity of institutional actors 65–66
  mutual deference 69
  mutual support 68–69
  nationality, cases against the state of 124n.96, 125–26
  OAS General Assembly 36–37
  reappointment of judges 122, 125–26
  Rules of Court 36
  sanctions 35, 38*t*
  Sayán 39
  standards 38
  transparency 117–18
  Zaffaroni 39–40
Inter-American Human Rights System 112–13
Inter-American System of Human Rights 145–46
interdependence 97–98, 103–4
  institutional mechanisms of 66
interest groups 86–87
intergovernmental bodies 62
internal judicial independence 41–46
International Association of Judicial Independence and World Peace 11–12
International Bar Association (IBA) 11–12
International Court of Justice (ICJ) 14
international courts
  definition and scope of 13
  design of 6–7
  five criteria for 13
  functions of 14–15
  international law, adherence to 13
  international legal instrument 13
  legally binding outcomes 13
  new-style *vs* old-style 8
  origin of 6–7
  permanence 13
  rules of procedure 13
International Criminal Court (ICC) 8, 42–43, 44, 97–98, 112–13
  Assembly of States Parties 77–78
  Office of the Prosecutor 65–66
international judiciary x–xi
International Law Association (ILA)
  Study Group on the Practice and Procedure of International Courts and Tribunals 12–13
Ireland
  abortion rights 132
Italy 95, 145

judges
  accountability holders 35–37
  appointment of *see* judicial selection and appointment

judges (*cont.*)
  judicial accountability *see* accountability
  judicial activism 108, 128
  judicial career 11
  legal accountability 30–40
  as neutral third parties 19–20
  selection of *see* judicial selection and appointment
judicial conduct, standards of 31–34
  failure to meet, consequences of 34–35
  international codes of 46–51
judicial council model 41–42, 44–45
judicial dialogue 142–43
  epistemic and deliberative values 98–102
judicial discretion 22
judicial governance institutions 77–78
judicial independence principle
  conceptual vagueness 10–11
  as instrumental and relative 18–24
judicial nomination 104–5
judicial reasoning 125
judicial review 55–56, 130
judicial selection and appointment 103–26
  advisory expert panels 110–16
  context 103–5
  dissenting opinions 122–26
  legal framework and practice 106–10
  mandate 109*t*
  politicization 64–65
  reappointment 122–26
  tenure 122–26
  transparency 117–22
jurisdiction, definition of 66

Kavanagh, Aileen 54, 55–56, 67–68, 70–71
Keleman, R. Daniel 80, 82–83, 88
Keller, Helen 94
Keohane, Robert O. 23, 27, 29
Kosař, David 42
Kramer, Larry D. 58–59, 66–67
Krenn, Christoph 89–90
Kyritsis, Dimitrios 70–71

Larsson, Olof 127–29, 134
Latvia 145
'law and office' 8
legislative amendment 130–31
legislative override 127–29, 134–36
  see also political override
legitimacy 85–86
  authority 8, 15, 18–19
  concept of 19
  democratic 80–83, 86–91, 105, 125, 126, 131
  normative ix, 19
  perceived 8
  sociological approach 19
  unwarranted 62
liberal democracy 52
  see also democracy
liberty 58–59
Limbach Report 87–88
Lisbon Treaty 110–11
Lithuania 145

Maastricht Treaty 132
MacCormick, Neil 60–61
Mackenzie, Ruth 3
Madison, James 56–57
Madsen, Mikael Rask 136–37
Mahoney, Paul 5
Mak, Elaine 50–51
Mance, Lord 119
mandate 15
margin of appreciation doctrine 66–67, 137–38, 145–46
Maués, Antonio Moreira 101
McCorquodale, Robert 62–63
McGregor, Ferrer 97–98
McIntyre, Joe 3
members of parliament (MPs) 85–86
Menem, Carlos 142–43
merit 106–7
merit-based bureaucracy 11
Mexico 101
migration 134–35
misconduct 35
  see also serious misconduct
mixed model 36–37
Montesquieu, Charles Louis de Secondat de 53–54, 55–56
Montréal Universal Declaration on the Independence of Justice 11–13
moral character 40, 113, 118–19
Morales, Evo 40
Moreno Rodríguez, Diego 114–15
Mt. Scopus International Standards on Judicial Independence 11–13
Muir, Elise 134–35
multilateral cooperation 6
multilateral treaties 62
multilevel approach 23–24
mutual deference 69
mutual recognition and respect 101, 138–39, 142–43
mutual respect, duty of 67–68
mutual self-restraint 67–68, 69
mutual support 67–69

naming and shaming tactics 40
nationality 36, 125–26, 134–35
Naurin, Daniel 123
neofunctionalism 75, 92
New Delhi Minimum Standards on Judicial Independence 11–12
Nollkaemper, André 93
non-compliance 29, 90–91, 127–28, 134, 139–43
see also compliance; political override
non-discrimination principle 88–89, 134–35
non-governmental organizations (NGOs) 7–8, 40, 112–13
normative approach x, 19, 23, 99, 104

O'Cinneide, Colm 140–41
Open Society Justice Initiative 112–13
optimal degree of independence 148
Organization of American States (OAS) 16
  Chiefs of Missions to 32–33
  CVs 117–18
  General Assembly 36–37, 38*t*, 78–79
  judicial selection and appointment 106
  Secretary General 39
over-constitutionalization 134–35
override *see* political override
oversight functions ix, 41–42, 51

Paraguay 145–46
Parliamentary Assembly of the Council of Europe (PACE) 84–85, 87, 88–89
parliamentary institutions 84–102
  deliberation 86–91
  democratic legitimacy 86–91
  regional and domestic parliaments, role of 84–86
  transparency 86–91
peace and security 14–15
pecuniary sanction 35
persuasiveness 99–100
Peru 39
  Amnesty Law 141–42
Peters, Anne 27
Plenary Court 49–50
Poland 145
political activity, prohibition on 31–32
political constraints 129–30
political integration courts 22
political override 103–4, 127–43
  context 127–28
  forms of 128–43
  legislative override 134–36
  structural 136–39
  substantive 136–39
  treaty amendment 131–33
political science approach 17–18
politicization 42, 45, 64–65, 86–87, 106–7
politics and law 3, 5, 24, 146–47
Pollack, Mark A. 123, 125–26
popular sovereignty, principle of 140–41
Posner, Eric A. ix–x
preliminary reference 10, 68–69, 94–96
principal-agent dichotomy 77
prisoners' voting rights 90–91
privacy, right to 94, 120–21, 142–43
private parties, rights for 6
professional activity, prohibition on 31–32
professional knowledge and skills 49
proportionality principle 145–46
public authority 14–15
public confidence 50
public management theory 33
public opinion 51, 86–87, 104
'purely judicial' model 36–37
'purely political' model 36–37
pushback 136–37

qualifications 33
qualitative approach 17–18, 148
quantitative approach 17–18, 148

Rawls, John 140–41
reappointment of judges 110, 122–26
recusal 34, 35–36
regional economic integration organizations (REIOs) 16
Regional Judicial and Legal Services Commission 45–46
regional power constraints ix, 18, 22–23
remuneration 34–35
reprimand 35, 40
reputational cost 6–7, 119
res judicata 93
resilience 66–67
Rodríguez Mejía, Carlos 114–15, 118–19
Romano, Cesare PR 7, 13
rule of law 15, 58–59, 62–63
  backsliding crisis 11–12
  concept of 20
  international rule of law, definition of 20–21
Russia 15

safeguard arguments 101
Saldías, Osvaldo 98
sanctions 35, 38, 46, 50, 51
Sands, Philippe 3
Saunders, Cheryl 56
Schmidt, Susanne K. 134–35
secrecy of deliberations 33

Seibert-Fohr, Anja 11–12
selection, judicial *see* judicial selection and appointment
self-restraint 69
separation of powers principle 53–56, 59–60, 70–71
  see also checks and balances approach
  institutional design 56–58
  institutional roles 54
  pure doctrine/model 54–55
  role-based approach 55–56
  US constitutionalism 56–59
serious misconduct 34–35, 38*t*
Shany, Yuval 14–15
Shapiro, Martin M. 8
Shetreet, Shimon 9, 53–54
Slaughter, Anne-Marie ix–x, 6, 66, 103
sociological approach 19, 75, 92, 104
soft law instruments 11–12
sovereignty *see also* state sovereignty
standards of conduct: vague definition 34
standing 14
state consent
  compulsory jurisdiction 5, 7–8
  dependence on 5
  IC decisions, enforcement and compliance of 5, 9–10
  international courts, origin and design of 5, 6–7
  principle of 7
  reach of 5–10
  relevance of 5
state control, mechanisms for 6
state sovereignty 6, 10, 62–63, 141–42
statistical analysis 17–18
Steering Committee for Human Rights 119
Stone Sweet, Alec 94, 127–28
Strasbourg Observers 40
Strasbourg Panel 119
structural override 136–39
Sub-Committee on the Election of Judges 87, 88–89
subsidiarity principle 137–38, 145–46
substantive override 136–39
suspension 35

tenure 11, 110, 122–26
territorial scope 15
trade unions 86–87
transparency 30, 45, 46, 48, 50, 83, 86–91, 106–7, 108–10, 117–22, 125, 126
treaties 6–7
  amendment of 131–33
  override 128–29
Treaties of the European Economic Community 16
Treaty of the Functioning of the European Union (TFEU) 84–85, 110–11, 132–33
trial without unreasonable delay, right to 21–22

Ukraine 15
ultra vires 85–86
unanimity 107, 108–10, 131, 137
undue influence 4, 28, 55, 125–26, 129–30, 138–39
United Kingdom (UK)
  Brexit 16
  Hirst v the United Kingdom, reaction to 68
United Nations (UN) 32–33
  Basic Principles of Judicial Independence 11–12
  General Assembly 11–12
  institutional framework 41
  treaty bodies 77–78
United States (US)
  Constitution (1787) and separation of powers principle 56–59
  domestic courts 66–67
  federalism 56
  judicial review 55–56

values-based approach 70–71
Venzke, Ingo 14–15
vertical integration 59–60
veto power 131–32
Vile, M. J. C. 54
Voeten, Erik 96, 104–5, 124
Voigt, Stefan 17–18
von Bogdandy, Armin 14–15, 81–82, 89
vote trading 108–10

Waldron, Jeremy 53
Weber, Max 19
welfare benefits 134–35
Wiebusch, Micha 136–37
World Conference on the Independence of Justice 11–12
World Trade Organization (WTO) *see* Appellate Body of the World Trade Organization (WTO AB)
World War II 15
  judicial councils 41–42

Yoo, John C. ix–x

Zimmermann, Dominik 22–23